To
Nancy & George
+ family

From
Leonard, Sharon
Donny, Bobby
Natasha + Lenny

Jan. 31, 1979

May God continue
to Bless you in your
much needed work!

Thanks for all your
help + listening
"ears" + visits!

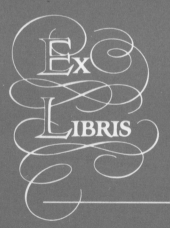

Ex
Libris

Daily Guideposts, 1979

Daily Guideposts, 1979

Guideposts
Carmel, New York 10512

Foreword

This book has but one objective: to aid you in your personal quest for spiritual growth and development throughout the coming year.

This is the third annual volume of daily devotionals to be offered exclusively to Guideposts subscribers. Many readers of our two previous volumes have written to tell us of the help and comfort they derived from *Daily Guideposts, 1977* and *Daily Guideposts, 1978*.

The book you now hold in your hands—*Daily Guideposts, 1979*—is like its two predecessors in that it offers heartwarming episodes from everyday life to point up inspirational messages. But it is different in that this year the whole family of Guideposts writers was asked to participate—and seventy-five of them did.

You will find no name at the bottom of each selection, only initials. Sometimes the initials belong to famous and beloved Christian authors like Catherine Marshall, Marjorie Holmes or Norman Vincent Peale. Sometimes they belong to people you may never have heard of, but a glossary on page 317 will enable you to identify them.

We sifted over 3,000 devotional items to select the 365 you will find here. We offer them in the hope that they will help the Holy Spirit bring you to a more perfect companionship with our Lord and Savior.

May God bless you this year, and all the years of your life.

THE EDITORS

Introduction

Let's begin this book by asking a question: what is the year of our Lord 1979 going to mean to you? The answer isn't difficult. The year is going to give to you just about what you give to the year. If you love life, life will love you right back. Complain about life and life will give you something to complain about. Run away from life and it will run away from you.

So move into the new year with this thought fixed firmly in your head: *Things will be fine in Seventy Nine*.

How do you go about making things fine in '79? First, affirm to yourself that with the help of the Lord Jesus and the Heavenly Father and the Holy Spirit it's going to be the greatest year you ever lived. Affirm it and believe it!

Next, make up your mind to get rid of a lot of stale old destructive thoughts and habits. How long have you carried the same old negative attitudes around? Have you had a new thought lately? Do you think about people in the same old critical way? Do you think about God in the same old tired, desultory manner? What about those old fears, old anxieties, old hates, old resentments?

If you carry all that dead wood forward into 1979 you might as well forget about its being a good year. If you want to make it a terrific year, you must cast off the old worn out things.

So right now, before you read any further in this book, sit down and make a list of any grudges you are carrying, any fears you are nurturing, any prejudices you are harboring about people, any secret sins—large or small—that you are concealing. Then take that list and tear it up as a symbol of your determination to be rid of all those things.

Finally, ask God to go with you into the New Year. If you sincerely ask Him, He will. And when He does, it means you are going to be renewed and revitalized in your life, because God is not only goodness and morality and honor; *God is life*.

Take His hand and things can't help being fine in '79!

Our Heavenly Father, help us as we go forward into the days and weeks and months of this coming year to serve You every minute of every day, all the way.

NORMAN VINCENT PEALE

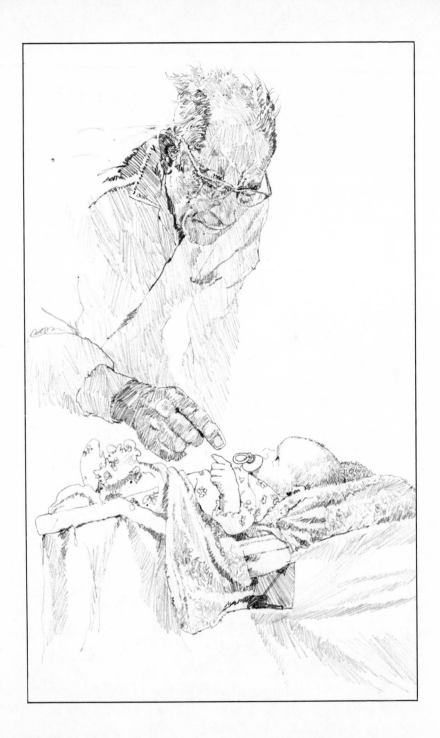

JANUARY 1979

S	M	T	W	T	F	S
	1	2	3	4	5	6
7	8	9	10	11	12	13
14	15	16	17	18	19	20
21	22	23	24	25	26	27
28	29	30	31			

1.

This is the day which the Lord hath made; we will rejoice and be glad in it.

Psalms 118:24

A long time ago we ran an article in Guideposts about a famous obstetrician who delivered babies with great professional skill, and with a beautiful flourish all his own. This doctor talked to babies. From the moment he first touched them he would smile at them and soothe them with soft words of welcome.

"Hello, little one, now don't be frightened. This is a wonderful world, and you are *so* wanted. The loveliest things are prepared for you. Your folks love you already and have made great plans for you. So don't be afraid, child. We're all tremendously glad you're here . . ."

Soft words of welcome. Surely that's the way to greet all new things—a baby, a stranger, even a brand new year. And that's the way I'm determined to greet 1979, not holding back as though its twelve uncharted months were something to be feared, but striding forth to meet it with a Christian's assurance, and a Christian's generosity of spirit.

Welcome, 1979, now don't be frightened . . .

This is the year that You have made for us, Lord. I will rejoice and be glad in it.

V. V.

2.

Trust no Future, howe'er pleasant!
Let the dead Past bury its dead!
Act—act in the living present!
Heart within, and God o'erhead!
Henry Wadsworth Longfellow

Lose ten pounds by Easter. See old friends. Do more for my church. Read the Bible through.

Resolutions. Whatever happens to them? Some never get off the ground, others die by March. How can I keep them?

Pondering this question, I thought of a young wife and homemaker I knew, mother of two schoolchildren, teacher, active community participant, frequent hostess, and decided to try her guiding rule: Take one step at a time, and take it now!

To lose ten pounds by spring, I must refuse chocolate cake *today*. For lunch next week with an old classmate, I need to set the date *now*. I can't do more for the church without being an informed member which means getting to the Sunday service *this coming Sunday*. If I read four chapters a day, I'll finish the Bible in 12 months, but I must read the first four *tonight*.

Humanly, I may not keep every resolution, but if I want to journey into richer tomorrows I must take the first step today.

Lord, in my search for You, let me remember that eternity begins today.

M.B.D.*

3.

All people make mistakes; that's why they put erasers on lead pencils.

Author unknown

My new typewriter has a wonderful feature—a correcting tape. Now when I make an error, my page isn't ruined. All I have to do is flick a switch and backspace over the wrong letters, and they are lifted off the page without a trace. I can then type in the correct characters, and the person reading my typing doesn't even know I made the mistake.

I have an automatic correcting power in my life, too. Nobody's perfect; I know I'm going to make mistakes. But Christ came to correct the sins in my life—to eradicate them, as if they never had been. I need not feel that my whole life is ruined because I have erred.

I am the one who must flick the switch. I must first acknowledge my sin, then ask His forgiveness. Then my life is cleared, like a blank page, to be re-typed, this time more carefully.

But the best part of all is that Christ isn't a machine to break down, wear out, or become obsolete. He is steadfast and true, always ready to forgive you and help you begin again.

Call on Him today, confessing where you have erred, and let Him give you a fresh start.

Father, I have sinned today. Forgive me, and help me to be more like You.

B.R.G.

4.

Many receive advice, only the wise profit by it.

Publilius Syrus

Jerry, our friendly garage man, closed the hood of my new car. "Remember now, the way you drive can shorten or prolong this baby's life."

"How's that?" I asked.

"Don't race the engine; don't drive fast until you've gone at least five miles; don't foul alignment by bumping the curbs when you park; don't make 'jack-rabbit' take-offs and don't ride the brakes downhill."

"That's sure a lot of don'ts," I said.

Jerry chuckled. "Yeah, I suppose so. But I'm telling you, if people regularly practiced these simple little tips, they'd get much smoother performance and far fewer repair bills."

It's the same way in my relationship with God. If I'd regularly follow more of the little tips He's given me in the Bible about daily living, my Christian life would be a lot more fulfilling: Don't overtax yourself unnecessarily; don't rush into a day without a purpose; don't get into arguments that put relationships out of alignment; don't rush to judgment; and don't be so stubborn that you cannot accept the inevitable with equanimity.

Lord, make me a good driver in every sense of the word.

R.H.F.

5. Our prayer and God's mercy are like two buckets in a well; while the one ascends, the other descends.

Mark Hopkins

Tomorrow we'll take our Christmas decorations down. I'll bundle our tree decorations to the attic. But I won't put Christmas away. Not since my friend Leta Fischer told me how to use Christmas cards long after the trappings have been packed away.

"We enjoy our cards during Christmas," Leta told me a few years ago. "But after the holidays we put them in a box beside our dining room table. Then each morning we draw out one or two cards and pray for the senders. We do this until every friend who has remembered us is remembered by us before God. We pray until the box is empty."

What better way to keep Christmas alive?

Stay close to our friends, dear Jesus.

H.B.F.

6. And from my stricken heart with tears two
wonders I confess:
The wonders of redeeming love and my
unworthiness.

Elizabeth C. Clephane hymn

My 14-year-old son's greatest delight seemed to be teasing his
sister Jana, who was 11. The taunts and comments led to bicker-
ing and frequently to tears.

One day when the teasing became too much for her, Jana
screamed in a voice loud enough to be heard throughout the
house, "I love you, Alan. Sometimes, you try to keep me from it.
But you can't stop me from loving you." With tears streaming
down her face, she fled to her room, leaving Alan speechless and
different.

Sometimes, God speaks loudly to us in order that we stop and
listen. I think of the death of Jesus on the cross as a silent scream
of God in which He says, "I love you that much, no matter what
you do."

*Father, I am left speechless with the wonder and depth of Your
love.*

R.D.R.

7. Therefore . . . be ye steadfast, unmoveable,
always abounding in the work of the Lord . . .

I Corinthians 15:58

That morning I invited an acquaintance to go to church with me
and she was angered. "I don't need church," she snapped. "I've
better things to do!" Then I was offended and I vowed I'd never
have anything to do with her again.

That afternoon my son saw a stray kitten in the yard, and asked
me to help him catch and save it. We worked over three hours.
The kitten was too frightened to be lured by food. We stalked it
around buildings till I was breathless. I crawled under some
bushes after it. Once I came near enough to reach for it. It ripped
me with vicious claws. Still, we persisted. That kitten was cold,
wet and starving. It needed us, know it or not. We'd help it, like

it or not! We did catch it, when it climbed a tree and my son climbed after it. When it had been warmed, dried and fed, it cuddled contentedly in his arms, purring happily.

"Now he's glad we kept after him, isn't he?" my son asked. I had to agree.

Sometimes people don't like us to remind them that they need Jesus' saving power. They don't like to hear that their lives are negative without God. But telling them is a part of our serving God. I knew that I was going right back to that acquaintance and tell gently and lovingly of God's wonderful provisions. Maybe some day she will be glad.

Please, Father, keep me willing to tell everyone I talk to about Your wonderful love.

L.C.

8. . . . A broken and a contrite heart, O God, thou wilt not despise.
Psalm 51:17

I heard a kind of parable-story the other day that I think I'm going to remember a long time:

A wealthy man, who was very sick, was determined not to die. When he recognized the Angel of Death near his bed, he cried out, "I'll do anything not to die. Anything!"

The angel took him to a huge place full of lighted candles of all sizes and of varying brightnesses. The angel explained that each candle represented a human life. Their sizes corresponded to human achievements and stations in life, while their flames showed how well the person they represented had served God.

"Notice how some of the shortest candles give the brightest light," the angel said.

"But where is my candle?" the dying man asked.

The angel pointed toward one of the tallest candles. Yet atop it guttered only a tiny flicker of flame.

"At the end of another year," the angel asked, "do you think your candle would give more light?"

The man wept. "I don't deserve another year. I've done so little."

"Your contrition has just earned you another year," the angel said. "Use it well.'"

Lord, it's a comfort for me to know that, no matter how small my portion, my "light" can burn brightly.

M.A.

9.

The Lord will perfect that which concerneth me.

Psalm 138:8

Yesterday morning, my ironing was interrupted by a telephone call, and, when I returned to the task, my mind was still on the phone conversation. I ran the iron over half a shirt before I realized that the wrinkles were not smoothing out, in spite of my efforts. Of course I discovered, then, that I had forgotten to plug the iron back in.

How often we try to smooth out the wrinkles in our lives with an iron that isn't plugged in to the Power Source. We struggle and push against our problems, hoping to iron them out by our own efforts, but the stubborn creases remain. Yet all the time we have access to a power that can smooth out the troubled places in our lives if we will only keep the connection intact.

If there is a problem worrying you today, take a few minutes to sit quietly with closed eyes and plug in to the presence of God. Don't fill up the silence with pleas for help. Just sit in the stillness until you feel the current of God's power coursing through you. Then return to your daily routine. The problem will still be there, but now the power to cope with it will be moving through you, smoothing the way for a solution.

Charged with Your power, Lord, I know I can cope with my problem.

M.M.H.

10. Have Thine own way, Lord, have Thine own way,
Thou art the Potter, I am the clay.
Mold me and make me after Thy will,
While I am waiting, yielded and still.

Adelaide Pollard

In order to raise money to build our new church, we had to get pledges. Our circle decided to make little bricks, with pins in them, and give them to the members to wear, to remind ourselves that it takes money to build a church.

Several of us spent most of one evening making row upon row of perfect little bricks, from a clay mixture. We formed each one by hand, carefully put the pins in, and set them away to dry. When I looked at them a few days later, all the bricks were lopsided, warped and crooked. The pins wouldn't open or close, and I was so disappointed I almost cried, when I thought of all the time my friends had spent making them.

I carried them home from the church basement, sat down at my kitchen table, took each brick, one by one, and scraped, and scraped, and sanded, and scraped some more. Little by little, they started shaping up, until they were looking like they were supposed to look like again.

I did a lot of thinking in the four hours I sat there scraping; and the thought kept coming back to me that God had made each one of us lovingly and carefully, with a perfect plan in mind for each individual. Then, somehow along the way, we warp a little here and there, or we get a tiny bit crooked, or our thinking gets lopsided, and, oh, how we must disappoint our Creator.

Thank God, we are not just lumps of clay . . . we might have been, though, if it were not for His loving-kindness. He sent Jesus to guide us back to Him. With tender, loving care He smoothes a bump off here and there, He awakens a conscience, He forgives us our lopsidedness, He straightens us out again.

Dear Lord, thank You for sending Your Son to us.

P.S.

11.

. . .For the Lord seeth not as man seeth; for man looketh on the outward appearance, but the Lord looketh on the heart.

I Samuel 16:7

A month after my 19-year-old son was killed in an automobile accident, I waited sadly on a bench in a crowded mall for a younger son to finish his shopping. My depression deepened as I became aware of the hundreds of unfamiliar faces passing by.

It would be impossible for me ever to get to know even this small segment of the world's population, I thought. How can God possibly care what happens to each person in the entire world? On a planet filled with natural and man-made disasters, it seemed incomprehensible that God could concern himself with the heartbreak of one mother crying for her son.

But even as tears began to blur my vision, I remembered what God had told Samuel. He does not see men the way we do; he looks on the heart. I blinked away the tears and tried to picture the heart of each oncoming shopper through God's eyes. Was that sour-faced man worried about his job? Could that whining child need attention? Had that solitary woman also lost a loved one?

My own pain lessened as I felt myself wishing I could do something to bring comfort to all those solemn strangers. By the time my son joined me I knew that, incredible as it seems, God actually does consider the hopes and the fears of each one of us. For I learned that evening that when you look at the heart through the eyes of God, you see with compassion and love.

Lord, as I look on the outward appearance of others, help me to look also on their hearts.

R.H.

12.

. . .Know ye not that your body is the temple of the Holy Ghost which is in you, which ye have of God, and ye are not your own?

I Corinthians 6:19

Temples. I've been thinking about temples ever since the Mormon temple was opened briefly to the public here in Washington, D.C. People lined up for blocks. I thought of Solomon's magnificent temple; the temple where Jesus taught.

A temple is awesome. Reaching up toward heaven—as if man, poor little guy, is striving to touch God with his soaring arches and spires. And man makes his temples beautiful with all the artistry he can afford (and usually a whole lot more). He adorns it with gold and silver, paintings, precious things. He fills his temple with music from mighty pipe organs and choirs; he makes it fragrant with incense and flowers.

There are other kinds of temples as well. "Temples not made with hands." How about trees? They too soar toward heaven, so majestic and yet so simple, richly adorned. Their buds in spring, their dancing beads and blossoms, and then the gradually opening parasols of the leaves, a dozen shades of green in summer and a blaze of gold and crimson in the fall. Even in winter they stand proud, their branches soaring like temple arches toward the sky.

The Holy Spirit must be there, the very breath of God dwells there among the trees.

And if a tree is a temple of God, then my body—this body, how much more! Shouldn't I keep it as beautiful as I can for Him, inside and out? Its flesh firm and glowing, its bones supple and strong. Its every part—every organ, tissue and cell, every drop of flowing lifeblood—are they not more precious, more remarkable than anything the finest man-made temple could contain? The sound of my own voice speaking, or laughing, or mourning, or lifted in song—isn't that more remarkable than the finest musical instrument?

Then how dare I do anything to defile or soil or damage this temple entrusted to me? How dare I neglect it, let it go to waste? For the spirit of God dwells there too, within me. The Holy Spirit breathes with my every breath.

My body is God's temple, His true temple, given freely to me but to be returned to Him one day. "Ye are not your own." I am not my own.

Thank You, God, for this magnificent creation, my body where my spirit dwells. Let me cherish it, care for it, keep it always clean and strong and well.

M.H.

10

13.

Often the greatest talents lie unseen.

Plautus

"I can't do a thing with that child," I complained, speaking of a little boy I once taught in grade school. Kenny would not respond at all. For hours a day, he'd just sit and watch what the other children were doing.

"You've got to find the glory in him," my mother advised me. "It's there somewhere. That's what you must work with."

It was a long search, but one rainy day I gave the children a heap of small colored shells, and invited them to make necklaces for their mothers. I didn't expect Kenny to participate. To my surprise, he edged into the group and began sorting and choosing shells. His finished necklace was a beautiful thing, the shells perfectly matched, the colors subtly blending. Was this Kenny's glory? Was this the gift God had given him, a splendid talent for fashioning beautiful objects with his hands?

Today, after time and training, Kenny is working happily and successfully as a craftsman in a small gift shop.

What an adventure each day can be, Lord, finding the glory in each person I meet.

L.C.

14.

When I consider Thy heavens . . . the moon and the stars, which Thou hast ordained.

Psalm 8:3

Becky brought it home from college—that one stunning fact, that one incredible bit of news that within the area outlined by the bowl of the Big Dipper, there are 10,000 galaxies, and that each of those galaxies contains approximately 10^{10} stars. That's ten followed by 1,024 zeros, enough to fill this page!

"O Lord, when I consider Thy heavens . . . the moon and the stars, which Thou hast ordained." It boggles my mind! I cannot *think* in terms of ten to the tenth power, much less times ten thousand.

But I didn't have to *think* in those terms. *Thy* hands created . . . ordained . . . fashioned the stars, by whatever process, and flung them into space. *Thy* hands! And when I consider it, then sings my soul. My God! How great Thou art!

Amen, Amen.

J.C.

15 *Your Spiritual Workshop for January*

LEARNING TO EXPRESS LOVE

Sometimes we are unaware how self-centered we are, or how whining and fault-finding. Sometimes we want to show more love for people close to us, but are too shy or inhibited to do so. Perhaps these guides will help you to *demonstrate* your love this month.

Love without words: If you are inarticulate when it comes to open expressions of affection, try loving with your eyes. Don't be impersonal like the mother who is so busy with her household tasks that she gives orders and rebukes without turning from the stove. Look into other people's eyes; say silently, "I love you. I love you."

Touch: Simple touch can quiet the rebellious words of a child, bring a feeling of warmth to an elderly person, cool the anger between brother and sister. One father found that communication with his son improved when he put his hand on the boy's shoulder. A mother learned that something extra flowed between her and her daughter when she held the girl's hand in her own. But the use of touch *must* be done with sensitivity and sincerity.

Saying the words: The language of love is vital, though many people dislike trite expressions. "I love you" is a cliché, but nothing better expresses deep caring. If the words stick in your throat, go off by yourself and practice. Sounds silly, perhaps, but no one hesitates to practice for a speech. Is a talk to the PTA more important than communicating love to a mate, a child or parent?

Doing the unexpected: Some people approach the sending of greeting cards in such a machine-like manner that these so-called "mementos of love" could be handled by a secretary. Aren't there more creative ways to show love—a single red rose brought home to a wife, a telephone call from a son at college *not* on Mother's Day?

Knowing the real source: If you worry about having too little love to give, pray about it, draw as close to God as you can. "*We love Him because He first loved us*," said John. (I John 4:19) Think about this. Truly, His love is so abundant that it can fill you and flow through you to others.

E. St. J.

13

16.

Casting all your care upon Him; for He careth for you.

I Peter 5:7

Some time ago a good friend spoke to me of her burden. Her older son was estranged from her. He had written his mother a terse, shattering letter cutting off all communication. "Don't even send me a Christmas card or a birthday card," he wrote.

"Why don't you let Jesus help you?" I asked her. "Why don't you simply tell Him that this problem is too much for you, that you want Him to take over the government of your life, including this—and He will."

My friend did just that, relinquished the whole problem to Jesus, the Burden-bearer, including any resentment about her son's attitude and actions.

A year and a half later, the son came to see her. There was a reconciliation. Why? Because my friend was changed. Because surrendering to Jesus had made her a different person—more loving, more understanding, more selfless. And her son knew it.

Lord, what great news, that You actually want to bear my burden. And now I want to talk to You about it and give it to You. Thank You for listening, Lord.

C.M.

17.

**Jesus, Thou art all compassion,
Pure, unbounded love Thou art.**

Charles Wesley

Our television operates by remote control. From a spot across the room, I can press a button to turn the set on or off, change channels, reduce or increase volume. The machine responds perfectly to these controls except when I run the vacuum cleaner over rugs nearby. By some electronic fluke, although no one has touched the buttons, the set by itself clicks on, switches channels, distorts the picture with broken lines of light.

There are times when my own life is like that television set. I, too, go haywire when Jesus' control of my life is broken. If I turn on anger when my neighbor's dog digs up my new rose bush, if I turn off generosity when the church needs me for a committee, if I switch to resentment when I hear my daughter's latest water-color criticized, distortions streak my days. But if I remember to "walk in love as Christ loved us" (Ephesians 5:2), my life snaps back into focus.

Oh, Lord, keep me always in Your control.

M.B.D.*

18.

**Let me live in my house by the side of the road
And be a friend of man.**

Sam Walter Foss

When I was a girl I used to think I'd be a missionary. But things didn't work out that way. Now, 30 years later, I sometimes feel a twinge of regret when I read of others who had the courage to serve the Lord in this way.

One day I confessed that secret longing to an elderly friend in our neighborhood. Mr. Braxton, nearly crippled with arthritis, and no longer able to work, spent his days in the front yard, smiling and waving a cheery hello to each car that passed his door. When he heard of my unfulfilled dream, he said, "Shucks, what's to stop you?"

"Oh, it's too late now," I replied. "I'm too old, and there's my family to consider. I couldn't leave now."

"My dear," he said, "don't make the mountain higher than it is. Christ said, 'Go ye into all the world. . .' but don't you know, the rest of the world begins just outside your door."

Frank Braxton was a missionary. He spread Christ's love over a bend in Old Mill Road. But he also taught me that if each person who felt this love took it a little farther on and gave it to someone else, that love could cover the globe.

I can do that. You can, too.

Father, help me to serve You wherever I am.

B.R.G.

19.

I will not leave you comfortless; I will come to you.

John 14:18

My husband and I were tempted to throw the tiny blue and gold grandfather clock out with the trash. It wouldn't keep the right time. In spite of all the careful adjustments made on the delicate two-inch pendulum and the meticulous balancing of the little weight fastened to its stem, the independent miniature time-piece seemed to tick off the minutes as though it couldn't wait for tomorrow. It was always fast in spite of my best efforts. On one occasion, as I attempted still another adjustment, the pendulum fell off and I left it in disgust, ticking like a frightened child's heart. Before the next hour had passed the silly little clock had recorded over three and a half hours!

And then my husband became seriously ill. His hospitalization lasted many weeks and for a while it seemed that he might never come home again. At first the loneliness of my days was unbearable. While I waited, praying desperately for God's help, the little clock continued to tick gaily along. It seemed to be racing ahead, singing out "It won't be long . . . he'll soon be home . . . it won't be long!" As I prayed, the cheerful sound comforted me and gave me courage.

My husband recovered and is home again. The willful little clock still doesn't keep time. However, I wind it regularly for the sound of its ticking has become a source of hope for me and a reminder that God, who is never far away, sometimes uses strange devices to comfort His suffering children.

Thank You God for Your many voices. May I always listen for Your presence.

D.H.

20.

Courtesies of a small and trivial character are the ones which strike deepest to the grateful and appreciating heart.

Henry Clay

Would you like some real fun today? Well, ask the Lord to put somebody in your way today whom you can help. God may surprise you.

Yesterday I prayed for this. Later, as I was buying a pair of shoes, the young clerk writing the sales slip looked tired and discouraged. So I said, "I've been watching you write that slip. I'm impressed by how beautifully you write."

The clerk looked at me in surprise. "Nobody ever told me that before."

You should have seen his face. His shoulders straightened, his whole attitude changed. As I left, he waved to me. Now, it was a very simple remark based on the fact that he did have nice handwriting. But it raised his ego and gave *me* a lift that lasted all day.

Dear Father, there are so many people who hunger for a kind word, who need assurance from another person. Put one of these persons in my path this day.

N.V.P.

21.

Just as I am, without one plea,
But that Thy blood was shed for me,
And that Thou bidd'st me come to Thee,
O Lamb of God, I come, I come!
Charlotte Elliott hymn

Not long after we were married, my wife and I purchased an antiqued pine dining room table. It was our favorite piece of furniture. We admired the honey-toned richness of its smooth surface and polished it lovingly.

Then the children came, and we began to discover how soft pine really is. I remember one night when our eight-year-old son did his arithmetic homework on the table. To our dismay, the set of problems were inscribed through the paper into the table top. Through the years there were more calamities: dents from hurled toy building blocks, tracks from miniature cars, scratches from sewing machines and typewriters, a burn from a sizzling Christmas dinner plate. But it's still our favorite piece, because it carries the signatures of family living.

It seems to me that life is a bit like that table. All of us carry marks of living, dents and scratches from sorrows, mistakes, disappointments, often our own foolishness. How comforting it is to think that God doesn't mind those scars; He expects and forgives them. He doesn't want us in some sort of cosmetic perfection; He wants us to come to Him just the way we are, scars and all.

Heavenly Father, give us the wisdom to turn to You without worrying about past mistakes or errors.

R.H.S.

22.

. . . Weeping may endure for a night, but joy cometh in the morning.

Psalm 30:5

One morning a few years ago I happened to be watching a television talk show where the interviewer was a woman. Her guest that morning was Sister Margaret Mary, the young and attractive dean of an exclusive women's college in the East.

For some reason, the hostess on the show was inclined to badger the nun, questioning her persistently about her way of life. The nun conceded that, because of her vows, she could not smoke or drink alcoholic beverages or eat certain foods on certain days; she could not marry and have children; she could not go to parties or restaurants or the movies or the theater or even watch television without the permission of her superiors.

Finally the hostess said to the nun, "I suppose what I am trying to get you to say is that you have given up all the pleasures of life."

"Perhaps I have," replied the nun serenely, "but I have kept all the joys."

I never forgot the distinction the nun made between pleasures and joys. What did she mean? I think she meant that pleasures are momentary and transient, but joys are lasting. That pleasures appeal to the physical senses, but joy dwells in the heart. That pleasure is mostly self-oriented, but that true joy comes from putting self aside.

Today why not pause in your search for pleasure and reach out, instead, for joy?

Father, the pleasures of life we seek for ourselves. The joys of life come from You. Help us always to know the difference, and to choose only what pleases You.

G.D.K.

23.

Can a woman forget the infant at her breast, or a loving mother the child of her womb? even these forget, yet will I not forget you.

Isaiah 49:15 (NEB)

Recently Guideposts sent me to interview Dr. William Wilson, noted psychiatrist, professor and pioneer in the field of Christian medicine at Duke University. Seated with his wife Elizabeth at their kitchen table, he took particular delight in recalling his favorite illustration of God's love.

"When I was an intern," said Dr. Wilson in his soft Carolina drawl, "I delivered many babies into this world. The process of birth is a whole chain of miracles, but one thing never failed to amaze me. No matter how long the mother was in labor, no matter how much she suffered, the first thing she wanted to see and hold was the baby itself, the very thing that had caused her so much pain. A new mother loves her child instinctively. She wants more than anything to take it in her arms and hold it to her breast.

"It's difficult," he smiled, "to imagine a love so strong. But God's love is even stronger. We are His children, and He loves us unconditionally. No matter how much sorrow we cause Him, no matter what our weaknesses, He waits for us with arms outstretched. And best of all, He waits forever."

Oh, Heavenly Father, help me come to You today as a little child, trusting, obedient, innocent, and with absolute confidence that You will take me by the hand and lead me in Your will.

K.B.

24.

Blessed are they that mourn: for they shall be comforted.

Matthew 5:4

All the hardships that I thought I had faced in my life were insignificant when compared with the death, a few years ago, of a friend whom I had loved dearly and deeply: Like many people who suffer loss, I felt that God had singled me out for punishment.

Then another friend, watching me sink into self-pity, brought me a passage written by a psychiatrist for people who have lost dear ones. It read: "All your trials . . . are gifts to you . . . opportunities to grow. You will not grow if you sit in a beautiful flower garden . . . but you will grow if you are sick, if you are in pain, if you experience losses . . . and if you take the pain and learn to accept it as a gift with a specific purpose."

Pain a gift? I wondered. But then I realized that it was true. Hadn't another friend rushed to comfort me? And, in my grief, wasn't I more aware of the suffering for others? I was growing as a person. God was giving me new insights and new friends to make up the loss I felt. And I came to know God better than ever because I needed Him to help me through my grief.

Your plan is perfect, Lord, I know. Thank You for the opportunities that every event brings into my life.

C.H.

25.

Nevertheless I am continually with Thee; Thou hast holden me by my right hand.

Psalm 73:23

Noon. The towering downtown buildings spewed forth a torrent of office workers, and the sidewalks suddenly became crowded. At a corner I stopped to wait for the signal to cross. Ahead of me there was a mother and her little son, perhaps four or five years old.

The light changed. Without looking up the little blonde boy reached his mittened hand upward. The mother kept her eyes on the light as she reached down. Their hands met and clasped tightly and they proceeded to cross.

Because they had reached for each other so many times, each knew the exact distance to be spanned. God knows us that well, too, and His hand is always there when we reach for it.

God, how comforting it is to feel Your hand in mine.

M.B.D.**

26.

In My Father's house are many mansions: if it were not so, I would have told you. I go to prepare a place for you.

John 14:2

Everyone called him Old Brother Randall. Not Mr. Randall. Or just Brother Randall, but Old Brother Randall. Even at 85 he still had a full head of hair, though it was snowy white. "The Lord says He's numbered every hair on our heads, but so far, He's let me keep most of 'em," Old Brother Randall used to say with a twinkle.

One day he telephoned to ask if I'd pick him up for church. He lived, it turned out, in a run-down, sagging house that had not stood the test of time as well as he had. Nonetheless, somewhat at a loss for words when he greeted me on his drooping entrance porch, I said, "My, what a pleasant old house!"

He was obviously pleased, for compliments about this house must have been scarce indeed. But then he cocked his snowy head to one side and said, "Oh, this is a nice house all right, but my Father's building me an unbelievably beautiful home in my next neighborhood!"

At first I was too startled by the idea of this ancient man having a father to grasp his real meaning. But then I understood. What a wonderful way to claim the promise of a Christian life! What better dream than that of looking forward to living in a house built by the Master Carpenter Himself?

Though Old Brother Randall was partially blind, his spiritual eyes were much more seeing than mine! I'm thankful God has dotted our world with elderly children like him. Their vision is an inspiration.

Father, open my spiritual eyes that I may also grow mature in You. Then use me to be an example and encouragement to Your younger children.

I.C.

27. For where two or three are gathered together. . . .

Matthew 18:20

Late one Saturday evening my husband and I relaxed before retiring for the night. It'd been a busy week anyhow; then we ended it that day by sawing and stacking firewood on a section of our rural property. In fact, the fire in the fireplace was a result of some of our work.

I said, "The fire has burned itself out. And so have I! It'd be nice to sleep late in the morning. I'll probably be tempted to forget about getting up and going to church."

John agreed as he absentmindedly poked the dying embers into a pile.

Moments later those same embers burst into flame. Then, since we were heading for bed, he took the poker and scattered the pile of embers and the fire died.

"You know," he said, "I think the Lord's children are like those coals. We 'turn on' with the encouragement and help of each other. But we 'turn off' and tend to grow cold when we don't have fellowship with others of His people."

John was right. The Lord surely knows we need one another. How this thought helps me resist the temptation of staying home sometimes!

Heavenly Father, I'm glad I'm a part of the family of God! I'm warm when I keep close to my brothers and sisters and cold when I'm apart from them. Help me to always remember that!

I.C.

28.

Not with the hope of gaining aught,
Not seeking a reward;
But as Thyself has loved me,
O ever-loving Lord.

Anonymous

One Sunday morning, as I checked out library books in the hallway of our Sunday-school building, I felt an arm encircle me from behind. I turned and looked into the kind, sweet eyes of Mrs. Havener, an elderly member of our church. "I just love you," she said, pressing her cheek to mine. And then she was gone, on down the hall to her class.

A warm glow enveloped me from my head to the tip of my toes, even as I stared after her, puzzled by her action. I'd done nothing to solicit her love, nor had she asked anything of me in return. I had only to accept her free gift. It made my whole day. And then I could not rest until I'd given it away to someone else.

Christ's love is like that—unsolicited and freely given—no strings attached. He loved you and me enough to die for us. He asked only that we accept His love to have eternal life. And once we have felt that divine love, we are compelled to share it.

Lord, send me someone to love today, that I may share Your wondrous gift with one who needs a friend.

B.R.G.

29.

The race of mankind would perish did they cease to aid each other.

Sir Walter Scott

I once saw a cartoon of four men in a rubber life raft on the ocean. There is a leak in one side of the raft and two men on that side are busy bailing out the in-pouring water. One of the two watching men on the opposite side of the raft asks his companion, "Shall we help them bail?"

His companion replies, "Why should we? The leak is on their side of the raft."

I never forgot that cartoon because the point was so plain: We are all in the same boat. No person anywhere can be hurt without all other people being diminished or endangered.

I find that I need to be reminded of this constantly. The memory of that cartoon really helps when I'm tempted to waste gasoline, or squander electricity, or even throw a chewing gum wrapper on the sidewalk. We are all fellow passengers on the very frail spaceship known as the planet Earth.

Jesus knew this, too. When He commanded all people to "Love thy neighbor," He was asked, "Who is my neighbor?" (Luke 10:29)

His unforgettable answer was the story of the good Samaritan, saying, in effect, "Your neighbor is always any person who needs your help. You must help him just as he must help you."

Lord, teach me to love my neighbor, even before I know him.

M.A.

30.

Earth has no sorrow that heaven cannot heal.
Sir Thomas More

Everyone knows the remarkable story of Helen Keller, who became blind and deaf when she was 19 months old, but then went on to graduate from Radcliffe College *cum laude*. For over 60 years, as a teacher, newspaper reporter and author, she brought a lovely radiance to the world.

Then, before she died in 1968, at 88, she was asked if she believed in life after death. "Of course," she replied quickly, "that's when God will let me see and hear."

Helen Keller needed only her heart to see and hear. How I wish I could use my heart as well!

Lord, give me also a seeing and listening heart.

S.F.

31.

Let your light so shine before men, that they may see your good works, and glorify your Father which is in heaven.

Matthew 5:16

When my son, Tommy, was five he visited a Roman Catholic church with a friend and saw his first stained-glass window. The lives of the saints were depicted in glorious reds, blues and golds. That night at dinner he bubbled over with the experience telling me that he "had seen the saints." Since we had never discussed the saints, I asked him what a saint was. "It's a person with the light shining through him," he answered.

Tommy's beautiful simple definition has stayed with me for years because until that moment I had thought of the saints as those men and women of ancient days who were stoned or pierced with arrows for their faith, not as men and women I might meet today who let God's light shine through them.

Oh, Lord, although I am far from being a saint, let Your light shine through me also.

A.S.

FEBRUARY 1979

S	M	T	W	T	F	S
				1	2	3
4	5	6	7	8	9	10
11	12	13	14	15	16	17
18	19	20	21	22	23	24
25	26	27	28			

1.

Now the day is over, night is drawing nigh,
Shadows of the evening steal across the sky.
Sabine Baring-Gould hymn

Each day, somewhere in the busy late afternoon hour between five and six o'clock, comes a pause, a few moments of quiet that I cherish. I'm speaking of the time when I drop whatever I'm doing in the kitchen and go into the darkening living room and turn on the lamps.

The soft lamplight restores beauty to the scarred furniture, worn carpet and faded slipcovers on the wing chairs, and a mist of serenity settles over the room. The day is almost over. The children are all in. Supper is in the making. A huge basket of clothes, scented with the fresh outdoors, has been brought in from the lines. And the one who loves us and works for us will be home soon.

For these few minutes I try to shut out the weighty worries of the outside world. They will come again soon in an early evening news broadcast, but for this brief span I stand in a small patch of peace. I add another log and gaze into the fire a few minutes or stand at the window and watch the daylight surrender to the dusk. Gratitude wells up within me.

Lord, thank You for the extraordinary blessings of an ordinary day.

M.B.D.**

2. Let the beauty of Jesus be seen in me,
All His wonderful passion and purity.
Oh Thou Savior Divine, all my being refine,
Till the beauty of Jesus be seen in me.
Old hymn

Browsing recently through a magazine, I came upon a full page advertisement concerning diamonds. "The wonderful thing about small diamonds is that the magic of a large diamond is duplicated in beautiful miniature. They come in all sizes—all beautiful and with a wide range of designs. Little windows full of light," I read, entranced. *What a description of the true Christian!*

"The true beauty can never be revealed until a diamond is cut and faceted by the expert. Each facet must be cut at precisely the right angle to bring out the fire and sparkle that nature hid there." *Oh, Thou Savior Divine, all my being refine!*

"Most diamonds," I read on, "have a tinge of color which adds warmth; in many cases it is so slight only the expert can find it. The total harmonious effect is what you see." *Only the expert can find it . . . like the God Who made me and knows me through and through.*

"All diamonds, whatever their individual characteristics, are precious and unique and every faceted gem catches the light." *Each one of us is precious and unique and God loves every one of us.*

Lord, help me today to be a little window full of Your light.

H.B.F.

3.

And being in an agony He prayed more earnestly. . . .

Luke 22:44

The voice of my friend over the telephone asked for my prayers for her husband in the hospital. With a little sob in her voice she said, "I've never prayed so hard in all my life before."

I appreciated the fact that she had felt free to call upon me for prayer, and joined her immediately. But I felt a twinge of guilt, asking myself why it is that we pray hardest only in the face of crisis.

This troubled me so much that later on, in my Bible reading, it was very reassuring to come upon the passage which told me that even Jesus "prayed more earnestly" in his human agony of Gethsemane. It seems very human to neglect the power of prayer until we are brought face to face with some emergency. Surely our Heavenly Father understands.

Father, hear my prayer today, forgive my neglect, and give me daily guidance in meeting my problems.

R.C.I.

4.

Thou preparest a table before me in the presence of mine enemies.

Psalms 23:5

That Sunday it was snowing fiercely, and the weatherman promised that at least four more inches would be added to the already heaping drifts. *Surely God will understand if I don't struggle out to Mass today*, I thought. I was reluctant to leave my warm kitchen at all, in fact, but I dragged out boots and winter gear, and went outside to fill my bird feeder. Back inside, I fixed a cup of tea and sat down to watch for my friends the birds to come and feast.

None came.

An hour later I looked out. Still no birds. It was so lonely without them.

So lonely without them. The words stabbed my heart. I looked at the kitchen clock. The priest would be offering Communion now. The offering was there, but I hadn't gone out to take it.

How often had I failed to take the portions that God had waiting for me? How often had He looked and not seen me there? Next Sunday, I resolved, I would be in church, snow or no snow.

God, forgive me for the times I fail to turn to You for nourishment and flounder so foolishly on my own. Today, especially, keep me close to You.

M.S.G.

5.

But whoso hearkeneth unto Me shall dwell safely, and shall be quiet from fear of evil.
Proverbs 1:33

The alarm jarred me awake. 5:30. I lay, feeling annoyed, trying to get my mind together to face the day. As usual, I did a quick evaluation of my life. It always seemed so bleak in the early morning. I picked up last night's paper from the nightstand. The headlines glared at me. They made things worse.

"The Strangler Claims Another Victim." *I must remember to always lock my car doors at night. And I'd better call the locksmith today to put that deadbolt lock on my door.*

"Cost of Living Up 8% in Last Six Months." *Perhaps I should begin looking in the Classifieds for a part-time extra job. I could take in some typing to supplement my income. Thank heaven I have my own typewriter!*

"High Speed Chase Ends in Fatal Crash." *An innocent motorist was killed. It really would be safer for me to take the bus to work.*

Depression darkened my mind. *It's all so hard*, I thought despairingly.

A sudden light thud on my blanket stopped my thoughts. My little white-and-gray kitten stood on my stomach for a moment looking at me. Then she walked up to my chin, sniffed at my face and curled up on my chest purring. I put my hand up and touched her protectively. I knew she was hungry. Suddenly a new thought came. *Wasn't I something like that kitten?* If I came to Jesus Christ with love and trust, would He do less for me than I would do for her? Or would He gently lay His hands on me and keep me safely in His care?

Oh ye of little faith, I thought ruefully as I crawled out of bed. My first act of the day was to feed my kitten.

Forgive me, Lord, for expecting less of You than I expect of myself. Let me hold tighter to my mustard-seed faith, and to Your hand. If I do that, I know I need never be afraid.

D.'H.

6.

Love bears all things, believes all things, hopes all things, endures all things.
I Corinthians 13:7 (RSV)

In 1962 when my mother suffered a stroke, I had a difficult time accepting it. Mom had a strong faith, and during my whole lifetime I had witnessed her devotion for God. It didn't seem fair that He would afflict His faithful follower like that. Then my father stepped in and took over. He insisted on taking care of Mom at home. For six years, until her death, he cared for her, waiting on her hand and foot, cooking, cleaning and doing all that was needed for her comfort. But most of all he loved her, and the love showed.

Watching this love in action, I saw my father in a new light. A new respect for him surged in me, and my own love increased. I became fully aware of what a blessing it is to have a father like mine. The joy of that discovery compensated for the sadness I felt for Mom; and it united our family in a stronger bond.

St. Paul said, "All things work together for good to them that love God." (Romans 8:28) Both my parents loved God; and because of their love even tragedy was turned into good.

Dear Lord, I praise Thee for all my blessings, those I recognize and those I can only try to understand.

B.R.G.

7. That best portion of a good man's life,
His little, nameless, unremembered acts
Of kindness and of love.

Wordsworth

On a gray afternoon I left the supermarket, my arms full of grocery bags. I was tired. The check-out cashier had been grumpy, the crowds pushy and surly. *The human race*, I thought, *needs humanization shots. We have all forgotten how to be civil to one another.*

Then I noticed a piece of paper sticking under my windshield wiper. Not a parking violation! No, it was a note, obviously scribbled in haste. It said: "Pardon me for intruding, but I noticed an oil puddle under your car. I thought you'd want to know, I hope it's nothing serious." The note was unsigned, but the friendly warning which a stranger had taken time to write saved me from a breakdown on the way home.

How seldom we encounter a truly anonymous act of kindness! Yet Jesus said: "Therefore when thou doest thine alms, do not sound a trumpet before thee . . ." (Matthew 6:2). Today, why not try to do something for someone without letting anyone know who has done it? The reward, as my unknown benefactor knew, will come in the secret knowledge that you have eased another's burden, not in recognition or praise for the deed.

Lord, help me to keep an attitude of caring, both for the nameless stranger or the friend in need.

C.H.

8. The Age of Miracles is forever here!

Thomas Carlyle

On my study wall is a sign a friend once sent me: EXPECT A MIRACLE! It's the first thing I see when I enter, and it gives off a radiance of its own all day. "Good vibes," as the kids would say. It fills me with something very important to miracles—a childlike expectancy.

Expectancy is like breathing to a child. Each day holds all the elements of a big adventure: He will find a penny . . . a violet . . . a four-leaf clover. He will ride an elephant . . . discover buried treasures . . . be invited by an astronaut to help explore the moon. . . . And more days than not, delightful things do happen, simply because he expects them to. No, not usually the precise stuff of his dreams, but many a dream's first cousin.

"Except you be as little children," Jesus reminded us, the kingdom can't come. We can't receive the wonderful things God has in store for us unless we believe in them!

So I do believe in miracles; they are always happening to me. And I know that for anyone who'll watch for them and be expectant enough to work for them, they will happen too. Big miracles, or little daily miracles that are often overlooked. The secret behind having a miracle happen to you is simply to be open and ready to receive.

Lord, thank You for the expectancy that is back of every miracle. Keep me always filled with that eager, trusting, childlike expectancy.

M.H.

9.

Love is not arrogant or rude.
I Corinthians 13:5 (RSV)

"He's the only real Christian I know," my grandmother always said whenever the name of Walter Tyson was mentioned. I myself always thought of him for his white whiskers and the Snickers bars he brought me every time he came to our house. Mr. Tyson was a stalwart in his church and his generosity apparently went far beyond Snickers bars, for he was always busy in community projects and, though a moderately wealthy man, he died a very poor one. It was said that he spent his money secretly helping others.

Yet to me the most memorable thing about Mr. Tyson was that he refused to call himself a Christian. One day I heard him explain this to my mother. "If you mean," he said, "that I accept

Jesus as my Lord and Savior, then I'm a Christian and proud of it. But as I live each day, I'm afraid I can't call myself a Christian. I can only say that I'm trying hard to be one."

It's something to think about.

Father, never let me be so certain of my faith that I forget to work at it.

V.V.

10.

Man shall not live by bread alone, but by every word that proceedeth out of the mouth of God.
Matthew 4:4

Browsing through a shop in the North Carolina mountains, where Scottish chauvinism rides high, I came across this old verse:

A Scots Toast

May the best you've ever seen
Be the worst you'll ever see;
May the mouse ne'er leave your girnal
wi' a tear drop in its e'e.

I don't know the exact translation for the Gaelic word *girnal*, but taken in context it must mean *cupboard* or something close to that. Imagine the poor mouse crying because he found the cupboard bare! What a colorful way to say "May you never go hungry."

"Give us this day our daily bread," Christ taught us to pray, mindful of the body's needs. But He also spoke of a spiritual famine that can destroy the soul.

What's the state of your own spiritual cupboard these days? Is it stocked with faith, with knowledge of the Bible, with love and loyalty to your church? Take a look today, and make sure that it's not bare.

Break Thou the bread of life, dear Lord, to me.

M.R.

11.

Sitting at the feet of Jesus, O what words I
  hear Him say!
Happy place, so near, so blessed, may it find
  me there each day.

Old hymn

Do you ever wonder what Martha served in that special meal
that she prepared for her beloved guest—Jesus? I'm sure that
nothing was too good for this occasion—nothing! What were the
"things" Scripture tells us she was so busy about? Why, dishes, of
course—fish, meat, breads, vegetables, fruits—*dishes*, maybe
as many as ten!

But Jesus said to her, "Martha, Martha, you are anxious and
bothered about many matters, when there is need of but one
thing (dish)." (Luke 10:41, 42 MLB)

Like Martha, it is easy to be too extravagant, to work more
than is needed so that we end up exhausted, fretful, and tense,
and too tired to enjoy our times with the Lord. Jesus says to me,
to you: "Don't. Live simply. Then there will be plenty of time to
sit at My feet. Work, yes, but not so much that you have no time
for fellowship with Me." Programs, meetings, clubs, and purely
social activities can never satisfy the longing heart. "Take time to
be holy; speak oft with thy Lord." Only one dish is needed!

*Lord, today I would live simply and walk quietly, restfully
listening to Your voice and learning to say "no" to whatever
stands in the way of my being my best for You.*

H.B.F.

12.

You may fool all the people some of the time;
you can even fool some of the people all the
time; but you can't fool all the people all the
time.

Abraham Lincoln

Not long ago a church friend was telling me a story he used to
make a point in his Sunday-school classes. It's about a movie

director who was looking for a derelict to play a key scene. After a long search, he found just the man in a slum.

But by the time he appeared on the set, the derelict had bathed, shaved and changed clothes. He had done everything he could to make himself look presentable, not realizing that his efforts made him unusable for the part for which the director needed him.

My friend points out to his classes that you make the same mistake as the derelict when you put up a false front, either to your fellows or to God. God already knows your faults; all He wants is for you to come to Him, just as you are.

Father, thank You for Your everlasting, loving arms that are always there to support me, faults and all.

I.C.

13. Not as the world giveth, give I unto you.
John 14:27

In our last foreign service post my son, Brian, attended a school where he was the only American child in his class. Normally this would not upset him, since he is bilingual and has lived much of his life abroad. But in the third grade in Venezuela he ran into a problem he could not understand.

He had spent the night before Valentine's Day writing cards for every classmate in his new school. But when the school bus dropped him at home on the afternoon of the 14th, he was near tears. "Mommy," he said sadly, "they wouldn't take my cards."

It turned out that Valentine's Day is not celebrated in Venezuela. Brian's classmates had been embarrassed and confused by his gifts, especially since they had nothing to offer in return. But Brian was miserable. He had something to give, and no one wanted it.

Brian's rejected gifts gave me pause. If someone wants to do me a favor, and I won't let him, I stand in the way of the blessing he would receive in his giving. Then I wondered, what must God feel like when He offers everlasting life to all of us, and, through carelessness or indifference, some of us refuse to accept it?

With a grateful heart, dear Lord, I accept Your gift of life today.
B.R.G.

14.

(Valentine's Day)

My little children, let us not love in word, neither in tongue; but in deed and in truth.
I John 3:18

When I answered the doorbell on Valentine's Day, there stood my neighbor with her two small daughters. The children had a precarious grip on a paper plate that held two cupcakes, iced in white and decorated with tiny red candy hearts.

"These are for you from us," the older child said. "We helped make them."

"Yes," the youngest piped proudly, "Mom only stirred a little bit." Their eyes were glowing with excitement as I thanked them and, as they left, I heard the older one say, "Giving is the best way of loving, isn't it, Mom?"

Giving is the best way of loving, I thought, looking at the little cakes. If that were the only lesson that young mother taught her daughters, it would be more than enough.

Lord, remind me to show my love to another today by giving something of myself.
R.C.I.

15 Your Spiritual Workshop for February

ARE YOU AFRAID?

If you have some fear that is interfering with your work or your sleep or making you avoid social gatherings, try confronting that fear now with these five steps.

1) *Name it*. Write your fear down on a piece of paper. Give specific details. A fear that may seem enormous bottled up in your mind can assume quite normal proportions when put in words before you.

2) *Relax*. Psychologists report that fear produces tension which can block creativity. You need a relaxed body before you can have a relaxed mind, so sit in a chair and let your body go limp. Breathe deeply, slowly. Think of peaceful things. Continue this exercise until you're sure the tension has drained out of you.

3) *Search your Bible* for passages like: "God hath not given us the spirit of fear; but of power, and of love, and of a sound mind." (II Timothy 1:7) And Joshua 1:9; Matthew 28:20. And, of course, the wonderful 23rd Psalm. The Bible verses go on and on, giving assurance that God can handle your fear, that He wants you to be free of it. He asks, yes implores, you to give Him your burden.

4) *Trust Him*. Believe, with all your heart, Proverbs 3:5: "Trust in the Lord with all thine heart; and lean not unto thine own understanding." Regardless of what goes wrong, you must believe that He loves you and cares what happens to you.

5) *Surrender it*. Take the sheet of paper with your fear written on it. Offer up a prayer like this: "Lord, I have brought this matter to Your attention. I know now that while I am unable by myself to throw off this fear, You can do it for me. I put my trust in You."

Then tear up the paper and let the pieces fall into the waste-basket.

N.V.P.

16.

**Were the whole realm of nature mine,
It were an offering far too small;
Love so amazing, so divine,
Demands my soul, my life, my all.**

Isaac Watts hymn

Last winter I was very ill with flu and, of course, I went to my doctor. He gave me a shot and some pills, telling me to take four of them every two hours. Back at home, I decided it was too much medicine. I decided that I would take two pills every four hours. Soon I was feeling a little better. Days passed, though, and my illness dragged on. I didn't feel too badly, but I wasn't well. I returned to my doctor. I told him my opinions about taking so much medicine. He was disgusted with me.

"If you had followed my directions, that much medication would have killed those germs. You are just making them mad and giving them a chance to build up immunity against the pills. I can't help you, if you won't trust me and follow my directions exactly!"

We must also give ourselves to our Lord and Master completely, holding nothing back, if we would have the most joyous, successful life, the life God means for us. God wants us to trust ourselves to Him, body, mind and soul. When we fully dedicate ourselves to Him, then we reap the full, joyous benefits of God's love and blessing.

Father, help me to find Your plan for my life in every detail.

L.C.

17.

It is more blessed to give than to receive.

Acts 20:35

One of my babies had the colic for three months. Since she cried most of the time for those weeks, I could get no rest. I dragged myself through long days and nights, getting more tired all the time. Finally I scarcely knew what I was doing. Then two friends came to me, beaming with happiness at their planned surprise.

They proposed to take care of the baby nights for a while, so I could get some sleep.

"Oh, I couldn't let you do that!" I protested. "It's so much work!" I saw all the glad light die in their eyes. They looked so dejected, so disappointed.

"I really do need your help so much!" I confessed, relenting. "Please do help me." And they did. They really enjoyed those long, dark hours they had the baby, and cared for her with love and tenderness. Their joy was beautiful to see—the joy my pride had nearly robbed them of.

As Jesus said, it is better to give than to receive. Giving is marvelously rewarding. Yet for every giver, there must be a receiver. Jesus received the loving hospitality of Mary and Martha. He accepted the grateful woman in Bethany who anointed Him with precious ointment. Our own salvation depends on our humbly accepting our Lord's gift. Let's give all we can. And let's receive graciously and thankfully, too. It's a precious part of the richness of living.

Dear Father, let me give of my best. And help me to let others know the glory of giving generously, too.

L.C.

18.

Love your enemies . . . pray for them which despitefully use you. . . .

Matthew 5:44

I have a friend who works in a bank in our home town. Bill's boss is a skinny little man who keeps bicarbonate of soda in his desk to soothe his churning, angry insides. "The boss used to take his feelings out on me," Bill told me once. "I hated to go to work. Until, that is, I learned a secret for handling difficult people."

Since I know a few such people myself, I perked up.

"One day when the boss was being unfair, I mumbled a '*Bless you!*' under my breath. I meant to be sarcastic but right away I thought that I heard the Lord's voice whispering, '*That's the idea! Ask for a blessing on your boss.*' "

The next morning Bill decided to try an experiment. Whenever his employer got angry, Bill would ask God to bless him.

At first the experiment seemed to fail. For instance, one morning Bill arrived at the bank ten minutes early. The boss greeted him with, "Decided to get to work on time for a change?" ("Lord, thank You for this man and bless him," Bill prayed.) Later the boss criticized Bill in front of a customer. ("Lord, bless my employer and bring him peace.") On and on the experiment went, always with the same apparent failure.

But then an interesting thing began to happen. Bill accidentally learned that his boss had a painful back problem which he never talked about. Later Bill also learned that the boss' wife was an invalid who constantly nagged him.

Suddenly Bill's "Bless You" prayer had a new focus. His feelings began to shift. The boss was still a bit testy but then he did have a lot to put up with!

"The secret," Bill told me, "was not that the boss changed; I changed. I started to see him as a needing, hurting man. And when that happened I began wanting—really *wanting*—God to bring him His best."

Keep me mindful, Lord, that being kind to others is also honoring You.

J.L.S.

19.

Let this mind be in you, which was also in Christ Jesus.

Philippians 2:5

During the terrible winter of '78 I was commuting to New York City to do research on a book at the microfilm section of the public library. After reading the pale green images all morning, everything seemed unreal. I got up dizzily to go to lunch. The writing hadn't been going well. I trudged through the snow-covered streets to a small Greek restaurant, the only cafe in the area. The place seemed lively: two quick, dark countermen and one older waitress, who was humming a song I didn't know. I ordered ham and eggs, and presently a very old man came in. He was a messenger, carrying three or four bulky manila-wrapped packages under his arms. He sat down with a long sigh.

"Hi, George," the waitress said. "How's the back today?"

"Not so good, not so good," he said. He took off a cheap vinyl cap and rubbed a leathery hand over his face and gray-black hair.

"How about some nice stew, George?"

He considered this a long moment, and I saw his hand feel in his pocket for change. "Just give me a glass of milk, my stomach ain't so good today."

The waitress went away, and came back with his milk and a steaming bowl of stew. She set the stew in front of me and drew a large soup spoon out of a tray with a flourish.

"Excuse me, Miss," I said. "I ordered ham and eggs."

"Didn't you say the special?" She turned around to the grill. "Oh, right, Eddie's got your over-easies on. Sorry." She started to take the stew away, and then turned back. "George, could you take this, else I gotta throw it out."

The old man considered for a moment, and then said, "Okay, I'll take it off your hands."

"Thanks, George," she said, "it goes against my nature to throw things out."

I went back through the cold streets to the cold green images, strangely warmed.

Lord, help us to do as You would do.

G.S.

20.

And whosoever shall give to drink unto one of these little ones a cup of cold water . . . he shall in no wise lose his reward.

Matthew 10:42

Sunday's edition of our local newspaper carried one of those tests which I invariably take—and flunk with equal regularity. This was no exception. ARE YOU CREATIVE? the title inquired. 1. *When did you last stuff a pillow?* (I never did!) 2. *Did you add*

your signature to a recent painting? (Signature? I can't paint!)
3. *Do you frequently, seldom,* or *never make pot slings?* (I'm not
even sure I know what they are.) I called a time-out before I
became despondent.

But it was a few minutes well spent, because I decided to
make a little test for myself. And I've had a wonderful week,
because here was one test I could pass. I passed it because,
knowing the questions in advance, I crammed!

1. How long has it been since I called _____ _____ (new
   name each day)?
2. Have I maintained a positive, cheerful attitude today?
3. Did I send out at least one thank-you note this week—
   even if it is "just for being my friend"?
4. Have I said (in *words*) to each member of my family: "I love
   you"?
5. Have I shared something with a person I knew was unable
   to reward me?
6. Have I prayed for my friends?
7. Have I given my most precious gifts: an encouraging word,
   a smile, a moment to listen to their needs?
8. Have I given graciously—without reserve?
9. Have I received as graciously as I have given?
10. Have I done all these things in the name of Jesus?

*Lord, teach me to add beauty to the lives of others with little
daily acts of kindness. Let the joy of serving be my reward.*

J.M.B.

21.

. . . And the fruit thereof shall be for meat,
and the leaf thereof for medicine.

Ezekiel 47:12

In 1952, Dr. Selman A. Waksman won the Nobel Prize for the
discovery of streptomycin. Shortly after that, I had the privilege
of interviewing Dr. Waksman in his laboratory at Rutgers University. The conversation went on longer than I expected. As
twilight fell early on the wintry afternoon, Dr. Waksman wandered over to a window and looked out at the fields beyond.

Then he asked: "Are you aware that the cures for all of man's ills are under our feet?"

I suggested: "Because you found streptomycin in rotted leaves?"

"Everything is there," he said, still gazing out the window. "Did you know that the name of the first man, Adam, is derived from the Hebrew word 'Adamah,' meaning earth? And do you know the verse from Ezekiel about medicines created out of the earth?"

"You make it sound so simple for the scientists," I said. "Just look down."

He turned and looked at me and shook his head. "That's what you do second," he said. "First you look up."

Lord, whatever man's ills, physical, mental or spiritual may be, help us always to remember that in seeking cures we must first of all look up.

G.D.K.

22.

Draw Thou my soul, O Christ, closer to Thine; Breathe into every wish Thy will divine!
Lucy Larcom hymn

The clock radio on the headboard of my bed will play for an hour and then shut off. What a delightful way to drift off to sleep.

Last night I climbed into bed, snapped the radio on, stretched and slipped down under the covers. The music faded. I reached to turn up the volume, but before I touched the radio the sound became louder. I moved my hand away; the music grew faint. Testing, I reached toward the radio again, then away. The swell and fall of the sound was in direct relation to the distance of my hand.

I don't understand much about electronics, but I realized that my moving close to the radio somehow increased its volume. To give out a truly clear, strong sound, the radio had to have my hand very close to it.

How like that radio our lives are. Once we are removed from the loving presence of Jesus, how weak and ineffectual we become! But by staying very close to Him we can, in some inexplicable way, draw strength and power from Him.

Father, help us to stay close to You, to draw strength from You and to be heard in Your behalf, strong and clear.

D.D.**

23.

Are not two sparrows sold for a penny? And not one of them will fall to the ground without your Father's will.

Matthew 10:29 (RSV)

Outside our window during the past winter was a feeder filled with seeds. Sparrows, especially, considered it their neighborhood hangout and came in flocks—chilled and famished—to the tray. When I replenished the supply, they fluttered to nearby, naked bushes, patiently waiting in hungry, huddled little humps.

Sparrows don't have brightly colored coats—just dingy, speckled, dirty-looking ones, I thought. *And their only song is "cheep-cheep." But the Lord surely must love them, He made so many.*

Now the little brown birds are poking piles of untidy grass and sticks into any open spot in garage or barn or under eaves. Some people find them a nuisance and shoo them away. Not me. They're my inspiration. I can't sing it like Ethel Waters, but I try. "I sing because I'm happy, I sing because I'm free, for His eye is on the sparrow, and I know He watches me."

I can't feel sorry or sad or insignificant when I know the King of Kings is watching over me.

Thank You, Lord, that You care about me, that I'm special and You never lose sight of me!

I.C.

24.

A certain Samaritan, as he journeyed, came where he was: and when he saw him, he had compassion on him.

Luke 10:33

Much has been written about the healing of memories, but it seems there is something to be said for unhealed ones. For instance, a friend was deeply humiliated as a child by never having proper clothes, and her wounds are still there. But out of this has come great compassion for every child she sees in rags.

So, ten years ago she opened the Perris Closet in three rent-free civic rooms, and contacted local churches for good, used clothing. They responded, and so did my church and several others here in nearby Sun City (California), which still contribute clothing, food, money, and most of the volunteer help. We clothe whole families, and in emergencies supply bedding and kitchen equipment. But children are still our main interest. Due to the desire of my friend to spare them the heartache she suffered—and still suffers through unhealed memories—thousands of them have been outfitted in new jeans and sneakers and shirts and dresses.

So if you have painful memories, believe now that your wounds have served their purpose in making you a more caring person. Your memories will remain, but they will no longer hurt. And you'll have in your heart the peace that Jesus promised.

Lord Jesus, let me remember that even the hurts of the past can work for good in the present.

L.R.

25.

Father, forgive them. . . .

Luke 23:34

Victor Hugo, the great French writer, once wrote a poem describing an episode in the life of his father, a general in the Napoleonic wars. One evening just at dusk, followed by a single gigantic hussar who was his personal aide, the general was riding across a battlefield in Spain. Dead and dying soldiers were everywhere, and from one badly-wounded Spaniard came a pitiful cry for water.

The general stopped, dismounted, and held a canteen to his enemy's lips. As he did so the man whipped out a concealed pistol and fired it in his benefactor's face. Incredibly, the bullet missed, passing through the general's hat. The hussar, enraged, unsheathed his sabre, but the general stopped him. "Give him a drink anyway," he said.

It's half a century, now, since I first read that poem, but I still remember it sometimes when I feel that I have been wronged or taken advantage of. To forgive someone who has clearly and unmistakably tried to hurt you is probably the most difficult of all spiritual disciplines. But Christ said we must do it. Not just once. Not just seven times. But seventy times seven.

Think about your worst enemy today. See if you can make a little progress toward forgiving him, or her.

Father, You forgave Your enemies here on earth. Show us how to forgive ours.

A.G.

26.

Jesus saith . . . , 'I am the way, the truth, and the life: no man cometh unto the Father, but by Me.'

John 14:6

Looking for a friend's home in a strange city, I became so turned around I finally stopped at a filling station to call him. "Stay where you are," he directed. "I'll come show you the way." Fifteen minutes later he appeared, waving and calling, "Follow me!"

As we wound our way through the complicated city I saw several tourist attractions I would have liked to stop and explore, and a large department store's "Going Out of Business" sign was almost irresistible. But convinced that without my friend to follow I'd get lost once more, I stayed close behind.

While we were stopped for a light, my eye caught his yellow bumper sticker: *I have decided to follow Jesus.*

Following Jesus is a lot like following my friend. As we wind our way through life, the way is unknown and frequently complicated. Tempting side trips beckon, suggesting we give up following Him for a moment here, a day there, a month or a year. Some of the world's bargains are almost irresistible! But our Leader calls, "Follow Me!"—And only He knows the way home.

Dear Lord, help me to follow You closely today.

P.H.S.

27.

Lord, who throughout these forty days,
For us didst fast and pray,
Teach us with Thee to mourn our sins,
And close by Thee to stay.

Lenten hymn

Last year about this time I dropped into a friend's house and discovered Sue's large canning kettle, steaming atop her stove. "*What* are you canning in February!"

"Actually I'm cooking glassware," Sue said. It seems she'd been reading about a process of heating and cooling called "annealing."

"Supposedly it softens glass and makes it stronger and less brittle. I'm annealing our drinking glasses—maybe they won't break so easily."

After I returned home, Sue's words still stuck in my mind. *Annealing makes things softer, stronger and less brittle.* During last Lenten season I'd been mentally wrestling with the merits of self-denial. *What good does it really do to give up favorite food or deny myself of something special?*

Giving up, denying myself and doing without for awhile could be my process of spiritual annealing to make me softer toward God, stronger in my faith and less brittle in my attitude toward others. (And it turned out it did.)

Tomorrow is Ash Wednesday—the first day of Lent. I'll humbly acknowledge and accept its annealing process in my life.

Father, my self-denials are small, but I ask You to use them and make me softer, stronger and less brittle toward You and Your children.

I.C.

28. (Ash Wednesday)
Surely, surely, he hath borne our griefs and carried our sorrows.

Isaiah 53:4

The young priest departed from the usual Ash Wednesday ritual by handing out sheets of paper with drawings of empty suitcases on them. After a prayer, he explained that all of us were weighted down with too much luggage. "What's in this luggage?" he asked. "Our mistakes, our regrets."

How well I understood him. My own shoulders seemed to be sagging with the weight of past errors. Then the priest asked us to write down our regrets. I wrote down 12.

We placed the sheets of paper in a metal container, and the priest lit them with a match. As the flames leapt up, I watched, and let each of my blunders dissolve in the smoke. My spirits lifted. With God's help, I had shed my burdens. As each of us approached the altar, the priest touched our foreheads with the blessed ashes and said, "Come to the Lord with all your heart; leave your past with the ashes."

For me, the Lenten season had begun.

In these next forty days, Lord, I cleanse my heart for the months ahead.

M.S.G.

MARCH 1979

S	M	T	W	T	F	S
				1	2	3
4	5	6	7	8	9	10
11	12	13	14	15	16	17
18	19	20	21	22	23	24
25	26	27	28	29	30	31

1.

. . . Christ is the head of the church: and He is the saviour of the body.

Ephesians 5:23

Seat belts—that was one of the minor battles a friend of mine used to wage with his rebellious teen-age daughter. Owen used them, but "They're too much bother," Sally used to say, priding herself on finding ways to outsmart their built-in buzzer.

Last summer in Vermont, I saw Sally again after a long time. What a change in her! She was married, she and her husband had a new baby, a new house, and had just joined a church. Getting into their car, I couldn't help but smile when I saw Sally ever so carefully strap the baby in the carseat and then automatically reach for her own seat belt.

I thought about that automatic gesture of hers this morning when a curious little item in the newspaper caught my eye: "Motorists who don't use seat belts are likely to be non-churchgoers," the article said, and then described a survey conducted at the Johns Hopkins School of Hygiene and Public Health. Non-seat-belt-users were found to neglect their physical as well as their spiritual welfare; they were less likely to visit

51

dentists and doctors. The report also noted that for one given year nearly 80 percent of motor vehicle fatalities involved the occupants of a moving vehicle. "Most of these," it said, "could have been prevented by the use of seat belts."

I wonder, Sally, when did you change your mind about seat belts? Was it when you were married? When the baby came? Or was it when you began to take your faith more seriously? When did you find out that people who love God value His creation; that people who like themselves, take care of themselves?

Lord, sometimes I am too careless with my life. I forget that it is not really mine, but Yours.

V. V.

2.

The Lord gave, and the Lord hath taken away; blessed be the name of the Lord.

Job 1:21

The letter lay, fragile and stained, on top of the pile. It was hard going through my mother's things. Missing her was still so new. I looked at the date. It had been written by a friend to my mother in 1939, shortly after my father died.

"Dear One," it began. "It hurts so terribly, doesn't it? Accept the pain if you can. Say, 'Yes, because I have loved and now lost, I must cry for a while. I must hold this ache of loneliness within myself and say, this is the price I pay for having loved. I will accept this price and pay it in gratitude for the love I was blessed to know, for I would not have wanted to be without that love. I will pay this price, God, and I thank You for the wonderful years we shared.'

"I think He must have cried on the day that His Son hung dead on the cross, don't you think so? Don't you think that because He, too, is familiar with tears, dear friend, He is especially close to you right now?

"I weep with you, and my love surrounds you. Please write and let me know your plans, and if there is anything at all I can do to help."

I folded the letter and slipped it back into the envelope, grateful for this healing message from the past. Thank you for the wonderful years, Mom, I whispered. Of all the women in the world, I'm so lucky *you* were the one God gave me. Yes, it was worth the price.

Thank You, God, for giving her to me. And for giving me Your Son. Such gifts are eternal.

D.H.

3.

. . .Whereby we cry, Abba, Father. The Spirit itself beareth witness with our spirit, that we are the children of God.

Romans 8:15,16

Recently I discovered that *abba* is one of the few Aramaic words known to have been actually spoken by Jesus Christ. That Jesus addressed God directly at all must have been shocking to His Jewish contemporaries, who held the name of the Lord so sacred and awesome as to be unspeakable. To use the word *abba*, as Jesus did, was *unthinkable*.

Abba is the familiar term used by Jewish sons and daughters in addressing their father, corresponding more to "daddy" than to the more formal "father." In addressing God as Abba, therefore, Jesus not only claimed His Sonship with God, but did so in the most intimate way! As children in Christ, it is our wonderful privilege—and obligation—to follow His example.

Dear Abba, I love You. How wonderful to be Your child.

K.B.

4.

All good gifts around us
Are sent from Heaven above;
Then thank the Lord, O thank the Lord
For all His love.

Matthias Claudius hymn

The blustery day only added to the high spirits of the children, making them as restless as the wind. The day worsened as the older boys, four and six years old, fought or begged to go to the beach and the baby fretted with teething difficulties.

For the tenth time, it seemed, I said, irritably and too loudly, "Please go outside." Then as they finally did go, I yelled after them, "But stay close to the house." We lived beside the large parking lot of a grocery store and I worried about their safety.

Thankful for the peace, I hurried about catching up on chores. Suddenly I realized that things were too quiet. I ran to the door and saw all three boys playing quietly in a large box which was not there earlier.

"Look, Mom," Clay shouted. "Jesus sent us a box."

At first I was tempted to explain that the wind must have brought it from the store. Then I was ashamed. How seldom I give Jesus credit for the everyday pleasures of life. A child's expression of gratitude caused me to say a prayer as I went back to my work with a light step.

Thank You, Jesus, for children, the wind and boxes.

R. D. R.

5.
See to it, then, that all your seeds
Be such as bring forth noble deeds.
John Oxenham

Did you ever notice how, when one car breaks the speed limit, other motorists tend to follow suit? Just last week I noticed that I began to creep up over the limit after I had been passed by a fast driver.

Sometimes I'm tempted into the false notion that what I do is my business alone—"If I want to speed, it's my business, and I'll bear the consequences." But it's *not* my business, alone. If I break the law by speeding, I might not get caught, but someone else nearby, by imitating me, might. Or, if he were an inexperienced driver, my bad example could result in an accident.

Jesus said, "Let your light so shine before men, that they may see your good works, and glorify your Father which is in Heaven." (Matthew 5:16) I try to test all my acts against this command. I may not be responsible for all the actions of others, but I am responsible for those actions that my behavior influences.

Father, let my light shine today, and every day.

B.R.G.

6. When one door closes, another opens but we often look so long and so regretfully upon the closed door that we do not see the one which has opened for us.

Alexander Graham Bell

As a child, Evelyn Sass had a promising singing voice and was often called upon to sing the solo parts in church and school productions. With her teacher's encouragement, she began to dream of a musical career.

Then, suddenly, in her early teens, through a series of illnesses, Evelyn lost her hearing totally. The dream of becoming a singer died. She became depressed and withdrawn, spending long hours alone, until one day her teacher came to visit.

"You know, Evelyn," the teacher said, "God gave us five senses. You still have four of them. I challenge you to concentrate on one of these. See if you can't develop it beyond the norm so that what you gain in one offsets the loss in another."

Evelyn did. She chose sight, and she worked and worked at it until she had developed such a remarkable skill at lipreading that in 1930 she won the National Lipreading Tournament held in New York City. In addition she went on to have a successful business career, married, and bore a daughter—me.

I'm proud of my mother—and I know what she went through because I also have a hearing problem and rely on lipreading. And like my mother I have come to know that there are many doors in this life. What a waste of time it is to keep on staring at a door you know cannot be opened. And how exciting it is to find the one that God swings wide for you!

Father, thank You for opening my eyes to the thrilling opportunities You set before us.

E.V.S.

7.

. . . I am the light of the world.

One day I took my small daughter to a bookstore where she bought a little luminous flower for her bedroom. "It lights up in the dark," I assured her as she held this treasure securely in a box. "Before you go to sleep, look at it and it will be glowing."

But the following morning she stood beside my bed with the flower in her hands. "It didn't shine," she whimpered, her face crestfallen . . . "not once!" And I remembered we had forgotten to "charge" it. That morning we placed it in the warm sunlight outside and all day it absorbed the sun. The following night the flower glowed on the table beside her bed.

Often I remember that morning. It taught me a deep lesson. I must lift everything up to Jesus Christ—my marriage, children, friends, health, finances, my church, missions, our country's President—even the impossibles I must "expose" to Him, so that His light will lend them His radiance.

Today, Lord, I know You are "the God Who is enough" for everything. There is no place where Your light cannot shine.

H.B.F.

8.

Sufficient unto the day is the evil thereof.

My husband's job had taken us to a strange city where neither of us knew anyone. I had left behind wonderful friends, a cozy home, a job I loved. Even my furniture looked uncomfortable in the midst of all this unfamiliarity. Home alone, I was falling into a deep depression.

As I sorted listlessly through the morning mail, I came upon the alumnae magazine of my old college. In it was a meditation by an unknown author.

"There are three days in the week," it began, "about which I never worry. One is yesterday. Yesterday with its cares and worries, its pains and aches, its mistakes and failures, has passed forever beyond my recall. It was mine; now it is God's.

"The second is tomorrow. Tomorrow with all its possible blunders, its burdens, it dangers, and promises, is as far removed from me as its dead sister yesterday. Tomorrow is also God's, because it is still in His keeping.

"There is left for myself one day in the week. *Today*. Anyone can carry the burdens or resist the temptations of one day. It is only when we add the burdens of those two eternities, yesterday and tomorrow, that we break under the pressure of daily living. It isn't the experiences of today that bring frustration. It is the remorse for what happened yesterday, and the fear of what tomorrow might bring. These are God's days. Let's leave them to Him."

My depression lifted instantly. *Of course*, I thought, *how true!* And I felt a surge of gratitude to the Lord Who always has a way of sending a message when I'm down.

Each day that I live in Your name, Lord, I know that You'll never give me more than I can handle. Today I give thanks for this blessed assurance.

M.S.G.

9. And He walks with me, and He talks with me . . .

C. Austin Miles

The afternoon before my daughter's school play, Karen was suddenly seized by an attack of stage fright. I thought of suggesting that she study her lines some more, but I changed my mind. We went for a silent walk, instead. We agreed not to talk, but we stopped to pet a dog, picked up a few unusually pretty stones on a graveled road, smelled some lilacs and watched the sky turn from a bright glare to a soft, restful pumpkin color. When we got home, Karen was relaxed. The stage fright was gone, the play went well and she had discovered a very effective tranquilizer—one that can't be purchased in any pharmacy.

If you're feeling nervous about something today, put on your coat, tell your family or co-workers you'll be back in a few minutes and take a walk with Jesus. As you walk, meditate on His words, "Peace I leave with you, My peace I give unto you." (John 14:27) Silently repeat the words over and over as you walk, letting their truth flow gently through you. Try it. You'll be surprised at how self-composed you'll feel when you get back to your daily tasks.

As we walk together, Lord, teach me to know, in my very bones, that the only peace that's lasting is the peace that comes from You.

M.M.H.

10. . . . Be ye not unwise, but understanding what the will of the Lord is.

Ephesians 5:17

Whenever despairing patients ask Dr. Samuel Rosen of New York City if he can restore their hearing, he always says, "If God is willing."

Once, asked why he used that phrase so constantly, he replied, "When my parents prayed, their prayer always ended with 'If God is willing.' That became a cornerstone of my faith and my work."

Dr. Rosen, the son of immigrants, developed the surgical technique that eliminates otosclerosis, a form of deafness. The search took ten years of tenacious and often frustrating effort. In the end he succeeded.

"If God is willing" is a phrase of great power. Try using this expression of faith the next time you are faced with some important task or undertaking. It puts you in partnership with the Eternal.

Lord, give us the wisdom to seek Your will and then do our best to follow it.

S.F.

11.

Doing an injury puts you below your enemy; revenging one makes you but even with him; forgiving it sets you above him.

Benjamin Franklin

Thirty years ago a family in our church suffered a great loss. Their seven-year-old son was hit and killed by a car. The child had run without looking into the car's path.

Deeply distressed, the young driver forced himself to come to the funeral home. There, overcome with grief, he broke down in tears. The bereaved father, tears also flowing down his cheeks, walked over and embraced the driver. "Don't blame yourself," he said, "it wasn't your fault."

I was just a young girl at that time, but I never forgot that scene. How often in life I've seen people "getting even" with others, sometimes for deliberate injuries, and at other times for unintentional slights. Jesus knew that grudge-holders hurt themselves more than anyone else. That's why He said, "If ye forgive not men their trespasses, neither will your Father forgive your trespasses." (Matthew 6:15)

Father, teach me the healing lesson of forgiveness.

B.R.G.

12.

No legacy is so rich as honesty.

William Shakespeare

The little old lady ahead of me at the drugstore check-out counter must have been approaching 80. She explained that she had purchased a small book for twenty-five cents the day before and now had come back to buy another for a friend. As the clerk wrapped the package, the lady noticed the price was thirty-five cents. "But I only paid a quarter yesterday," she said. The clerk was kind but firm. "No ma'am, the price has been the same all week."

The old woman dug into her ancient handbag and came out

with the correct change. "I'm sorry I was such a bother," she smiled at the clerk and left.

I stepped forward to pay for my purchase when suddenly the lady reappeared. She looked at me and apologized saying, "I'm sorry to interrupt you, but I still owe the store a dime for the book I bought yesterday."

"Oh, no, that's all right," the clerk said, trying to refuse the dime. The old lady was insistent. "It's the only honest thing to do."

"That's right," I said, "it always pays to be honest."

"Oh, no," the lady answered. "It costs to be honest. It just cost me a dime." Then she added, "But Jesus loves us when we're honest."

How right you are, little lady, how right you are! The more it costs me when I'm honest, Lord, the more I know You love me.

J.B.

13.

Call unto Me, and I will answer thee. . . .
Jeremiah 33:3

Mrs. Baxter and I were waiting while our 16-year-olds took written tests for driver's license learner's permits. We'd known each other casually from numerous PTA meetings over the years.

"My husband and I always worry when they first start driving," she said. "We just tell them one thing: Call us if you get in trouble. Doesn't matter how late it is. Just call us. We'll come and help."

I nodded. "We say that in our house, too."

Our kids finished their tests and walked out together. Mrs. Baxter and I followed, acting braver than we were about having another teen-age driver in the family.

A moment later we came to the corner and saw the sign on the church's outdoor registry:

"God is your Heavenly Father. Call home."

Mrs. Baxter and I looked at each other. "No matter how late it is," I murmured.

Mrs. Baxter smiled. "Yes," was all she said.

Our fledglings fly, Lord. Life moves on—as it should. How comforting to know that no matter what point we arrive at in life, You are already there.

C.A.

14.

Therefore if any man be in Christ, he is a new creature: old things are passed away; behold, all things are become new.

II Corinthians 5:17

There's a legend behind Leonardo Da Vinci's painting of "The Last Supper" almost as fascinating as the famous masterpiece itself.

According to this story, Da Vinci searched for and interviewed hundreds before finding a suitable model for Christ, whom he wanted to paint first. Finally a 19-year-old with an innocent face was selected. This figure took six months to complete.

During the next six years the great painter chose other models to represent each of the 11 apostles, saving space for Judas in the picture because he was unable to find a hard, callous face which looked like a betrayer of the Son of God.

Eventually a Roman dungeon furnished such a man. Using this prisoner's evil face as a model, Da Vinci finished his famous painting. As the prisoner was led away, he cried out, "Oh, Da Vinci, how low I've sunk; I am the *same* man you painted seven years ago as the figure of Christ!"

Sin allowed in a life shows in the face. And yet Christ allowed in a life also shows in the face.

Father, help me make the moral choices that will reflect the glowing evidence of the Holy Spirit within.

I.C.

FIVE STEPS TO MORE EFFECTIVE MEDITATION

We all yearn for quiet moments of reflection in which we can grow spiritually. Why not consider these five "P's" as you work out your own meaningful program of meditation.

PREPARE: Choose a time and place where you won't be interrupted. Be comfortable. Choose a topic carefully. Any Scriptural episode from Jesus' life is a fruitful choice, for instance. The selected passages should never be long, just three or four verses, if the deeper levels of meaning are to come forth. If your mind sparks to the concrete rather than the abstract, choose an object rather than an idea; a flower, a snowflake, a star. See it as the creation of God which will contain hints to His nature.

Do not meditate for less than 15 minutes. Your attention span will increase with practice.

PONDER: To be true meditation, your thoughts must have direction and pattern; they should not wander. If you are meditating on a flower, observe not only color, form and height, but ask who planted it, how the seedling made its way to the light, whether there is purpose to beauty. If it's Scripture you're pondering, take the significant words one by one until each yields its less obvious meaning. Ask God for His special word to you as revealed in the particle of truth you've just been examining.

PERSIST: The hardest thing about meditation is keeping your mind from wandering. When your thoughts roam, try to bring them back without fuss, for annoyance with yourself is just another distraction.

PRAISE: Thank Him for your new insights, the deeper love you feel for Him.

PROMISE: At some point in your meditation, God may well call you to action by moving you to write a letter, call someone, apologize to a friend. Promise God that you will act on these things. Your meditation will not be complete unless you do.

E.S.

16.

Through the storm, through the night
Lead me on to the light.
Take my hand, precious Lord,
Lead me home.

Thomas A. Dorsey hymn

Did you ever notice how a happy cat isn't satisfied unless it's touching you? Baby, our new chocolate brown Burmese, is no exception. He came to us when a friend was transferred abroad to a country with strict quarantine laws. We agreed to give him a new home. Lonely for his old family, and afraid of his new surroundings, Baby wouldn't come near us for two days. He'd hide under the sofa, until we pulled him out and stroked him time and again, convincing him we were friends. Now he isn't content to sit alone under the sofa. He must rub against our legs, or curl up on top of us, rubbing his head against whatever part of us he can reach. The contact is his way of saying, "I like you."

People need the security of a touch, too. If I visit a sick friend in the hospital, she may be glad to have company; but if I hold her hand, the bond of friendship is much stronger. Some of my strength may flow through the touch and help her to feel better. I can stand up straight and tell my son that I love him, but if I stoop to put my arm around him, he knows I mean it. Sometimes a simple touch can heal hurt feelings or straighten out a misunderstanding without a word.

Jesus went from town to town touching people—healing them, encouraging them, loving them. One woman found new life by touching merely the hem of His robe. His arms are ever outstretched to you and me. Take His hand today, and that of someone near you, and let His love flow through.

Lord, help me to draw near enough to touch someone today so that Your love can be felt in the touch.

B. R. G.

17.

(St. Patrick's Day)
Holy, holy, holy, merciful and mighty!
God in Three Persons, blessed Trinity.
                                    Reginald Heber hymn

"There are a lot of things that I know, but that I don't understand," a friend said to me one day. "And one of them is the Trinity. How can God be three separate beings and yet remain a single entity? It staggers my mind!"

It staggered my mind, also. In fact, it continues to do so—trying to comprehend how the Father, the Son and the Holy Spirit—completely different—can be God, Omnipotent, Omnipresent and Omniscient.

It helps to read about Ireland's patron saint. Apparently St. Patrick's students had expressed the same concern. In explanation he plucked a shamrock and said, "The Trinity is like this shamrock." He pointed to its three leaves, each one distinct and separate yet all growing from a single stem.

I think of St. Patrick's shamrock whenever I wonder about the Three-in-One. Its simplicity gives me faith to believe in the mysterious complexity of the Trinity—something I know, but don't understand.

Father, thank You that You never said we had to understand Your ways—which are too much for our human comprehension. All You asked us to do is to faithfully believe Your marvelous words and leave the rest up to You.

                                                        I.C.

18.

I will bless the Lord at all times. . . .
                                    Psalm 34:1

Philip was not the brightest boy in my Sunday-school class, but his imagination was fired by the stories of King David. Full of enthusiasm he set out to write his own life story of the shepherd king. Sadly, his abilities were not up to the task. For a long time he chewed his pen; then his face cleared.

"A *lot* of things happened to King David," he wrote. "But no matter if they was good or bad he went strate off and made up a plasm about them."

Philip's spelling left much to be desired, but his artless words made me wonder: Do *I* bring all the happenings of my life— good and bad—to God? Only as I learn that He cares about the ups and down of my every day, can I begin to turn prayers into psalms.

Father, a lot of things happen to me every day, just as they did to King David. Help me bring them all to You, just as he did.

G.K.

19.
Turn your eyes upon Jesus,
Look full in His wonderful face
And the things of earth will grow strangely dim
In the light of His glory and grace.
Helen Howarth Lemmel hymn

I don't know anyone who loves children more than my sister, Hazel. She just bubbles whenever she is near any small child. No one could have been more thrilled than she was when her first son arrived. And the children she comes in contact with are drawn to her like pins to a magnet. She doesn't do anything special, but they seem to sense something that makes them want to be near her.

I used to wonder what that special something was, until one morning I watched her feed cereal to her two-year-old son, Bobby. She was talking to him with each bite, the same as I did with my own children. But all of a sudden Bobby put his finger on Hazel's magic. He stopped eating and pointed at his mother. "Mommy," he said, "I see Jesus in your eyes."

When we truly love someone, it can't be hidden. It shines out in our eyes for all to see. When Christ is in our heart, His love shines out to the world. Bobby saw Christ's love in Hazel's eyes.

What reflects in my eyes today, and in yours? Are we letting God speak to others through us? Or by our actions, are we turning Him away? We can let His love shine out, just by letting those around us know we care.

Dear God, let Your love shine through me today, so that others who see it may claim it for themselves.

B.R.G.

20.

. . .I am the Lord that healeth thee.

Exodus 15:26

Some years ago in Washington, D.C., I developed a very severe case of asthma. Whenever we had a day of heavy air pollution, I could barely breathe. We finally had to get an electric-pressured inhalator which forced medicated air into my lungs. I tired very easily. Even taking a walk became almost impossible.

One day after having done all I, or the doctor, could do, I knelt beside my bed. "All right, Lord," I said. "I've done all I can. If I must have asthma, okay. But please give me a sweet and cheerful disposition to go with it. Help me not to burden my family or friends with complaints. I accept whatever You send me."

Hard to know when it happened, but I needed the breathing machine less and less. By that summer, I could swim several widths of a pool again, and my doctor found no wheezing on subsequent check-ups.

Looking back, I suspect Jesus has a sense of humor. Faced with the request of granting a sweet disposition or healing an illness, He, in my case, found the latter an easier task.

Seriously, I've been deeply grateful for that answered prayer. Now when friends ask what became of my breathing problem, I answer, "I gave it to Jesus."

You've made it clear to me, Lord, that to receive Your healing power we must first turn our problems over to You.

M.S.G.

21.

There is one glory of the sun, and another glory of the moon, and another glory of the stars: for one star differeth from another star in glory.

I Corinthians 15:41

Do you remember the first time in your life when you found you were different from other people? Did you like it? The particular moment I recall was back in the first grade, and I didn't like it one bit. The teacher had asked us to bring our own jars of paste to school. Trouble was, every other kid had a jar with a blue label on it, but somehow my mother had bought me a different brand, one with an orange label. It sounds silly, but suddenly I was out of step, different, and to my youthful mind, inferior. It was painful.

I thought of this recently as I talked with the lovely singer, Princess Pale Moon. How much worse it was for her. Pale Moon is a Cherokee Indian whose family chose to bring her up in the city of Asheville, North Carolina, rather than on the large Cherokee reservation nearby. The kids at her school, with that cruel streak that children can show, often taunted her for being a "redskin." For hours she'd stand before the bathroom mirror trying to scrub the color out of her face. As the years passed, she suffered increasingly from the terrible pain of being different.

Then Jesus came into her life, and the hurt went away.

"You see, I had it all figured backwards," she told me. "When other people did not accept me, I thought I was not accepted by God. But once I knew that Jesus loved me, it didn't matter what other people thought. I was free, free even to love those who didn't love me. And from that time on, being a Cherokee Indian has been my special glory."

Oh, to be able to go back to the first grade, to stand up in Miss Jean Simenon's class and say, "Look at what I have, a very special orange-labeled jar of paste!"

Thank You, Father. How exciting it is to be the person You created.

V. V.

22.

How to have a good day: "Sprinkle" some love and faith on the clothes you are washing and ironing.

Norman Vincent Peale

Sometimes, when I hear my friends complaining about the ironing they have to do, my mind goes back to my childhood and the afternoons I spent watching my mother iron. I remember the clean, cosy kitchen and the smell of freshly-laundered clothes.

I'd sit quietly on a stool watching my mother's deft hands turning a mundane task into a thing of love and beauty.

There—she's ironing my slip now—look how gently she handles it. First long, expansive sweeps of the iron on the flat part and then careful little pats on the delicate lace. There's Grandmother's tea apron—how stiff each starched ruffle is. And now Dad's shirts—magically turning from a rumpled heap into a crisp, rectangular stack, each fold love-patted into place.

From the way Mother ironed, I knew she loved us because I could see that love flowing through her iron into the clothes we wore. To this day, that picture of Mother ironing reminds me that love can be expressed in countless ways as we go about our daily tasks.

Lord, let me "sprinkle" a little love today.

M. W.

23.

Having then gifts differing according to the grace that is given to us. . . .

Romans 12:6

At a recent orchestra concert, I sat next to a writer friend whom I hadn't seen for several years, and I'll have to admit that I felt a bit of a twinge when she named off some of the prestigious publications her work had appeared in. We aren't in competition because our areas of writing are different, but I still felt a little overawed by her outstanding success.

As the music started up again, though, with the inspiring strains of Bach's "Jesu, Joy of Man's Desiring," I felt soothed. I knew that the conductor had the complete score in front of him and knew exactly what each player should be doing in order to blend perfectly with the whole. Yet each orchestra member had only one part in front of him—his own. The players didn't look to one another for their cues or compare parts. They watched only the conductor, so that each contributed his own special tones, according to the composer's plan.

How foolish I had been to compare my writing achievements

with someone else's! If I can just keep my attention focused on Jesus, my own special notes will contribute to the harmony of the whole. That's all I need to do.

Lord, You've given me a unique part to play in this world—and I'm grateful.

M.M.H.

24.

For this my son was dead, and is alive again; he was lost, and is found.

Luke 15:24

"My son is a nonbeliever," a mother told me, sadly. "He's spiritually lost, and I can't reach him. Please pray for him."

I promised I would pray for him, and I did, in a rather desultory manner. I was praying for him as I waved goodbye to her, as I later washed dishes, and in my regular prayer time.

But I remembered a day when my first-born was physically lost. He was only a toddler. He had been playing on the porch. I suddenly realized that he was gone. I didn't know how long he had been gone, or what direction he had taken. Immediately, I thought of a hundred places where he could get hurt. I called for all the help I could get, and began to search. None of the work I had to do mattered now. All was forgotten. I could think only one prayer, and I prayed it over and over, with an awful urgency. I didn't stop for a moment until I found my son. He had come into the house and gone into a closet to play in a big box there. He was asleep, curled down in the box.

My son was lost for nearly a half hour. Her son, unless He receives Jesus as Savior, will be eternally lost. Many people, like him, seek direction, seek answers, in this world of turmoil. They hunger for a better way of life, and we Christians can tell them how to find it. Many might be saved if their neighbors put forth some effort. Many wait, needing personal, concerned testimony.

Suddenly I felt a tremendous urge to go into a quiet room, to fall on my knees, and to really pray, to pray for that boy as desperately as I had prayed for my little lost son.

O my Father, if there is one word I can say, one thing I can do, to help a lost soul, help me to say it. Help me to do it.

L.C.

25.

Work, and thou wilt bless the day
Ere the toil be done;
They that work not, cannot pray,
Cannot feel the sun.

J.S. Dwight

It was Sunday. I was trying to get ready for church. My two-year-old son had just spilled his dump truck load of dirt onto my newly-swept kitchen floor. The baby was crying. The phone rang. My sister-in-law calling to say she was dropping over (at dinner time). My Saturday ironing was still piled on the ironing board in the living room.

The floor had to be swept. Again. I didn't want to sweep it. I won't, I decided. Once is enough! Defiantly I put a kitchen stool over the little brown pile so it wouldn't be tracked into my carpeting.

I frowned at my four-year-old daughter as she bounced through the door, returning from Sunday school.

"Look," she cried happily. "Look what I got." She held up a partly-crayoned picture of Mary, mother of Jesus.

"It's a picture of a Mommy. Just like you!"

I looked down at a smiling young woman in flowing dress, sweeping a little pile of wood shavings outside through her curtained door. My angry thoughts were silenced.

"No, honey," I answered. "Not like me."

Returning to the kitchen I looked at the small mound of dirt. Carefully I swept it into the dustpan.

Lord, thank You for honoring me with this home and this family to love and care for.

D.H.

26.

Rejoice in the Lord always: and again I say, Rejoice.

Philippians 4:4

For years a couple in my home town talked about a trip they planned to the Grand Canyon. But each year, for one reason or another, they kept putting it off. They delayed and delayed until finally the husband became too ill to travel. Result:They never got to go at all.

Isn't it unwise to keep postponing the things we really want to do? Of course it is! And I've learned that the same is true of knowing Jesus Christ. It is not enough to say that one day in the future I will find the time to receive the blessings of His presence. If I am to live my life to the fullest, I must know, serve and enjoy Him every day, beginning now.

Teach me, dear Lord, not to take chances with my own eternal life.

D.D.**

27.

Whosoever drinketh of the water that I shall give him shall never thirst. . .

John 4:14

The mighty Amazon begins in the Andes and, with its many tributaries, drains the largest land mass in the world. Its force, as it flows 2500 miles to the sea, is one of nature's wonders.

In their small boats, Brazilian fishermen sometimes venture far offshore. During World War II, the story goes, two fishermen, out of sight of land, sighted a drifting lifeboat—evidently the result of a submarine attack.

As they approached the lifeboat the lone occupant aboard moaned and whispered, "Water . . . water!"

One of the fishermen climbed into the lifeboat, filled a bucket from the sea and held it up to the parched lips. The emaciated man's eyes were filled with both gratitude and wonder, for the water was cool and sweet. Salvation had been at his fingertips all the while he drifted. For the Amazon flows far out into the

Atlantic Ocean, its volume and force pushing aside the salt water.

So it is in all aspects of our lives. When we need Jesus Christ most, He is as near as our reach is long—whether on the vast expanse of His seas or in the quiet of our room.

All you need to do is to lower your bucket.

Father, teach us to know that Your healing presence is always available to us, no matter what the situation may be.

W. H.

28.

I know a place where the sun is like gold
And cherry trees burst with snow. . . .
Old song

At the bottom of our farm and across the levee there is a sheltered nook beside the creek where the first violets, anemones and deer-tongue lilies bloom. There is moss there and grapevine swings for the children; and wild birds and squirrels build nests there. My young husband and I discovered it long ago and christened it "Fairy Land," and each of our four children was introduced early to the charmed spot when the snow had melted and the earth was warm. Now that they are grown they come trooping back when the first violets show. We pack a lunch and set off in a wagon behind the tractor to rediscover "Fairy Land" and almost-forgotten dreams.

Is there such a favorite place in your own memories? If the days seem dark around you, why not revisit it in your imagination and visualize yourself meeting Jesus there. Just share the whole scene quietly with Him. Imagine yourself sitting at His feet. Peace and tranquility will flow to you. His light will chase your shadows away.

Lord, we could not have found You if no one had told us of Your love. Thank You for radiant Christians who light the way for others.

M. M.

29.

The setting sun is reflected from the windows of the almshouse as brightly as from a rich man's abode.

Henry David Thoreau

As I prepared the ground for my zinnias last spring, I unearthed an Indian arrowhead. "Look at my treasure," I cried, "I found it on our own land."

"Our land for now," my husband said. "Yesterday it belonged to the Indians. Tomorrow it will belong to somebody else."

Back outdoors on my knees in the soil, I pondered this business of ownership. What did anyone *really* own?

A wren began warbling just then, over and over again from the neighbor's yard. I sat back on my heels listening to the concert. Suddenly a new thought: That little wren's song belonged to me, even though it came from my neighbor's yard. Bird songs belong to all who hear them. The grace and sweep of all the stately trees and the scent of all the luscious flowering blooms belongs to those who behold and smell them. Sunshine warming my back belongs to everyone it shines upon. And rain and wind and snow and rivers and oh, so many many wonders! They're all mine!

All of God's creations belong to all of His creatures. Actually, for as long as we are on this earth, we each own the whole universe.

Help me, Heavenly Father, not to let deeds and fences trick me into forgetting the glorious bountifulness of Thy all-inclusive plan for my sojourn here on earth.

R.H.F.

30.

Ye are our epistle written in our hearts. . . .

II Corinthians 3:2

At a recent prayer retreat, we were asked to meditate on a passage of Scripture and then share the personal message we got from it. When I told what God had said to me through the passage I'd read, the lady next to me said, "I read the same one and got a completely different message!"

When she shared her insights, we agreed that both were valid. How could that be? Was it possible that there could be more than one right interpretation of a Bible passage? Then it hit me: Of course! The Word is alive! It is God speaking to me now. He may say one thing to me and another to you in the same passage, and that's all right! How much more personal the Bible seems to me now. It's like getting a letter in the mail written just for me, instead of a form letter that says the same thing to everyone.

The next time you find yourself questioning someone else's interpretation of a Bible passage, remind yourself to be thankful that God doesn't send form letters.

Thank You, Lord, for Your personal message to me.

M.M.H.

31.

For mem'ry has painted this perfect day
With colors that never fade,
And we find at the end of a perfect day
The soul of a friend we've made.

Carrie Jacobs Bond

Want to have a perfect day today? These six short rules have worked for me; you might wish to follow them today:

Try to strengthen your mind by reading something that requires effort, thought and concentration.

Try to do somebody a good turn and not get found out.

Try to do a task that needs to be done, but which you have been putting off.

Try to go for one full day without finding fault in anything.

Try to have a quiet half hour by yourself. Think of God, read the Bible; you'll get a little more perspective in your life.

And finally, don't be afraid to be happy, enjoy what is beautiful, believe that those you love, love you.

You'll have a perfect day. I'll guarantee it.

Dear Father, please help me concentrate on today and not worry about tomorrow or yesterday. Help me follow these rules for a perfect day.

N.V.P.

APRIL 1979

S	M	T	W	T	F	S
1	2	3	4	5	6	7
8	9	10	11	12	13	14
15	16	17	18	19	20	21
22	23	24	25	26	27	28
29	30					

1.

Consider the lilies of the field, how they grow. . . .

Matthew 6:28

"Aren't they beautiful?" I gazed at the lilies-of-the-valley carpeting my father-in-law's garden, their fragile white bells scenting the air.

"Dratted things have taken over the place; can't keep 'em down," Dad grumbled, showing me the tough, invasive roots. "Still, may as well bunch some for market."

Each year after that the flowers made a nice sum of money which Dad put straight into his church offering. Oh, there was one spring when the whole crop was spread in profusion around the room of a sick child, and once they graced the church for a family wedding.

Dad's been in Heaven some time now, but recently I passed the block of shops that replaced the old home. And there in the concrete loading-bay was something green, thrusting through a crack.

"Can't keep 'em down," Dad had said. *Like love*, I thought. Or kindness, or generosity—any of the lovely virtues that sweeten life with their beauty.

Thank You, Lord, that Your love thrusts even through the hard heart. Let it bloom there, to answer another's need.

G.K.

2. How beautiful to walk in the steps of the Saviour, stepping in the light . . .
E.E. Hewitt

Do you remember that old hymn? Whenever I hear it I think of my childhood on the farm and how, when Daddy did the spring plowing, I'd follow him down the furrows, gingerly placing bare feet in his wide damp-earth tracks.

I remember how one day in particular Daddy was trying to finish a field in preparation for seeding cotton the following day. My legs were aching from the long back-and-forth journeys and my eyes were heavy as we watched the sun set with a last burst of brightness. Twilight came and it was harder for my legs to match Daddy's steady stride, but, doggedly, I kept at the task of "helping Daddy finish." And then it was dark! My father had one last round to make, but I was unable to follow. Our faithful plough horse knew the way and Daddy let the lamplight of our kitchen guide him. "But I can't see your tracks," I sobbed.

"Honey," he said, "just follow the lamplight. You'll know which way I've gone."

The little incident has remained a spiritual lantern for me all my life. Jesus, too, "put His hand to the plow" to prepare the earth for seeding and harvest. It's up to us to follow His tracks in the light of His example—remembering all the while that others are following ours.

Lord, lead us to the many mansions of Your perfect love; and let our ways create a path of light.

J.M.B.

3.

God is our refuge and strength, a very present help in trouble.

Psalm 46:1

A man, a thief, was executed for his crimes. To his amazement, as he hung on a cross wracked with pain, mocked by a jeering crowd, he turned and found the Son of God right there beside him on the next tree.

Sometimes God feels very far away. We've gotten so out of touch with Him that we assume He is out of touch with us. But when we turn, we discover that God is right there, next to us wherever we are, sharing our pain and inviting us Home.

Thank You, Lord, for being near us even when we ignore or betray Your love.

P.H.S.

4.

. . . The sheep follow him; for they know his voice.

John 10:4

Someone gave my youngest son an orphan baby lamb. Since he works and goes to school, too, the chore of feeding Cuddles became mine. One night when the lamb was about three weeks old, my husband, Rex, and I were going out for the evening. I was rushing about trying to do my work and get ready to go. The lamb was crying for her bottle from her pen.

"We'll be late!" Rex warned.

"But I'm not ready, and Cuddles is starving. I have to take her a bottle."

"Give me the bottle. I'll do that," he said impatiently. He strode to the pen, hurriedly thrusting out the bottle of warm milk. "Here, lambie; here, lambie," he rumbled.

But his was not the right voice. The small sheep stopped in her mad dash to reach the bottle. She shook her head in anger and suspicion, stamped small impatient feet. When Rex held the bottle closer to tempt her, she retreated just as far as she could. She ate only when I came and called her with the right voice.

Jesus is my Master. I long to respond as faithfully to His voice. Other voices speak to us, some of them well-intentioned, but only His leads us to eternal life.

Thank You so much, Father, that You keep calling until I hear You.

L.C.

5.

And as they came out, they found a man of Cyrene, Simon by name: him they compelled to bear His cross.

Matthew 27:32

The obscure people that flash across the drama of the Bible always fascinate me. Simon of Cyrene was one—a visitor from a rural Roman province in Africa who happened to be in the big city of Jerusalem during the events of Christ's passion. Simon was a family man, Mark's gospel suggests. A country boy, perhaps. Simon wasn't really "anybody" until the unexpected moment when the cross was thrust upon him.

Some people look to heroic figures like Peter or Paul to show them how to lead a Christian life. Yet somehow I feel closer to Simon, because I know that like him, in a far smaller way, I too will be called upon to carry crosses from time to time. Unexpectedly. Without warning. And I pray that I may bear these small crosses—the ordinary, humble burdens of life—as well as I'm able.

Dear Lord, when life's crosses weigh us down, give us the courage to bear them—as Simon did—for Your sake.

E.G.

6.

And we know that all things work together for good to them that love God....

Romans 8:28

Recently I attended a meeting where the speaker passed around pads of paper and asked us to chart our life lines.

"Draw a straight, horizontal line," he told us, "for those periods when your life has run smoothly." Then we were told to dip the line to show the low times, when life had lacked zest, caused perhaps by illness, separations, disappointments, conflicts. Conversely, graduations, weddings, travel, achievements—euphoric moments—were to be shown in peaks.

I half-shielded my paper with my arm as I drew because I discovered so many downs in my life. Somehow I thought that other people would have more peaks and fewer depths than I. When we held up our finished papers, however, I was surprised. All our graphs zigged downward with considerable frequency!

That little experiment reminded me that, of course, I was not the only one to run into a lot of bumps along the way. But it also made me think that if I didn't have the dips, then I wouldn't have those beautiful heights. Why, how utterly boring a straight line would be! And how comforting it is to know that whether my life be a matter of highs or lows or dull straight lines, all the lines come together for good because I love the Lord.

I am grateful, Father, for the mountains You have given me, and for the valleys, too.

M.B.D.*

7.

. . . It is finished. . . .
John 19:30

Typing the Good Friday bulletin for Epiphany Lutheran Church, where I work as secretary, I read the explanation of Christ's sixth word on the cross. For me, Good Friday has always been a day of sadness, a day to dwell on the suffering and death of my Savior, reserving joy for Easter. In my mind I'd pictured the nearly final gasp of a man in great pain as almost a whisper. But the bulletin said it was a triumphant shout of joy, more like "It's finished—completed! The work I came to do is done, and done well."

For the first time I could identify with my Lord's words and understand where the joy fit in. Twice I've felt a much smaller, but similar joy—giving birth to my two sons. It was a work I'd prepared nine months for, which I knew would mean pain, but which promised a reward worth all the effort. The few hours of labor sapped my physicial strength, demanding every ounce of energy in me, but with that final strain and eventual release, joy filled my soul as the baby's cry signalled life! In that instant all suffering and pain were blotted out. My job was finished, and it had been done well. My child lived!

How much more triumphant must have been Christ's cry on the cross at that moment He knew His labor on earth was finished, and because of it, all mankind would forever have life.

Lord Jesus, I rejoice with You and praise Your name today for the gift of life You have given me.

B.R.G.

8. (Palm Sunday)

Each year, I look forward to this week, the week of tragedy and triumph, the week in which Christ was crucified and rose from the tomb. I wish I had been there in Jerusalem when it happened. All my life I've been a reporter. And if I had been there, I wonder how I would have reacted to the stupendous events that were taking place.

Jesus had spent Saturday night at the home of the risen Lazarus at Bethany, two miles east of Jerusalem. News had spread that Jesus would go into Jerusalem on Sunday morning, probably His first visit there since boyhood. Few people of Jerusalem had heard Jesus preach, but they had heard a lot about His teachings, His miracles, His fulfillment of the prophecies. Excitement was intense.

It was the custom at Jerusalem for the people to greet important visitors by lining the steep road outside the city, waving palms and olive branches, strewing them in the visitor's path. Such was the welcome Jesus received. Most people hoped He would prove to be the King of the Jews who would free them from the Romans.

Did anyone recognize Him as the Savior?

Would I, as an objective reporter, have recognized Him as my Savior?

Do you recognize Him as your Savior?

G.D.K.

9. (Holy Week)

On Palm Sunday afternoon, Jesus stunned the city by throwing the merchants and money-changers out of the temple. With my reporter's eye, I can see the furious priests demanding, "Who is this country preacher who thinks He can come into the Temple of Solomon and take over?" What worried them most was the great crowd that had welcomed Jesus and followed Him to the temple. Would He, indeed, take over? The priests were determined not to allow this.

Jesus spent the rest of the day healing and preaching; then He returned to Lazarus's house for the night. The priests hoped that was the end of Him. But first thing next morning He was back at the temple. Something had to be done about Him.

In Jerusalem were a group of Greek scholars, then the intellectuals of the world, and they asked to speak to Jesus. To them, it didn't matter whether Jesus was the King of Jews or the Son of God or the son of a carpenter. They found Him to be a holy man, wise, gentle, and they were impressed with the way He used simple parables to clarify religious truths.

One such parable foreshadowed His death. Jesus said that a grain of wheat could either stay whole by not germinating, or it could become one with the earth to produce a great harvest. (John 12:24) He meant that His death would guarantee the growth of Christianity.

Trying to reconstruct these momentous events, I often imagine myself in the temple near Jesus, watching Him, listening to Him.

Would I have understood His great parable about the grain of wheat?

Would His words have taken root in my heart?

Have they taken root in yours?

G.D.K.

10.

(Holy Week)

The conspiracy against Jesus began on this day. The chief priests and the elders approached Jesus in the temple and asked Him many questions, trying to trap Him into admitting that He was a traitor, either against the government or against Jewish religious laws. Jesus evaded the questions by answering in parables, letting his interrogators draw their own conclusions.

Twice, however, Jesus was specific. Asked whether the Jews should pay tribute to Caesar or to God, He answered: "Render therefore unto Caesar the things which are Caesar's; and unto God the things that are God's." (Matthew 22:21). Asked which of the 3600 Jewish commandments was the most important, He answered: First, love God totally and, second, love your neighbor as yourself.

As a journalist, I've spent countless hours in courtrooms, taking notes as prosecuting attorneys tried to dismantle the accused's defense of himself. Sometimes my sympathies were with the attorneys, sometimes with the accused. But still my first obligation as a journalist was to report my observations impartially, and this was not always easy.

I wonder how I would have reacted to the cross-examination of Jesus that day in the temple. I probably would not have understood some of His parables any more than the priests and elders did. But I certainly would have understood His own two commandments.

I do my best to love God totally, because I know He loves me. I am aware that occasionally I act in less than love toward my neighbors, and I ask God's help in overcoming this.

What about you?

G.D.K.

11.

(Holy Week)

Often a reporter must dig for hidden facts to support events that have occurred openly. That week in Jerusalem, I would have dug. And I would have been shocked by what I found.

The high priest Caiaphas was determined that Jesus should die. Some interpreters of the Bible think that his agents approached Judas Iscariot and bribed him to betray Jesus. Many people still did not know what Jesus looked like, so Judas said, "Whomsoever I shall kiss, that same is He." (Matthew 26:48) And the authorities at the temple agreed that they would try Jesus for spiritual treason once He was brought before them. The verdict was already determined: Guilty.

Surely Jesus knew all that was going on, but He was unperturbed by it. He spent the day at the temple, healing, teaching. Before heading back to Bethany for the night, Jesus told a couple of His disciples to find a place in the city where the twelve could partake of the Passover meal on the next evening. Jesus knew very well that it would be His last meal.

How, I wonder, could anyone face imminent death with such calmness. Such dignity. Such courage. It was possible only because Jesus knew that all His life He had obeyed the Father's will, even to the Cross.

Each one of us in our middle years has experienced the death of loved ones. But we seldom think of our own death. When I think of mine, I am not so sure that I will have the calmness, the courage, the confidence that Jesus had.

Have I lived the kind of life that will make it possible for me to be serene at the end?

Have you?

G.D.K.

12. (Holy Week)

On this day, the Lord gave us the sacrament that is the very heart of our faith.

During the Passover meal, Jesus picked up some bread, blessed it, broke it into pieces, then said to the Apostles: "Take, eat: this is My body." Then He picked up a goblet of wine and blessed it and said: "This is My blood of the new testament,

which is shed for many . . . This do in remembrance of Me."
(Mark 14:22, 24; Luke 22:19)

That was Christianity's first communion service.

Today in untold thousands of churches around the world, Christians have gathered for a commemoration of the Lord, an expression of worship that unites all Christians regardless of any externals that may separate us.

My work as a journalist has taken me all over the world, sometimes to countries where I did not know the language. But during a communion service, I have always experienced the sensation that I was not among strangers, but that we were all together in the Upper Room with Jesus for the First Communion, suddenly brothers and sisters in the family of the Lord.

Later this morning, when I go to church to commemorate this sacred day, I know I shall once again experience this miracle of brotherly love.

Share the miracle with me.

G.D.K.

13. (Good Friday)

I was raised to believe that this is the saddest day in the history of the world. In many ways, it is. And yet I have discovered a certain joy in it, the greatest joy the Lord could give us.

I was not aware of this gift until a book assignment sent me on a long trip through Africa to study the work of missionaries. I was in what is now Tanzania when some missionaries told me about a very old man who lived nearby and who, since his own baptism years before, had come to the mission every day to teach religion to the school children.

The missionaries told me: "He is a saint. You must meet him."

He turned out to be a short man, lean, slightly stooped, his face all wrinkles, but his eyes and mind bright and alert. I could see he was a happy man. At one point, I asked him which aspect of Christianity he valued most. Without hesitation, he said:

"The forgiveness of sin."

The full impact of that answer did not strike me until the morning, months later, when once again I was reading Luke's account of this sad day.

Jesus was crucified between two thieves. One of them taunted Him to save Himself if He was truly the Son of God. But the other called to Him: "Lord, remember me when Thou comest into Thy kingdom."

Jesus replied, "Verily I say unto thee, Today shalt thou be with Me in Paradise." (Luke 23:42, 43)

It was as simple as that. By acknowledging Jesus as the Lord and indicating his belief in His mission, the Good Thief repented and received forgiveness. Only the Son of God could be that merciful.

Since meeting that African, I have never lived through this very special day without thinking of his words of joy. And I am sure now that if I had been able to observe Jesus during the last week of His life on earth, even if I had not been persuaded by His miracles and His teachings, I certainly would have given Him my life after hearing His burst of loving forgiveness on the Cross.

Maybe that is why we call this saddest day in history *Good* Friday.

G.D.K.

14. (Holy Week)

It was a strange day, a quiet day, a lonely day, a day of waiting. It was the Sabbath, and devout Jews did not work or socialize or travel. Housewives did their Saturday cooking on Friday so that they, too, could keep the Sabbath. The Sabbath was a day of prayer, reading of the holy books, going to the synagogue. But this Sabbath was something more.

A fierce storm had struck the city while Jesus was still on the cross. Buildings were damaged. Trees were uprooted. Graves opened up. So people were afraid and stayed in their homes. Even the Apostles were in hiding.

It was a day for doubt, for sadness, for guilt feelings, for reflection, for questions.

Who really was that man who died on the cross yesterday afternoon? What was there about Him that the wrath of God should show itself in darkened skies and raging winds? Would the King of the Jews have allowed Himself to be executed in such a lowly way, among thieves? Would the Son of God? What was going to happen next?

Jesus had already given them the answer. He once had said: "Destroy this temple and in three days I will raise it up." (John 2:19) The people thought He was talking about the great temple in the city that was the heart of their religion, and His words had been thrown back at Jesus by the priests and elders in the temple only last Tuesday. How, they demanded, could anybody rebuild the temple in three days? So they called Him a liar and a traitor, and they condemned Him.

This strange, unsettled day, then, was necessary for the fulfillment of the prophecy, for Jesus to prove to the people that He had been talking about Himself.

If I had been there, would I have predicted that He would rise from the dead?

Would you?

G.D.K.

15. (Easter)

It was the custom of the Jews that the dead should be anointed with oils and spices before being left to eternity. The women who had come with Jesus from Galilee could not anoint Him on Saturday, the Sabbath, but they were there before dawn the next morning.

They saw that the big boulder at the entrance of the tomb had been moved. They went inside. The body of Jesus was not there. The women didn't know what to make of it.

Suddenly two men in shining garments appeared to them and asked: "Why seek ye the living among the dead? He is not here, but is risen." (Luke 24: 5,6)

Astounded, the women ran to where some of the Apostles were gathered and told them what had happened. The Apostles didn't believe them. But Simon Peter wanted to see for himself.

Now, Peter was a huge man, tall, big-boned, heavily muscled from years of toil on the sea, a mountain of energy and power. It was not in his nature merely to walk to the tomb and take a look. He had to run. And he ran at top speed. He must have been quite a sight, this great hulk of a man pounding along the road, kicking up dust, his gaze eagerly straight ahead, his beard flowing behind him. I can see him now . . . I wonder what I would have thought if I had seen him then?

The Bible says that Peter saw the empty tomb for himself and went away in amazement. But he could not keep his amazement to himself. Like a gale, the unbelievable news swept through the city. Great crowds went to the tomb, peering inside, murmuring questions.

"Is it true? He is not there? Who has taken His body away? They say He has risen from the dead. Is that possible? Do you believe it?"

Would I have believed it?

Would you?

And would I, a working journalist then, have written what I write now?:

"Jesus, the Lord, has risen. Through Him, we all rise, in this world and the next. Hallelujah! Hallelujah!"

G.D.K.

THE GOLDEN KEY

"There is one method for getting out of difficulties that I've seen work over and over again," Dr. Emmet Fox once told a friend. The late author and counselor was referring to his "Golden Key" principle. Here's how he summed it up:

Stop thinking about the difficulty, whatever it is, and think about God instead.

As an experiment, bring the "Golden Key" into your Spiritual Workshop this month and try it out with one specific problem you face. Be creative as you focus your thoughts on God. Review everything you know about Him. Stretch your thinking.

One mother, alienated from her teen-age son because of his disobedience and rebellion, tried that principle. After the first attempt, her thoughts left God and were back on her son within a few minutes. She decided that she needed to work harder on the idea. "Some part of every hour I'm awake, my thoughts will go to Jesus Christ," she resolved.

Throughout the day she directed her mind to Him. She began picturing Jesus walking by the Sea of Galilee, talking to people, ministering to the sick. Next she brought Christ to the present and saw Him walking up and down the streets of her own community. Soon He was at the high school talking to young people, including her own son. She began to see her son through the eyes of Jesus.

After a week, there was a decided change for the better. "I was more relaxed with my son, and he was less argumentative," she admitted.

What is the explanation for such a change? As the mother became less fearful and nit-picking with her son, she became a more congenial person—and he responded with a greater sense of responsibility. But here is the important point: *Not until her mind was filled with thoughts of God were her fears about her son eliminated.*

"The 'Golden Key' calls for quiet persistence," Doctor Fox said. "It's the surest way I know toward harmony and happiness."

L.E.L.

17.

'Mid all the traffic of the ways,
Turmoils without, within,
Make in my heart a quiet place,
And come and dwell within.

John Oxenham hymn

We inherited an old-fashioned desk from my grandparents. It's as sturdy as a rock, but it had a murky look from several coats of old varnish, and it was so scratched and chipped that it was actually ugly. We attacked it with varnish remover and sand paper, and as layer after layer of built-up junk came off, the natural grain of the oak began to appear, and the desk was transformed into a beautiful piece of furniture.

Sometimes I'm like that old desk—so coated over with worries and fears, so marred by disappointments and guilts, that I actually feel ugly. But I've developed a way to get rid of that junk. It may help you, too.

Find a quiet place, sit with closed eyes, and visualize an opening in the darkness that is filled with thousands of tiny pinpoints of light, representing the transforming power of God. When a thought comes to mind—any thought—mentally pass it up through that shimmering space, totally surrendering it to God. Feel it being transformed, purified, perfected, as it passes through this divine filter and out of awareness. Repeat this with each thought that comes, and after 15–20 minutes you will feel completely renewed and your spirit will be singing.

Father, help me to strip off my layers of negative "stuff" so that the soul You created in Your image can shine through.

M.M.H.

18.

Rest in the Lord, and wait patiently for Him. . .

Psalm 37:7

It was springtime in the desert. Carol and I wandered along, enjoying the beauties of nature exuberant after an extraordinarily wet winter. We stopped now and then to examine closely a cougar track, a cactus bud. I bent over a straggly weed, attracted by the dainty blue flowers it bore. About a quarter of an inch across, each had five oval petals and a minute yellow center.

"I don't remember seeing these before," I exclaimed.

"Well," Carol said, "the paper says that some plants are up this spring that have been lying dormant for twenty-five years."

"Twenty-five years!" I could picture a tiny seed, hidden under hard earth, waiting twenty-five years for exactly the right conditions so it could grow. I'm impatient because I don't know what the Lord is going to do with me next month! Yet because the seed did not die, but waited, I could now enjoy this exquisite mini-bouquet on a warm spring afternoon.

What of the seed within my own deepest desire? I don't know what its flower will look like. But if I wait . . .

Lord, I tend to be impatient. Help me to live on Your time, not mine.

M.J.N.

19.

In all thy ways acknowledge Him, and He shall direct thy paths.

Proverbs 3:6

There just weren't enough hours in a day. No matter how I managed my time, I usually went to bed with chores left undone. I determined to work out a realistic schedule.

I ruled off seven days on a sheet of paper. Pen poised, I started to write the 9½ hours each day devoted to my job and commuting, but I hesitated. A message flashed inside my head: "Put God first." Well, I was willing to put God first, but, after all, I *had* to work.

Again I started to enter the 9½ hours, and this time the message was most insistent: "Put God first." Okay. I began each day reading a devotional. After some calculations, I entered "5 minutes—devotional" in each column. Seven blank spaces stretched beneath each entry. Five minutes. Was that all the time I gave God a day? My time was a gift from God. I could use 90 percent of it for my own affairs, but I should return 10 percent

to God. Five minutes a day was less than one percent. I began to
see that I had been giving God practically no time, and, as a
result, I never had enough. "God," I prayed, "please help me
solve this problem."

Instantly, I had an answer. I spent an hour a day commuting.
Instead of listening to the car radio, I could repeat psalms,
meditate, pray . . . The Bible said the more we give, the more
we get. Now that I am applying myself to this new schedule, it is
interesting to see how God reveals other nooks and crannies of
time that I can use to honor Him.

*Lord, thank You for showing me ways to turn my time into Your
time.*

L. P. E.

20.
Come and see the works of God. . . .
Psalm 66:5

When warm, sunny days follow a spring rain in our region, wild
morels leap up in fence rows, ditches and woods. These little
brown or gray mushrooms are delectable; and people roam
searching through meadows and woodlands for them. I remember the first time a friend, an old hand at hunting morels,
took me to look for them.

"Look for dead elm trees a-peelin' their bark," he advised.
"Lookee here!" He popped several morels into his plastic sack.
We walked for an hour. I peered over logs, around stumps,
through grass and weeds. Nothing. But he constantly stopped to
pick mushrooms where I'd already looked. His sack grew plump.
Mine drooped, almost empty.

"There's one!" He pointed down at my foot. "See it?"
"Where?"

"Reach down there." I groped. My fingers grasped the cool,
dew-covered brown spear of fungus before I saw it. With his
help, I found a few more, big old ones. His sack was nearly
bursting now, and he had harvested tiny ones, tenderest and
tastiest. I fumed about why he had seen so many that I could not.

"I've been hunting these little bits sixty years," my friend
comforted me, understanding my puzzlement. "You spot them

93

easy when you been lookin' that long."

Isn't the walk of faith a little like that? When you first begin to pray, you feel as if you are just groping. When you first begin to read the Bible, many of its truths elude you. A true faith takes time and patience and persistence. But, then, one day you reach out—and God is there.

Even when I don't see You Father, I know You are there.

L.C.

21. For God so loved the world. . . .
John 3:16

We were having a family gathering at Grandmother's house, enjoying visiting with relatives we hadn't seen for a while. Three-year-old Michael ran into the living room all aglow because an aunt had given him a small bag of candies. He went all around the circle offering a candy to each person. Everyone said, "No, thank you." With a puzzled look he slipped outside to sit in the porch swing.

My perceptive sister said, "That child is disappointed. He wanted to share and no one accepted his generosity." Presently he wandered back into the room and Lois said, "Michael, may I have a green candy?" Wriggling with delight, Michael poured the colored candies into his hand to find the green one requested.

Loving, giving and accepting are the very heart of Christianity. "For God so loved the world, that He *gave* . . . "

Father, teach me to give unselfishly, to accept graciously, and to love wholeheartedly.

D.M.

22. Thou shalt love thy neighbour as thyself.
Matthew 19:19

It was crowded at the Fourth Presbyterian Church in Bethesda, Maryland, that Sunday. My wife said she'd save a seat while I parked the car. I reached the pew to find someone else had taken my place. By squeezing over, my wife made room. But I resented the man jammed up against me. When we'd stand to sing, I'd turn my shoulder on him. I tried to think about loving people. I wanted that fullness of joy that comes from loving everybody. But somehow I could not get into that warm spirit.

At prayer time Pastor Halverson asked us to touch the person next to us and silently pray for them. Without really wanting to, I found myself touching the arm of the man squeezed next to me and praying for him. In that instant I suddenly felt warmth for him and the joy I sought flooded me.

But not until later did it dawn on me: God didn't ask us to love the whole world, just our neighbor.

Oh, Father, help us remember that it's the cranky woman next door, the garlicky man next to us on the bus, and the tired impatient salesclerk who are our neighbors.

R.H.S.

23.

All things bright and beautiful,
All creatures great and small,
All things wise and wonderful,
The Lord God made them all.

Cecil Frances Alexander

One morning when my son was just a toddler, I awoke to a glorious spring morning. All around me God's beauty abounded—golden sunshine, buds newly opened, trees clothed in fresh yellow-green. I wanted to sing, like the robin whose song caressed my ear, and to share the feeling inside me. So I gathered my son in my arms and stood at the window, "See, Honey," I said. "Isn't it lovely! Just look out there. Spring has come."

But Bruce didn't smile. His attention was focused on the glass itself, not seeing through to the beauty beyond. He stretched out his arm and one pudgy finger rested on a flaw in the window pane. No amount of coaxing could draw his eye from that distorted spot. By his own determination to focus on something wrong, he missed the joy I so much wanted him to share.

How often we are blinded by the flaws in our world! We're surrounded by poverty, sickness, crime. At times we can see nothing positive and then we hurt or despair. But God created this world and pronounced it good. (Genesis 1:31) And He chose us to share the joy of His creation. Today, let's resolve to look beyond the imperfections of life to the beauty He made for us all, and be glad with Him.

Thank You, Father, for Your gift of life, for the world and all the wonders it contains.

B.R.G.

24.

Train up a child in the way he should go . . .
Proverbs 22:6

I see by the newspaper that Christian Dior, the world renowned fashion designer, has announced a new line. This year he will be showing clothing for children. There will be tiny nightgowns for $30 each, toddler dresses from $40 to $50. "Dior realizes," says a company spokesman, "that parents who are well-dressed would like to see their children in fashions that reflect their taste and values."

I'm afraid I'm not in a position to purchase Dior's clothes, but I can buy his idea. I want my children to reflect my values, it's true, just as God our Father wants us to reflect His. He longs to see each one of us clothed beautifully in what exemplifies Him best—the garment of holiness. And that's the way I'll try to dress myself—and consequently my children—today.

Lord, help me each day to wear the clothing of the spirit that will glorify you.

P.K.

25.

I know not where His islands lift
Their fronded palms in air;
I only know I cannot drift
Beyond His love and care.

John Greenleaf Whittier

After weeks of wintry weather, the day was warm and sunny. Driving along, I spotted lots of cows and young calves and one pair, in particular, caught my attention. Coasting to a halt off the pavement, I stopped to watch.

Perhaps six weeks old, the calf somehow had managed to separate himself from his mother by getting through a small opening in the barbed wire. Now he was trying to return to his mother but was unable to get back into the pasture.

Roving up and down the fence row, again and again he pushed at the wire, only to be as many times rebuffed. The cow, ever watchful, softly called to him when he appeared to be straying too far and this quickly brought him running back to her. Standing as close to him as possible, she would lean over the fence, give him several comforting licks, and nuzzle him as if to say, "Even though you are in that 'far country' beyond the fence, I am still here, and we'll be together again and everything will be all right." And she kept at it until finally the calf made it back through the hole in the fence.

How like our loving Father this creature of His is, I thought. As that calf did, again and again we roam and stray; again and again He calls us back; cares for us; touches us with His forgiving love.

A moment's pause on a spring day became for me a precious reassurance, voiced so eloquently by the poet. However far we go, we "cannot drift beyond His love and care."

Heavenly Father, help us to remember always that nothing will be able to separate us from the love of God in Christ Jesus our Lord.

N.S.

26.

Life is a mirror for king and for slave,
'Tis just what you are and do,
So give to the world the best you have
And the best will come back to you.

Anonymous

Years before Salk vaccine conquered polio, that dread disease crippled the mother of a friend. But she occupies her wheelchair like the captain of a ship, and from it she lives and loves more fully than most people who walk freely through the world.

"I'm shut in," she makes it very clear, "but not shut out!"

She writes poetry, cards and letters. Her mail, coming and going, makes the postman groan. Her phone bill is enormous— she calls so many others far and near, to cheer them up.

She sews for the needy, makes costumes for neighbor kids. She coaches a boy in French, reads to two blind friends. Apart or together they are brought to her door every week. When they can't make it she calls them up and reads to them! She plays the guitar and sings.

And her mind is hungry for knowledge. She gets up at dawn so as not to miss the sunrise and to have her coffee ready for the educational classes on TV. "It's the best time of day to learn." She takes notes as she listens to debates and forums and talk shows.

She bears no bitterness at her fate. She has made it fruitful.

Shut-in? No. The only true shut-ins are people who imprison themselves behind self-pity, anger, resentment, self-concern. We may be physically active, free to move about, but if the spirit is locked away from love, then we are the truly crippled. The only way to be a shut-in is to shut love out.

Dear Lord, release my spirit from the bonds of self-pity. Whenever I feel thwarted, fretful that I can't do all the things I want to for myself and others, help me to remember this mother of my friend.

M.H.

27.

. . . Do that which is good . . .

Romans 13:3

Just as sure as April, came the weeds and grasses that flourished in a 4x7 bed across the street from my office window. Dandelions, purslane, buckhorn and ragweed quickly upholstered the plot, which was centered with a yellow fireplug. Collecting beer cans and paper, it was an eyesore in an otherwise attractive downtown intersection. Why, I wondered annually, didn't the mayor do something about it?

On a rain-fresh May morning ten years ago I walked past the weeds and suddenly remembered my mother taking me with her to the garden early in the morning after a rain. "Weeds pull easy now," she would say. Why not pull those weeds?

I was heaving at the growth, bringing up clumps of earth-matted roots when a voice said, "I can tell you were raised on a farm."

It was my friend Mary Louise Walk, who with her husband, Foster, owns a large dairy farm.

"Mary, why did God make weeds?" I asked wearily, giving up.

"Birds eat seeds and bees gather honey from weeds," she said.

"Bees gather honey from flowers, too," I countered.

"Then we must plant flowers," she said, hugged my shoulders and was gone.

The next morning I stood amazed beside the 4x7 bed. It was a festival of color. Red geraniums, blue ageratum, petunias bloomed gloriously in a bed of rich soil smelling slightly of the "black gold" of a dairy farm. Mary had planted flowers.

Every spring since, the yellow fireplug is surrounded by tulips and daffodils, then with summer flowers, and finally pillows of mums. She comes quietly in late day, tending, planting, watering. Her gift to the town is a joy to all who pass it.

Often, when I'm concerned about a situation I feel should be remedied I remember Mary's reply to my complaint. "Then we must plant flowers." It spurs me to do what she does. Do something beautiful—with love.

God, thank You for opportunities to do good. May we recognize them, and use them.

ZBD.

28.
Discretion shall preserve thee, understanding shall keep thee.

Proverbs 2:11

I heard the sound of breaking china and ran to the family room. On the floor lay the remains of a cherished old cup that had been in my husband's family for years. I began to make my feelings known. The object of my tirade stooped down to pick up the broken pieces. Onto the scene walked my 80-year-old mother. She bent down and helped the child on the floor hunt for the shattered pieces. When I stopped for breath, she lifted her head, looked at me and said, "Well, now, it's only a cup, you know."

It's only a cup. With new eyes I saw the dejected face of my child and realized that, after all, he hadn't meant to do it. I needed to keep things in perspective.

Ever since that day when something goes wrong, I think of my mother's statement: "It's only a cup." I try, objectively and calmly to evaluate my loss against the most important things of life. It always helps me regain a sense of perspective and understand what is really the most important.

Dear Lord, help me always to live with eternity's values in view.

M.T.

29.
Comfort ye, comfort ye My people, saith your God.

Isaiah 40:1

One Sunday the church's morning service was turned over to a young missionary returning to his mission field in Peru after a year's furlough in the States.

By chance, I sat beside his mother in the congregation. When our pastor and elders laid their hands on the shoulders of the couple and their four children to pray for their trip and subsequent ministry, my heart went out to the mother who was being left behind.

Two years before I'd been in her place. I remembered my feelings during my son's dedicatory prayer, then remembered his plane leaving—taking my precious child, his wife and my only grandchildren. I remembered thinking how they'd not be babies, but young ladies the next time I saw them. *If* I saw them again. . . .

I knew how she felt. I groped in my purse, blurrily looking for my Kleenex packet; then shared it with her.

After the service she turned to me and said, "The Lord must've arranged for us to sit together. You were such a comfort. I knew you really knew how I felt."

Sometimes God uses us to help one of His children by such a simple means as sharing a Kleenex.

Lord, give me the perception to know when one of Your children needs a comforting word. And the wisdom to know the right way to say it.

I.C.

30.

May you always find three welcomes:
In a garden during summer,
At a fireside during winter,
And whatever the day or season,
In the kind eyes of a friend.

Old Gaelic prayer

On the last day of April, it is the custom in some rural Wisconsin towns for the children to make tiny baskets out of brightly-colored paper and ribbons, which they lovingly fill with wild blue and purple violets, and soft green moss they have gathered. Then, on May 1st, they get up very early and hang the baskets on the front doorknobs of people they love. This is all done with great secrecy, whispering and a lot of tiptoeing.

One very cold spring, frost and snow had killed most of the wild flowers, or buried them beneath heavy drifts. Yet, on May 1st, when I opened our farmhouse door, I found several baskets which were much more beautiful than any I had ever received before. My eyes misted, and my heart brimmed over when I saw what was inside the baskets. The children had cut out bright paper flowers, and in the center of each had printed carefully a Bible verse, or a little prayer. One said, "Thank You, Lord, for my friend." Another read, "Jesus loves you, and so do I." The last one said, "I couldn't find any flowers, so I am going to pray for you tonight, before I go to sleep."

Sometimes, when my good intentions run into "frost and snow," I'm inclined to give up and stop trying. Not these children! They refused to let a setback cheat them out of a loving act.

Can't I learn to be like that?

Father, for the persevering heart You offer us, thank You.

P.S.

MAY 1979

S	M	T	W	T	F	S
		1	2	3	4	5
6	7	8	9	10	11	12
13	14	15	16	17	18	19
20	21	22	23	24	25	26
27	28	29	30	31		

1.

. . . Wherefore be ye not unwise, but understanding what the will of the Lord is.

Ephesians 5:17

Mother always seemed to be able to bring out the best in me, and, looking back, I can now appreciate what a difficult task this sometimes was. For instance, there was my brand new job with the local newspaper. I loved the work, I loved my own little corner near the City Desk, I loved typing my own news stories, and then one day I hit a snag. In tears I went home and told Mother I was quitting. A competitive paper had scooped us on a fast-breaking story, and my superior blamed me, the cub reporter, when I had had nothing to do with it.

"All right," Mother said rather casually, "leave if you like. But why not wait awhile? Right now, if you quit, they won't care. But if you hang on and make yourself really valuable, then they'll be sorry to lose you."

This "make 'em sorry" idea appealed to me mightily and I returned grimly to my job. But after a few weeks I got so caught up in the work that, when I was blamed for missing another story, I was too busy chasing the next one to fret.

One day a few months later I was thrilled to become a member of the Women's Press Club of Georgia. Going home that day, I finally realized what Mother had been up to. It wasn't that she thought that "showing them" was such a good idea. But she knew I'd be making a mistake to quit. So, instead of arguing, she had employed a little stratagem in order to keep a stubborn daughter on the right path.

Thank You, Heavenly Father, for the many ways our parents guided us, and help us who are parents now to be loving and wise in the lessons we try to teach our young.

M.S.G.

2. For he shall be as a tree planted by the waters. . . .
Jeremiah 17:8

Last Arbor Day, here in Illinois, our Department of Conservation explained what trees are for:

"Trees are for boys to climb, for cats to get caught up in, for bird watchers to hide behind and squirrels to live in. Trees are to catch kites, to hang swings in, to pitch tents under and to make houses and furnishings.

"Trees make a field a park, beautify streets, absorb sound, slow the wind, settle the dust, they are for picnics; they buffer raindrops, stop erosion and hold snow.

"Trees keep us warm and cool. Shade trees cool the summer breezes, and windbreaks temper winter freezes. A large tree cools the air by 20 degrees beneath its canopy, and the cooling power of a tree is equal to that of a ten-room air conditioner operating 20 hours a day.

"A full-size tree absorbs carbon dioxide and produces enough oxygen to offset the effects of one man's breathing, while 20 trees absorb the combustion by-products from five gallons of gasoline."

Trees stand very still and patient while being used, or they bow to the will of the wind, twisting, tossing, threshing, bending. Should they not bend, they would break with the force of this unseen power. But when the storm has passed, their limbs straighten and they stand tall and sure again.

Life brings storms to all of us, seeming sometimes to tear us apart, destroy us. But like the tree, we must bend—so we will not break. And when the storm passes we stand tall again, serve again.

When troubles strike, help us Heavenly Father to remember Your promise, "This too shall pass."

Z.B.D.

3.

Now I lay me down to sleep, I pray the Lord my soul to keep.

A child's prayer

Some years ago when I interviewed Robert Young for *Guideposts* he discussed the rewards that he and his wife, Betty, had gained from active church-connected service. One example: The evening when he knelt with his youngest daughter, Kathy, then just past her ninth birthday, to hear her prayers.

Kathy asked a blessing for everyone—her mother, her father, her sisters, the neighbors, her schoolteacher, the dogs. Then she started on her request list. That was pretty long, too. It sounded like an enthusiastic letter to Santa Claus. Suddenly there was a pause and Kathy said in a small, meek voice: "And now, dear God, is there anything I can do for You?"

Surely this is what Jesus meant when He said that we should all become like little children—not child-*ish*, but child-*like*.

Dear God, open my eyes this day so that I may clearly see if there's anything I can do for You.

E.St.J.

4.

When morning gilds the skies . . . may Jesus Christ be praised.

German hymn

This morning when I picked up the mail I was struck by the feel of the sun. It's one thing to see it framed in by a window; quite another to have it warm and golden upon my back. I felt a sudden delicious sense of lethargy—and yielded to it. Hugging my knees, I dropped my head and closed my eyes, on the slope beneath the front avocado tree. "I'm an unhatched egg," I used to say when I sat like that as a child.

"Are you praying?" a little girl's voice inquired politely. She went on before I had to come up with an answer. "What do you pray about?"

She looked about six, I thought as my eyes adjusted to the light. She carried a storybook and a Farrah Fawcett lunch pail. There was no time to dawdle, so she was moving toward the school as she went on with her conversation. "My gram'ma says God made this day and we'd ought to thank Him." The little creature skipped away.

I felt a little twinge of guilt. I'd been warming my body in God's beautiful sunshine, but I wasn't praying as my little friend had supposed. I resumed my position, and this is the prayer I said:

Thank You for the gift of the day which You have given me. Let me grow in the warmth of Your love. And, send me someone with whom I can share its glory—as You sent the little girl who showed me how.

J.M.B.

5.

The heavens declare the glory of God and the firmament showeth His handiwork. . .

Psalm 19:1

It was an Iowa night in May. I had gone back to help close up the house of our childhood; take care of those mundane yet memory-wracked details that signal a family's final chapter. Tired, yet unable to sleep, I went out and lay down on the grass. It prickled beneath my back; its sweet fragrance heightened the

108

aching. How often some or all of us would sprawl out under the stars like this, marveling at their mysteries.

Tonight only a few sparkling stars were scattered. Beyond the house a new moon curved, delicate, not dominating. Yet I was conscious of a whiteness beginning to grow, intensify along the northern horizon; then reaching up to claim the sky, splaying into its very center. Not sharp and swift like lightning, rather a leaping fountain of lights that crossed, entwined, vanished, then sprang up again brighter than before. As if some master craftsman were trying stage effects on an epic scale.

They spread like rays of the sun. They fluttered, fused into the shapes of winging angels. They danced like some heavenly ballet. What was happening? A vision? A sign? I watched in awed fascination, then ran excitedly to tap on the bedroom window, calling my sister-in-law to wake up and witness this astonishing display. I wanted her to share it, if only to confirm the incredible sight.

Her voice came back sleepily. "Oh, go back to bed, it's nothing but Northern Lights."

Northern Lights. Of course. We'd seen them as children (but surely never such a barrage of ethereal fireworks as this!) Our parents explained (wrongly) the phenomenon as the sun's reflections on the ice caps at the North Pole. . . . For a second I was disappointed. I really didn't want an explanation. I wanted the drama of the miracle, heavenly signs, to be witness to some blazing revelation.

Then I smiled. For how could anything diminish this mystery and marvel? That Arctic lights could travel so far and be soaring above me even now in such splendor! This too was God's signature on the sky reminding me of his glory.

How prone we are to seek the rare, the startling, the supernatural, while rejecting the daily miracles our Creator displays for us.

Thank You, God, for the magnificent revelations You offer us every day of our lives. In every work of nature, in the birth of every creature. Let me recognize Your hand behind them and worship You for them as I worshiped You that night.

M.H.

6.

All things are thine; no gift have we,
Lord of all gifts, to offer Thee;
And hence with grateful hearts today
Thine own before Thy feet we lay.

Offertory hymn

Recently, Corrie ten Boom, now 86, sturdy Dutch survivor of Nazi concentration camps, known for the book and motion picture THE HIDING PLACE was asked how she handled compliments.

"After all, Corrie," the questioner persisted, "you're beloved around the world. The public can really lay it on. As a Christian, how do you handle all that?"

Corrie, known to be impatient of all who try to elevate her to instant sainthood, made clucking noises followed by a snort. "Why, compliments are just like flowers," was her quick response. "And if they come my way, I gather them up throughout the day—one or two roses here, a few tulips there, a carnation or so, some daisies—a few stems here, a few stems there.

"Then at the end of the day, with a feeling of total gratitude I just hand the entire bouquet of compliments over to the One Who really deserves them. 'A bouquet of flowers for *You*, Lord. They all belong to You.' "

Lord, thank You for all the wonderful gifts You have given me.

C.M.

7.

. . .Simplify, simplify.

Thoreau

The lovely, old maple in the back yard of our farm in Pawling, New York, had died. Norman and I were both crestfallen as we surveyed it sadly one Saturday morning. "I guess we better call the tree man," Norman said, "it's too near to the house for comfort."

The tree surgeon came that afternoon, but instead of sawing through the trunk immediately, as we expected, he began by trimming away small upper branches. Then he sawed the larger limbs off until just the lower trunk was left. This he sectioned too, until his final cut when the tree base toppled harmlessly to the ground. "On difficult jobs like this," he explained, "we always tackle the easy part first. That way, the rest of the problem gets simpler and simpler as we go along."

Norman scratched his head thoughtfully and went back to put the finishing touches on his sermon. And sure enough, the next day, Norman told the congregation at the Marble Collegiate Church about what he had learned from the tree surgeon. Now, whenever we're stymied by a sticky problem, we think back to that Saturday. Instead of trying to cope with the whole dilemma all at once, Norman and I have learned to sort it out into little pieces that aren't so hard to tackle, after all.

When you're stuck with a problem that seems larger than life, you might want to think about our friend, the tree surgeon, too.

My problems, dear Lord, always seem to shrink once I've called on You.

R.S.P.

8. Oh, what peace we often forfeit,
Oh what needless pain we bear,
All because we do not carry
Everything to God in prayer.

Joseph Scriven

Studying in a deserted classroom one hot spring day, I was bothered by the buzzing of flies above me. They were angrily batting themselves against the ceiling in a vain attempt to escape. And only five inches below them was a window, open from the top.

Silly flies? Silly people. How often do we throw ourselves against a situation that will not budge, never looking for another solution?

Abraham must have felt trapped as he led Isaac up the hill of sacrifice. Moses must have felt trapped as he approached the

Red Sea. Philip must have felt trapped when Jesus said "Feed them." Helpless? Hopeless? Only when we insist on seeing things from a human point of view. When you feel hemmed in, trapped by a situation, remember: God has a better idea! Stop. Step back. Take another look.

Lord, let me take my anxieties to You and leave them there.

P.H.S.

9. Obey God because you are His children. . .
I Peter 1:14 (L B)

Recently I visited a young couple, the parents of a baby boy. At nine months, the baby inquisitively crawled around the floor of their home. Tiny little fingers grabbed the shag carpet or stretched out delightedly to touch furniture or scattered toys. As I watched, he moved slowly along a wall until he discovered something interesting—an electrical outlet. His hand reached toward it, but stopped when the deep voice of his father said, simply, "No." The child turned from the wall, and his mother gently picked him up in her arms. "Good, John," she said. "Don't play with that."

The child recognized his father's voice and had learned to respond to the word "no." He certainly doesn't know what electricity is, or what might happen if he plays with the outlet. But he has learned the right response to "No;" and he receives the praise and affection of his parents when he obeys.

Isn't that what our Heavenly Father wants at times in His relationship with us? From the Garden of Eden until now, some of God's commands have been difficult to understand. But if God says no, or tells us not to do something, He doesn't always expect us to understand why. He only asks us to obey. And then, like the child whose parents protected him from possible danger, we will find that God's commands are only for our own good.

Father, teach us to recognize Your voice and obey it.

L.W.

10.

**What is man, that Thou art mindful of him?
. . . For Thou hast made him a little lower than
the angels, and hast crowned him with glory
and honour.**

Psalm 8:4,5

The little gray feathers on the ground were the first sign of
another small tragedy. My short search turned up the lifeless
bird from which they had come, a yellow-breasted visitor who
had stayed too long in the yard where our big orange house cat
prowls and suns himself.

Suddenly I felt both anger and guilt for the cat, a charming
friend to man but a treacherous and deadly foe to small creatures. When I protested to my wife, who felt as bad as I did about
the destruction, she put it in perspective for me. "George is a
natural predator," she said. "He hunts out of instinct. You can't
blame him. He's just a cat, doing what cats do."

It was true, of course. The cat was incapable of either sympathy for its prey or remorse for its deed. It was a captive of its
own feline nature, a slave to its instincts.

Thank God, I thought, *humans are different.* Our Creator
gave us an ability to choose how we behave. We don't have to be
slaves to our desires and appetites. With God's help, we can
overcome selfish instincts that hurt others.

*Heavenly Father, thank You for the gifts of conscience and
compassion, and for the power to live as creatures made in Your
image.*

B. P.

11.

I would be true, for there are those who trust me.
Howard Arnold Walter hymn

My mother always loved lilacs. From the time I was old enough
to save my pennies for her birthday, she always had lilacs on May
11. Then, in her last year, after a long, downhill period of

suffering, her mind wandered; she didn't remember where she was or who I was. So when May 11th came around I thought, *Why bother? She hasn't responded to anything for days now.* But tradition prevailed, and I arrived at the hospital with a small spray of her beloved blossoms. As I arranged them in the vase on the bedside table, standing with my back to Mom's bed, a voice came forth clearly from behind me. "How lovely. It's my birthday. You didn't forget."

For that one brief moment, just two weeks before she died, Mom came back for one last visit.

Thank You, Lord, for this tiny miracle that never lets me forget to honor the living while they are alive.

N.L.

12.   . . . In the night His song shall be with me, and my prayer unto the God of my life.
Psalm 42:8

The other day, I was trying to get a message through to my friend, Betty. I'd called several times during the day and again in the evening, but I kept getting the busy signal. Since the message was important, I called back quite late that night and, this time, I got my friend out of bed.

I've found that God sometimes wakes me up at night to get a message through to me, too. My "line" is often so busy all day with external things that I don't have (or take) time to listen for His call. Only after I've dropped into bed are the connections open enough for Him to break through into my consciousness. Sometime the message comes as an image, or as words that seem to float across my mind, or as a creative idea that springs to life in the silence. Or it may just be the spiritual food of His presence that feeds a hunger I'd forgotten I had. Whatever it is, I'm always glad I answered the call, and insomnia is no longer something I dread.

When I have trouble sleeping, I remind myself that God may

be dialing my number. Instead of fighting to get to sleep, I try to still my thoughts and listen for His message.

When I can't sleep, Lord, let me use the quietness to listen for Your voice.

M.M.H.

13.

(Mother's Day)
God could not be everywhere and therefore He made mothers.

Jewish saying

I breathed my first breath because Mom was willing to suffer for me. I learned to walk and talk because she showed me how. I even learned to love when she first loved me. And most of all I found God by watching her example. But how quickly I forgot, so anxious was I to leave the nest, so rushed to get on with my own living.

Mother's Day isn't the only day to remember. Oh, how I wish that I had the whole year ahead to tell Mom how I care. Now that she's with God, I can only trust that somehow she knows I loved her.

If you are lucky enough still to have a mother to love, take time today to cheer her. It needn't be a great production; a simple phone call, a letter, a kiss or a hug can say, "I care." Choose some expression you know she'll cherish and let it tell her, "I love you, Mom, and thank you for my life."

Heavenly Father, thank You for the mother You gave me. Let my life be the monument to her memory.

B.R.G.

14.

Freely ye have received, freely give.

Matthew 10:8

The good sisters who ran the little Catholic charity in Atlanta, Georgia, were bewildered when George Bessada, an Egyptian foreign student, announced that he had arranged a fund-raising dinner for them. They knew well enough that they were desperate for money, but how would their friend George be able to help? After all, wasn't George from a poor country, and didn't he have money worries of his own?

Yet there they were, seated as guests of honor at an exotic dinner where some 200 persons had paid $10 apiece to be served course upon course of North African delicacies. Swirling in their midst were dancing girls clothed in glittering Egyptian costumes. It was like a scene from the Arabian Nights.

Later, when George presented the sisters with a check for $1100, they were barely able to stammer their thanks. Then one asked what had prompted him to arrange the gala. "Oh," George said, "you Americans are always helping my countrymen. My friends and I thought we'd show you that we're not always taking. We can make a contribution too."

A wise young man, George Bessada. Bessada knew that to maintain spiritual health there must be giving as well as getting in every life. And he knew, too, that it is the giver who knows the greater joy.

Help us to remember, Lord, that it is through giving that we receive the most . . . and become the most like You.

A.G.

THREE STEPS TO ENTHUSIASM

Too many people are defeated in life because they lack a very important quality: enthusiasm. Those who think of enthusiasm as a kind of superficial emotion should remember that the Greek words *en theos* mean "in God." George Matthew Adams puts it this way: "Enthusiasm is a kind of faith that has been set afire."

Just as the world loves a lover, so does the world love the person who is excited about life. If you are a person with no enthusiasm, or not enough, I suggest three steps which may help you.

Act As If: The noted psychologist William James said, "If you want a quality, *act as if you already have it*." For example, suppose you have an inferiority complex that you want to change. Start visualizing yourself, not as you think you are, but rather as you'd like to be—in this case a person confident, assured, able to meet people and to deal with situations. Then act as if you were that confident person. It has been proven that, in time, you tend to become what you *think* you are.

Ventilate Your Mind: Empty your mind of gloomy thoughts. Go over the day's unpleasant incidents: a sharp word, a disappointment. Review your mistakes, errors or stupidities. Hold them before you, drawing from them all the lessons they have to give. Then lump them together and mentally drop them out of your consciousness, saying these therapeutic words: "Forgetting those things which are behind, and reaching forth unto those things which are before . . . (Philippians 3:13)

Tell Yourself All The Good News You Know: Psychologists agree that you can condition a day in the first five minutes after you awaken. It was Henry Thoreau, the American philosopher, who used to lie abed for a while in the morning telling himself all the good news he could think of: that he had a healthy body, that his mind was alert, his work interesting. The same kind of technique can help you look forward to the day with eagerness. And the more good news you tell yourself, the more good news there is likely to be.

May God bless you, and may you feel the joy for living that He wants you to have.

N.V.P.

16.

To every thing there is a season, and a time to every purpose under the heaven.

Ecclesiastes 3:1

Calling on an old friend, I found her crouching among some peony bushes behind an old shed.

"Playing hide-and-seek with the grandkids," she explained, brushing dirt and leaves off her knees. "I can't run so fast, so I have to think of better places to hide. I'm in the autumn of my life now. I'm enjoying it as I thoroughly enjoyed every season of my life."

Seasons of life. I myself can remember the joys of childhood, the challenge and growth of teen years, the richness and business of young womanhood, marriage, motherhood. Now I'm living in the late summer of my life.

God gives us blessings and trials, successes and failures, joys and sorrows in each season. Each season is to be treasured and filled. God has been so good to me in each season. I know I can safely trust Him with the next. I only need to live well today. That will prepare me to live well tomorrow.

Thank You, gracious Father, for the privileges and blessings of living for You.

L.C.

17.

Remorse is regret that one waited so long to do it.

H.L. Mencken

"I want to show you this hammer," my friend told me, "because there's a moral attached to it. Years ago when I was a girl, my dad bought this hammer. He was proud of it.

"My sisters and I had been trying to put up a curtain in our upstairs bedroom, and borrowed the hammer. The window, never finished, had no sill and I dropped the hammer between the lath and weatherboarding. It fell all the way to the bottom.

"For years Dad hunted for his hammer. Finally he died without ever knowing what had happened to it.

"Yesterday I passed the tumbled-down homeplace, now used to store hay. I asked the farmer, 'May I pry off that strip of weatherboarding under the window?' Puzzled, he consented. I pulled back the rotting board—and there was the hammer.''

My friend shook her head sadly. "Had I told Dad the truth, he might have scolded, but it wouldn't have hurt nearly as much as these years of concealing it. I've thought about it so often and regretted it so much."

I felt sorry for my friend, but aren't we all like this? We sometimes avoid confessing our wrong-doings to our Heavenly Father, though He promised to forgive us and remember them against us no more. We suffer a lifetime with sin's burdens, when it could be so different.

Father, give us the wisdom to seek forgiveness; may Your will abide in us, directing us in all things.

Z.B.D.

18.

Long time therefore abode they speaking boldly in the Lord . . .

Acts 14:3

Ever feel inadequate to tell others your personal beliefs? If so, you can sympathize with my shy, engineer husband who was always too hesitant to share his Christian faith—until that night in the hospital.

Recovering from retina surgery with patches over his eyes, Louis was glad for the company of a newly-admitted roommate, Jim—a patient who was to undergo the same sight-saving surgery in the morning.

But Jim grew quiet after supper and started pacing the floor. Suddenly Louis heard his roommate open the closet door and start putting on his clothes. Then Louis knew that Jim was so worried he was ducking out of both the surgery and the hospital! *Help him,* Louis felt God urge, *"Pray!"*

Trembling, Louis mustered courage. "Jim, the night before my surgery I was really afraid," he said, "but people prayed for me and it helped. May I pray for you that way?"

After a weak, "Okay," came a strong, "Sure—go ahead!"

When Louis finished praying for Christ's hand to guide the surgeon's, he heard the closet door again and a shuffling of clothes. Shortly, he heard the shoes drop, one at a time as Jim climbed back into bed. They talked for a long time, with Jim sharing his faith, and the operation was successful the following day.

Father, when we are timid and fearful in Your behalf, give us the courage to speak up boldly for our Lord.

J.H.

19.

O speak to reassure me
To hasten or control,
O speak and make me listen,
Thou Guardian of my soul.

John E. Bode hymn

According to an old legend, after God created the Garden of Eden He went about naming the flowers. Then, cautioning each plant not to forget its name, He turned to leave. Suddenly, the small voice of a diminutive flower murmured timidly, "I don't have a name yet, Lord."

Smiling down at the frightened little blossom, the Lord said: "Since I almost forgot you—and to remind Me never to forget you—your name shall be 'Forget-me-not'." Thus the forget-me-not became a symbol of remembrance.

In every life there are times when things seem so bad, the way so dark, that we think the Lord has forgotten us. But He hasn't, really. If we simply have the courage and faith to call out to Him, as the little forget-me-not did, He will answer.

Lord, give me the faith to truly believe that when I call out to You, You will answer.

E.V.S.

20.

Teach me Thy way, O Lord, and lead me in a plain path. . . .

Psalm 27:11

Working on the needlepoint my son had given me for Mother's Day, I was perplexed. It was one of those painted canvases, with colorful yarn provided. This one was imported from Holland and the directions were written in several languages. I could see the design of the flowers emerging and had been thinking, somewhat contentedly, what a pretty pillow it would make.

But there, in the midst of the pale pink and rosy reds, it called for three big stitches of a dark brownish green. *That doesn't make sense*, I thought. *It will spoil the whole effect.* I tried reading the directions anew and started to ignore the green spot, thinking about covering it with red instead. But then I went ahead and did as directed, though I did it rather reluctantly.

When a large portion of that section was completed, I held it out to look it over. I had to smile when I saw the lovely lines of that bit of green—it formed a graceful stem, as if seen beyond and below the ruffled flower. It was far prettier than it would have been without the stem.

In just such a way the texture of our lives is woven. How often do I question following the directions God seems to give me. But if I have the faith to search out His will and follow His guidance, I'd be able to look back later and see the wisdom of those "dark green stitches" in life.

Dear Lord, I tend to object before You've had a chance to show me the wonder of Your plan for me. Help me today to do Your will.

M.S.G.

21.

. . . But a doer of work, this man shall be blessed . . . .

James 1:25

There's a dry wit among the "hill and holler" folks in the southern part of my state of Ohio. It's often more wisdom than humor. Recently a tine on my spading fork became badly bent. I was referred to a local welder and smithy. The grizzled, work-stooped owner wordlessly took the fork to his forge. In a few moments he handed it back as good as new.

"Will it work now?" I ventured, to make small talk.

He peered at me over his glasses, blue eyes twinkling. "It'll work if you will!"

As I drove home the smithy's salty words tugged at me. That very morning I had begged off from a church job I had been asked to do. *How easy it is,* I thought now, *for me to think of the church today, with its dedicated professionals, its sophisticated programs, its electronic tools, as something that really doesn't need my help.* But the old blacksmith made me see that somebody's got to do the work.

Lord, help me to realize that Your kingdom will come if we do some work and not leave it all up to You.

C.M.D.

22.

**Have we trials and temptations?
Is there trouble anywhere?
We should never be discouraged.
Take it to the Lord in prayer.**

Joseph Scriven hymn

As an only child I humanized everything. I talked to flowers (before it was the thing to do!); I talked to railroad tracks I walked on; I talked to my Sunday dresses—asking them to stay nice and unrumpled till after church. But, most of all, I talked to God. Mostly I thanked Him for my friends: flowers, railroad tracks and dresses that behaved. And I shared all my secrets—some things I decided it was unwise to tell my parents and lots of things I knew it was not good to tell my playmates. Parents might scold—and friends might laugh. But not God.

As I grew older I talked less and less to inanimate objects and more and more to God. As a child I would have said, "Dear Cake, please don't sink in the middle." As a wife and mother I said, "Dear God, please don't let my soufflé fall." I still talk to Him about little things. "I'm glad my hair looks nice . . . oh, help me find the paring knife . . . why did I do that, Lord?"

Childish? Maybe so. But there are all kinds of ways to communicate with God. This is mine. For me, it works. Because I know He listens.

Lord, thank You for the freedom to talk to You about anything and everything.

J.M.B.

23.

Experience is not what happens to a man. It is what a man does with what happens to him.
Aldous Huxley

On display in the French Academy of Science is a shoemaker's awl. It looks ordinary, but behind that little awl are both tragedy and victory. It fell one day from the shoemaker's table and put out the eye of his nine-year-old son. Within weeks the child was blind in both eyes, and had to attend a special school for the sightless.

At that time the blind read by using large carved wooden blocks that were clumsy and awkward to handle. The shoemaker's son, when he grew up, devised a new reading system of punched dots on paper. And to do it, Louis Braille used the same awl that had blinded him.

Tragedy will come into each of our lives, but we can choose how it affects us. When it strikes, some of us ask, "Why did God allow this to happen?" Others ask, "How will God use it?"

Father, even when we do not understand Your purposes, help us to seek Your will.

P.H.S.

24.

**One is nearer God's heart in a garden
Than anywhere else on earth.**
Dorothy Frances Gurney

One morning I saw my neighbor, outside in the spring sunshine, working in her flower garden. She looked up and waved to me, so I dropped what I was doing to run over and say, "Hello." I couldn't help comparing the giant-sized, glorious, multicolored pansies she was picking, with the sad-looking, little, anemic, stragglers in my own yard.

"They are so much more beautiful than mine," I said wistfully. "What is your secret, to make them grow like this?"

"The more you pick," she said, "the more you have—and the more you have, the more you can give away." Smiling, she handed me a sweet-smelling velvety bouquet.

Teach me, Lord, to be more willing to share love and joy with others.

P.S.

25. What the world requires of the Christians is that they should continue to be Christians.
Albert Camus

When the Cincinnati Reds won the 1976 World Series in four straight games, many people were predicting a baseball dynasty. It was the second straight world championship for the Reds, and with a fairly young team, there appeared to be no end to their success.

Yet the next year, the Reds were beaten in their own division by the Los Angeles Dodgers. The reason for their poor showing, Cincinnati manager Sparky Anderson said, was that his team did not play fundamentally sound baseball. They had become smug and careless.

I myself like to play baseball, and I know there's a reason for batting practice, for shagging balls—all the effort that keeps your game sharp. Surely the same is true of my Christian faith. A daily quiet time with God, prayers, study, fellowship with Christians—these are just as basic to Christians as batting and fielding practice is to baseball players. Only when we remain grounded in the fundamentals can our total Christian life be strong and complete.

Never let me become smug, Lord, in my relationship with You.

J.J.

26.

Lead, kindly Light, amid the encircling gloom,
Lead Thou me on!
The night is dark, and I am far from home;
Lead Thou me on!

John Henry Newman hymn

Every year at Guideposts we have a writing contest for high-school juniors and seniors. One of the prize winners I remember best was Tina Lafler of Tonawanda, New York.

One beautiful Saturday in May Tina set off on her quarter-horse, Reuben, to explore a wooded area near her home. She and Reuben strayed through the forest, unaware of time, until the sun disappeared and a chill drizzle began to fall. Soon she was in the midst of a raging storm, unable to find her way out of the woods. Frightened, lost, she was on the verge of hysteria when she suddenly saw a tiny sparrow dart in front of her.

All at once Tina became completely calm. "Father of sparrows and lost girls," she said aloud, "please take us home."

She dropped the reins. Reuben hesitated, then moved on. In an hour they were clear of the forest. The storm had ceased, replaced by a heavy fog. But Tina was no longer afraid. Reuben suddenly tensed, ears up. Tina heard a distant whistle. Her father's whistle. She raced towards it. When she reached her father, she leaped, laughing and crying, into his arms.

If you are lost today in indecision or trouble, in frustration or a forest, remember that there is a simple and infallible way home.

When I falter, Lord, guide me safely through my fears.

S.F.

27.

Remember the sabbath day, to keep it holy.
Exodus 20:8

Last week I ran into Roger Buffin, a student-scientist I know. He's experimenting with the feeding patterns of white rats. I asked how they were doing. He laughed. "Great! Especially on Sundays!"

"Sundays?"

He explained that one morning when he'd gone to the lab early, the cleaning lady was there. "I told her that the rats were fed only when they pressed the bars at the sides of their cages. As we watched them press, discover their pellets, eat them and return to pressing, she said, 'That certainly looks like work!'"

Roger continued with a grin, "The next Sunday when I stopped by the lab, I missed the pressing sounds. There were the rats, each with a pile of food pellets in front of it. On the first cage was a note: 'Everyone should have the Lord's day off.'"

Roger's little story has been nudging my conscience. For I've fallen into some bad Sunday habits, myself, cutting grass, ironing, washing the car. I've been raised to honor the Lord's day with quiet thoughtfulness and meditation. But somehow, I've been thrusting that old-fashioned truth into the background. God planned for me to use Sundays for healing my battered spirit with relaxation and inner reflection. And if I follow His plan, I'll reap the fruits of His wisdom.

Thank You, Lord, for the privilege of honoring You on Your day.
R.H.F.

28. She smiled and the shadows departed . . .
John Addington Symonds

There is an old story about a ragged little newsboy and a beautiful actress on a bitter winter's night. "Are you cold?" she asked him. And he said, "I was until you smiled at me."

What is this simple movement of human muscles that is able to work such magic? The first thing we watch for in a new baby: "Look, she's smiling!" and the one thing that comforts us at life's close: "He died with a smile on his face."

Why? How? We only know that it befriends the lonely, cheers the ill, soothes the angry, flashes signals of hope and joy. "The boss is smiling, looks like we'll have a good day." . . . "Dad can't be too cross about the car, he's smiling." . . . "Guess *what*? This boy *smiled* at me!"

A smile is a mystery; nobody knows its biological cause, only its emotional effect. For the person who smiles feels better himself. His smile is not only light to another's spirit, its curve swings inevitably back to light his own.

Few of us have the time or money to do as much as we want to for the poor, the sick, the lonely. But this one gift we can always bestow. Invaluable as it is, it costs nothing, takes no time, requires no sacrifice. A smile never wears out, and it is impossible to run out of smiles. The more we use them the more we have to give.

Smile today! Smile at a child, smile at a neighbor, smile at a clerk, smile at a stranger on the street. Smile at the person who looks so cross—for it is said nobody needs a smile so much as the person who has none to give; it may change his world.

Thank You, God, for this priceless gift. Remind me to smile!

M.H.

29.

**He who gives a child a treat
Makes joy-bells ring in Heaven's street.**
John Masefield

The motorcycles had passed. The flag bearers had gone. The first band was passing, and the clowns were in view. I had come early for my good spot along the parade route.

"Pardon me," a gray-haired woman said to a young mother standing next to me. "If you change places with me, your children will be able to see better."

With a bit of pushing and foot shuffling, places were changed.

"That was nice of you," I said.

"I've seen lots of parades," she said, smiling. "They haven't."

Father, teach us to recognize the ways in which we can make it easier for those around us to see the parade.

D.D.**

30.

A gift is as a precious stone in the eyes of him that hath it.

Proverbs 17:8

I remember my first primary school prize-day clearly because I had set my heart on the clockwork train.

Proud and important-looking it stood on teacher's desk with the other prizes; I could almost feel its shiny red metal in my hand.

It never occurred to me that the train was a boy's reward and that I would be handed a simpering-faced doll in a garish pink woolly dress. Tears of disappointment welled, but at that moment I saw my teacher's expression of shy pride. I instinctively knew it was she—a plain, lonely spinster—who had knitted the doll's outfit, and somehow I managed to smile a "thank you."

Strangely enough, I grew to love that doll dearly. And although I did not realize it then, that prize taught me one of life's great lessons—that a gift should be valued for the love which prompted it, love which graces both giver and recipient.

Lord Jesus, You gave Your life for me. Let me appreciate today all the efforts others make in my behalf.

G.K.

31.

Wisdom is better than strength. . . .

Ecclesiastes 9:16

Dale Carnegie used to tell the story of the farmer who was frustrated for years because every time he plowed one of his fields he had to work around a big rock lying in the middle of it.

Whenever he had to swing his plow around the rock, he muttered to himself, "Too much trouble to dig it up. It would take more strength than a man has."

One day, without meaning to, the farmer swung his plow too close to the rock, and hit it. To his astonishment, the rock moved. He put both hands against the rock and shoved. It moved. He hurried off to fetch a strong rope, tied it around the rock, and in a short time, pulled it to the side of the field, and permanently out of his way.

Wiping his brow, he growled to himself, "How was I to know it wasn't all that deep in the ground?"

Whenever I have a problem I try to remember that it is always wiser to confront a problem head-on than to step around it. That way I may move, not just a rock, but a mountain.

The Psalmist says, "It is God that girdeth me with strength, and maketh my way perfect." (18:32)

Give me that strength today, Lord.

S.F.

JUNE 1979

S	M	T	W	T	F	S
					1	2
3	4	5	6	7	8	9
10	11	12	13	14	15	16
17	18	19	20	21	22	23
24	25	26	27	28	29	30

1.

O taste and see that the Lord is good:
Blessed is the man that trusteth in Him.

Psalm 34:8

My tree house was high up in an old apricot tree in the yard of my childhood. The floor consisted of roof shingles, and the single piece of furniture was a gnarled tree branch that curved over the edge of the roof, on which I could sit. The roof, fluttering green leaves. And my kitchen, the sweet orange apricots tucked in branches near my fingertips.

When I had been spanked or scolded, I would climb my tree and sit in my little house, holding tight to the soft-bodied doll who was my best friend. Her painted smile understood my tears. High up and hidden, I found escape.

Recently I read an article telling of a man who lives high above the ground in a Douglas fir in British Columbia. His tree house cost less than $10 to build, and there are no taxes. Food grows in the forest around him and water gathers from frequent rains in two buckets hanging outside of his window. He has found a hiding place from the world's insanity.

Today I live in the middle of a big city. Inflation. Taxes. Unemployment. Panic. But I still have a refuge. It no longer nestles among leaves and branches. It is neither an escape nor a hiding place. Rather, it is a haven deep within me. Its floor, the everlasting arms of my Father; its walls, the love of dear ones; its roof, the promise of eternal life.

Whom, then, shall I fear?

Thank You God for the serenity my haven brings. I am so grateful not to have to run any more. So thankful that I know You are there.

D.H.

2.

Giving thanks always for all things unto God. . . .

Ephesians 5:20

When my mother died, I felt as if a door had slammed in my heart. The pain of loss just wouldn't go away until, in desperation, I asked God to bless my grief. That was a turning point.

So often in my life, when I've stopped fighting a problem and started blessing it instead, I find that I've touched the transforming power of Christ's love. Blessing rejected manuscripts has brought me guidance in revising them so that they sold; blessing my frustration when a new recipe flopped or the kids tracked mud on my freshly-scrubbed floors has smoothed out my tangled emotions; silently blessing a friend who criticized my living-room decor changed my hurt feelings to forgiveness; blessing my son when he was in trouble at school helped him grow to believe in himself. In little things and big ones, blessing problems brings forth the good that is in all things.

When you've tried to overcome a problem in every possible way, remember that blessing it may be just the light switch you need to dispel your darkness.

I bless today's problems, Lord, knowing that the very act of blessing them can bring me in touch with You.

M.M.H.

3.

O God, our help in ages past,
Our hope for years to come,
Our shelter from the stormy blast,
And our eternal home.

Isaac Watts hymn

What is mountain mystique? Is it that mountains are so solid, or that they seem old and wise, that they loom so far above the trivia of everydayness? Frequently I find myself yearning for them during trying times, and one of my favorite verses in the King James version of the Bible is: "I will lift up mine eyes unto the hills, from whence cometh my help." (Psalm 121:1)

But Today's English Version translators take a fresh look at that verse: "I will look to the mountains; where will my help come from?" The message here is that help comes, not from the mountains, but from the One Who created them.

All of us have "mountains," places or people who refresh us spiritually. But we don't have to actually be in those places or with those people to experience the kind of help they give. All we really need are a few moments of quiet with their Creator.

My help will come from You, Lord, Who made heaven and earth.

P.H.S.

4.

Bless them which persecute you. . . .

Romans 12:14

When I was a little girl, our small mining town was torn in two by a strike that sowed contention between neighbors. There were two factions—union and non-union or "scab." I was a union kid. Every evening at quitting time the union women and kids took a self-righteous stand along the roads and crowed at homecoming "scab" miners. But one of those miners was Mr. Polovich, who kept his cow in a pasture north of town and went past our house to milk her twice a day. He had been my friend. Now he was my enemy.

So I stood on Uncle John's porch and flapped my elbows and

crowed at Mr. Polovich and the rest of the "scabs" until one day my Uncle John, who was a little drunk and very angry, ordered Mr. Polovich off his sidewalk and fired his shotgun to emphasize his words. I was sure that when I opened my eyes my friend would be lying dead. But the charge had only kicked up a little dust, and Mr. Polovich was plodding on down the road.

That evening I sought out my friend, but I was too tongue-tied to apologize. He just smiled and took up our conversation from the week before as if nothing at all had happened. I went home that evening with a lighter heart.

I think of Mr. Polovich often. He was my first lesson in Christian forgiveness.

Lord, I know that You have overlooked and forgotten my sin. I need to practice forgiveness myself.

M.M.

5.

Come away by yourselves to a lonely place . . .

Mark 6:31 (RSV)

Coming to New York City for a summer job with Guideposts three years ago meant my first move away from my home in Milwaukee. For weeks the city seemed a strange, awesome place; and I was lonesome for family and friends. At times my imagination played tricks on me, and for a brief, happy moment a passerby would appear to be someone I knew. Only the mail kept me in touch with old friends. And although letters were temporary spirit-boosters, they always made me want to see the writer in person. Homesickness came in every envelope.

Then Pam wrote me. I had asked for news of our friends, but she wrote that she hadn't seen many of them. Then she said, "God seems to be encouraging me to study the Bible more. I'm getting to know Him better. I'm thankful God loves me so much He wants to spend time alone with me." Pam reminded me of the time Jesus told His disciples, "Come away by yourselves to a lonely place."

I've certainly done that, I thought. But I had never imagined that God had a reason for me to do it. *Did He want to spend time alone with me?* I wondered.

In the weeks that followed I, too, prayed and read the Bible more. And I was intrigued by the new insights I found. Back in Milwaukee I might never have had the time to get to know Him better. Gradually, as I became more aware of His comforting presence, I dwelt less and less on my homesickness. I began to make better use of the time God gave me in New York, getting to know and appreciate new people and places. I still thought about my friends back home, but I wasn't lonesome any more. After all, I was spending time with my Best Friend, Who lives with me wherever I go.

Comfort me when I am alone, oh God, so I may put such times to good use.

L.W.

6.
Look unto the heavens. . .
Job 35:5

My 12-year-old son brought home a report card marked with nothing but Cs. Disappointed at not receiving the B that he had been working for, he complained bitterly. "That's just mediocre! I wanted to do better than that." I thought about what he said. My life too, I feared, had been mediocre, and I felt an echo of his disappointment within myself. I also had wanted to do better.

But then I looked up the word and found that "mediocrity" comes from a Latin word "mediocris" meaning "halfway up a mountain." Rather than something to be ashamed of, I suddenly realized that it is really a resting place. It does not necessarily indicate that this is as far as you can go. All it says is, "This is as far as you have come." Halfway up the mountain is not a bad record at all. It's midway between the bottom and God, and on the way up!

All we have to do, then, is look up instead of down, and keep climbing. If we reach up our hand, God will reach down His.

Father, when I reach the halfway mark, may I be one of those who continue to climb.

D.H.

7.

Jesus Christ the same yesterday, and today, and for ever.

Hebrews 13:8

A strong scent of rain overpowered the smell of kitchen cleanser. Thunder rattled the metal sides and roof of our mobile home.

Suddenly, I was a child again. Nose mashed against the cool, water-streaked window pane, I watched the interminable rain. An arc of color gleamed through the bright green leaves of a pecan tree that shaded my parents' solid, 100-year-old home.

"Look, Mama, a rainbow!"

She quit scrubbing the sink and we admired the rainbow together.

"God set His bow in the heavens as a reminder that He cares about us," my mother said.

It has been a long time since I was a child. Everything is different now. I no longer live amid the lush greenery of the Deep South. The view through the window of my desert home reveals a rainbow arching across a treeless expanse, unbroken from horizon to horizon.

I saturate my mind with the beauty, and hear in memory my mother saying, "It's a reminder that God cares . . ."

Everything is *not* different, after all. God remains the same. Whether I see His symbols with the sharp eyes of a child impatient for the sun to shine or through bifocals, His message never changes: *I care; I will protect you*.

Thank You, Father, for the comfort I get when I see a beautiful symbol that assures me You care about us.

L. P. E.

8.

Trust in the Lord with all thine heart; and lean not unto thine own understanding.

Proverbs 3:5

Several years ago, I was struggling with a particularly stubborn problem. I'd prayed about it feverishly for several weeks, begging, pleading, but without any results. Then one evening I walked outside to get the paper and found my son Paul, who was a toddler then, trying to pull open the petals on a tightly-closed rosebud. He looked up at me wide-eyed and said, "Paul make pretty flower bloom."

As I heard myself explaining to him that you can't make a flower bloom by pulling on it, something clicked inside of me. I had been handling my problem the way Paul had handled the rose! By begging, pleading, trying to force an answer, I had been trying to manipulate God. I needed to take *my* hands off, wait patiently, and trust in the creative power of God to open up a right answer for me. When the answer did come, *it was not what I had expected. It was better.* So my interference really had been blocking God's perfect solution to the problem.

If you've been praying about something without results, maybe you need to take your hands off the problem so God can make His perfect answer bloom.

I have given You my problem, Lord. From this moment on, I will stop trying to force my answer but wait patiently for Yours, instead.

M.M.H.

9. **Though I speak with the tongues of men and of angels, and have not charity (love) . . . I am nothing.**

I Corinthians 13:1,2

The pipe organ, deep and vibrant, heralded the bride and her maids in their delicate gowns. Candles cast a gentle light over white chrysanthemums as the golden notes of "O Promise Me" soared through the church. Tears escaped my eyes. Tears for blurred memories of myself before the altar, so sure and full of hope. Tears for the potential still unrealized.

Then the majestic lines from First Corinthians fell against my ears. Although aware such perfection is beyond reach, I was uplifted. As fresh, young voices promised ancient words—"for richer, for poorer . . . in sickness and in health . . . till death do us part"—I renewed my own vows silently.

At the next wedding you attend, open yourself to the message of the ceremony. Let emotion take charge. Let the music sweep over you. Listen, really listen, to the words. You'll leave refreshed and rededicated. You'll leave thanking God.

Thank You, Father, for the power of ancient words, the language of music, the symbolism of Christ and church.

M.B.D.*

10. Thou anointest my head with oil . . .
Psalm 23:5

Phillip Keller, author of A SHEPHERD LOOKS AT PSALM 23, was himself an Australian shepherd. From his own experiences with sheep he is able to reveal the meaning back of every significant phrase in this most beloved of psalms. For one, he tells us sheep are especially troubled by a nose fly which attacks the head and nostrils and can drive them nearly mad.

At the first sign of flies among the flock, however, the good shepherd would apply an antidote of oil. "What an incredible transformation . . . gone was the aggravation, gone the frenzy, the irritability and restlessness. Instead, the sheep would start to feed quietly again, then soon lie down in peaceful contentment."

He draws an analogy between this and the irritations of our own lives. And how "there must be a continuous anointing of God's gracious spirit to counteract the ever-present aggravations . . ."

This analogy is so perfect I have adapted it into a little act of personal prayer and comfort that I want to share for whatever help it may be to you. Each morning and evening, after bath or shower, I draw the sign of the cross on my own brow with bath oil, saying: "In the name of the Father and of the Son and of the Holy Spirit." Then, "He anointeth my head with oil, my cup runneth over; surely goodness and mercy shall follow me all the days of my life and I shall dwell in the house of the Lord forever."

I realize this is very personal, but it is also so calming, so reassuring, so effective in driving away the swarms of worries and other mental miseries that bedevil us, that I can no longer keep it for myself.

Such little rites and symbols do help us keep closer to our Shepherd, and remind us that He does care and will look after us.

Dear Lord, my friend and shepherd—thank You that You know my troubled thoughts and have shown me this way to banish them.

M.H.

11.

Judge not, that ye be not judged.
Matthew 7:1

Impatiently I waited for the landscape architect. "Why must he *always* be late?" I fumed, thinking that he never returned a telephone call promptly, never arrived when expected. Although I admired his creativity, I wondered if we could work well together. A stickler for punctuality, I had little patience with tardiness, especially when it seemed habitual.

I was pacing the walk when he drove up, got out of his car and, smiling, approached me. "Good morning," he said.

"Oh, it's the late Mr. Jenkins," I sarcastically replied.

Instantly, the smile was gone, a lost, defeated look replacing it. In a voice devoid of life or sparkle he answered, "I *am* late, and I'm so sorry."

I was primed to lecture him on the virtues of keeping appointments when he added, "We've been having some difficulty with our fourteen-year-old daughter; yesterday she ran away from home and I've been up all night searching for her." Tears filled his eyes.

How quick I had been to judge; to condemn! Shame and remorse replaced all other emotions. "Oh, Mr. Jenkins, I didn't know; please forgive me!" I begged. And I prayed that day, and often since:

Dear Lord, help me never again to add to another's burdens by judging; by finding fault before I have the facts.

N.S.

12.

The Lord is my strength . . .

Psalm 28:7

My husband and I sat on our front porch watching our young son try to roller skate for the first time. Our driveway was his skating rink. He rolled a short distance, then fell. He picked himself up and tried again and again, skating a bit farther each time before he fell again. For over an hour he practiced, falling less often, as he taught himself balance and coordination. We couldn't help admiring him for his patience and perseverance.

Suddenly he surged forward. "Look," he shouted. He seemed determined to make it to the end of the driveway without stopping. Almost to the end, he tripped over a stone and fell forward. He began to cry.

My husband ran to him and picked him up. Our son's hands were scraped, and his elbows were skinned.

Minutes after his small wounds had been cleaned and cared for he was out practicing again. How proud we felt that he hadn't used his bruises as an excuse to give up.

This made me think of how our Heavenly Father must feel about us. He watches us, allowing us to learn, to experiment. But He is ready when we fall. There when we cry out. And after our wounds are cleaned and bandaged He surely expects us to continue to try to reach our goal. If we use our bruises as an excuse to give up before we have accomplished anything, how could He be proud of us?

Father, thank You for being there when we need You. And thank You for letting us learn.

P.E.D.

13.

**We're saved, saved to tell others
Of the Man of Galilee;
Saved, saved to live daily
For the Christ of Calvary.**

Arthur Woolsey hymn

It was both my husband's and my college reunion, and the memories came flooding back as we walked the campus for the first time in 20 years. The reunion had special significance for Dick and me because we had married at the end of our freshman year.

At a luncheon gathering our class president suggested that it would be interesting for each of us to introduce our spouses and give a quick sketch of important events since college. Our star wrestler got a laugh when he revealed he was now an orthopedic surgeon. There were the usual lawyers, teachers and executives. I listened proudly as Dick told about our travels related to his diplomatic assignments.

But the most moving announcement of all came when Stan Entwisle rose and said simply, "I'd like to tell you about my work in a moment, but the most important thing that's happened to me in these twenty years is that I found Christ."

There was a hush, and then a gentle murmur of approval. For all of us knew the most important thing we can do in life is to love Jesus. Before and after that, nothing else really matters.

I quietly vowed that I would align my priorities the way Stan had.

Father, let me not overlook an opportunity today to become Your gentle witness.

B.R.G.

14.

He hath made every thing beautiful in His time.

Ecclesiastes 3:11

There's a bridge at the foot of the falls about a half-hour's climb from our cabin in the Colorado mountains. From early childhood, I've spent countless happy hours there, dangling my feet over the edge of the rickety bridge, breathing in the clear, clean mist, listening to the echoes of eternity in the sound of the falls. But last summer, when I made my usual eager climb to the foot of the falls, an enormous round metal generating plant glared at me from the falls side of the bridge. Ugly! Monstrous! Beauty and charm sacrificed to technology. How *could* they?

Disgusted, I was ready to start back down the mountain when it occurred to me that I had a choice: I could either let the metal monster destroy my holy place, or I could sit on the creek side of the bridge and look at what was still beautiful. I chose the latter, and as the spray from the water-splashed rocks below tickled my bare feet, the changeless music of the falls soothed away my indignation. The magic was still there!

When you're disgusted about something you can't change, remember that you have the same choice: You can let it rob you of your peace, or you can "sit on the creek side" and look for what is still beautiful.

Help me, Lord, to love beauty more than I hate ugliness.

M.M.H.

15 *Your Spiritual Workshop for June*

FOR MALNUTRITION OF THE SOUL

Carol, an old friend visiting from California, had an unusual problem. Her marriage was happy, her health was good, on the surface things seemed fine, "But life seems to have palled on me," she said. "Nothing is much fun any more."

An hour and much talk later, I had a sudden inspiration: Could it be that Carol's trouble was spiritual malnutrition? Wasn't it possible that her inner spirit was starving to death?

Taking up my Bible, I sat down beside her and turned to the Old Testament story of Daniel in exile in the king's palace, how he "kneeled upon his knees three times a day, (his windows being open in his chamber toward Jerusalem) and prayed, and gave thanks before his God, as he did aforetime." (Daniel 6:10)

"We have three meals a day," I suggested. "Perhaps we need spiritual food three times a day, too." The word "vitamin" really means "life substance." And Jesus used metaphor after metaphor to tell us that His Spirit is our life substance. He described Himself as "living water" and "the bread of life."

So I challenged Carol to try taking spiritual food in the form of life-giving verses of Scripture, three times a day for one month. Together we took a concordance and started looking up words such as *strength, food, bread, water, hunger* and *thirst*. Eventually others came from studying Christ's words. After Carol left I created a box of index cards for such verses as: John 6:35; Psalm 107:8,9; II Corinthians 12:9.

There are endless ways to use such a "Vitamin Box." In our family we pass it around table before meals and let one of the children choose a card to read instead of the routine blessing. Housewives paste helpful passages over the kitchen sink, by the phone. Businessmen keep these cards in their desk drawers; students have them on book jackets.

The benefits will not come though if you simply try to use the Scripture passages which someone else has put together. Take the time to seek and assemble the verses which have special meaning for you. This is the way that Carol found to cure her spiritual malnutrition.

C.M.

16.

For as he thinketh in his heart, so is he . . .
Proverbs 23:7

My young son sits slumped on his Little League bench. The season is nearly over, but he has yet to get the nod from his coach to go to bat. Now his team is behind, and it doesn't look as if he'll get his chance today either.

Suddenly the coach shouts his name! At last he's sporting the plastic batter's helmet, determinedly staring at the pitcher on the mound. His grandmother and I straighten up and strain with his every move.

The pitcher takes an enormous windup and fires the ball. The bat sweeps around. Misses. Another pitch, another swing: strike two. I can't look. Another pitch and my son goes down swinging. Our hearts ache for him. But, look, he's smiling as he returns to the bench.

After the game he runs to us. "Did you hear when I ticked it, Mom? Next time I'm going to hit it over the fence! I know I can do it, and Coach says I can too!"

Look to the young for lessons in living, I thought to myself. Defeat is not measured by muffing a single chance, or even a dozen. My son had the wisdom to know that his experience, ticking the ball, would finally add up to eventual success in his next attempts. Even though he was a pint-sized little leaguer, he already knew that if you can always look to the future with hope, then you can never fail.

Lord, when I must taste defeat, remind me to think victory.
R.H.F.

17.

(Father's Day)
For whom the Lord loveth He chasteneth . . .
Hebrews 12:6

Fifteen going on sixteen is a difficult age for a girl—not quite a young woman, but more than a child. Of course, at 15 you think you've acquired the wisdom of the ages and your parents know nothing and you wonder how they've survived.

I remember an evening when I was that age. I had decided that I was too grown-up and too sophisticated for a midnight curfew. So there I was, standing in the middle of the living room, stating my case in ringing tones and at great length. One thing I knew for sure: I had the family's rapt attention. Mother stopped flipping through her magazine; Grandmother held the next play in her nightly game of Solitaire; Dad laid down his paper. All eyes were on me, but not a word was said . . . they listened.

At one point, when I paused for breath, Dad quietly got up from his chair, went into the kitchen, rummaged around a little, came back and put something at my feet, returning to his chair.

I looked down, and it was a box of soap chips. Soap chips? Soap box! A picture sprang to my mind of a street-corner orator standing on his soap box, haranguing a crowd. I raised my head and found all three pair of eyes were still riveted on me . . . but still nothing was said. And suddenly—I couldn't help it—I burst out laughing and ran over to Dad. Throwing my arms around him, I said, "Did I really sound that bad?"

His face broke into a broad grin, but, again not saying a word, he nodded.

I had been put in my place—but ever so gently—and with love.

Heavenly Father, help all fathers to try and understand their children so that when it is necessary to rebuke them it will be done with love and affection—or even humor.

M. W.

18.

There is no fear in love; but perfect love casteth out fear . . .

I John 4:18

I was clearing some weeds and brambles from our church cemetery one afternoon when a frisky, short-haired black dog bounded over to me. He crouched down, tail wagging, gave me a devilish sideways glance, and then dashed off into some brambles. By the time his master had come over, "Blacky" and I were already friends.

"Wonderful dog," I said.

"Yes," the owner said, "but he wasn't always that way. I found him near here a year ago. He'd been abandoned, and he was starving. When I brought him food, he would growl and snatch it away. It was three weeks before he stopped snarling and stayed by me to eat. Then the next week he came up to be petted, but reluctantly. But the week after that he began to wag his tail when he caught sight of me. One day he simply followed me home. Now he's a very loving dog."

Isn't God a bit like the patient man who kept offering love, while too often we are like Blacky, slinking in lostness and fear, afraid to trust ourselves to him? If Blacky had persisted in his snarling, perhaps the nice man would have given up.

God never gives up.

Lord, thank You for staying with me until I unconditionally accept Your love.

W.D.

19.

I will lift up mine eyes unto the hills, from whence cometh my help.

Psalm 121:1

Since the very time they were heaped by the hands of the Maker, it has been the ministry of the hills to lift men's hearts to God. Centuries ago they caused the thoughts of a lonely shepherd named David to ignite and flame into worship, and a psalm was born.

But God knew there would be times in our lives when, because of a weight in our hearts or on our shoulders, our eyes would be downcast. He wanted us at those times to be able to see a reminder of His love, and so He consigned to the shadowy valleys some of His most beautiful full-of-wonder creations . . . starlight reflected in a stream seen only by those with bowed heads; earth-hugging flowers so small that they must be viewed from a bent-knee position.

Look up, then, with gratitude—and look down with hope.

Lord, let Thy handiwork also remind us that we, too, were created to glorify Thee.

M.B.D. **

20.

**Praise God, from whom all blessings flow,
Praise Him, all creatures here below.**

Thomas Ken

One day my son and daughter were upstairs having an ear-splitting, uproarious squabble. When my nerves could take no more, I stormed up the steps, raging, "Can't you kids ever get along peacefully?"

I'll never forget my daughter staring quizzically at me, lifting her eyebrows high. "Of course we can," she said. "But you never notice us when we do."

And it was true. I was guilty of taking my children's good behavior for granted.

Too often, I realize, I take God's good efforts for granted, too. Sunshine, flowers, family, friends, love—I'm apt to expect and accept them all without a thought or praiseful prayer for God.

Lord, help me to learn how satisfying it is to praise You every single day of my life.

R.H.F.

21.

**Love ever gives—
Forgives—outlives—
And ever stands
With open hands.
And while it lives,
It gives.
For this is Love's prerogative—
To give, and give, and give.**

John Oxenham

The other day I heard a couple complaining. They had helped their son and his wife in a week-long stint of cleaning up a newly-purchased, but run-down house. By the time they left, it had been transformed, but the couple got no thanks from their son and daughter-in-law.

"We worked so hard," the wife said. "It really hurts, their lack of appreciation."

Now I'm no sage, but I remember reading a bit of wisdom along these lines that left an impression. It was this: Never do anything for thanks. Do it because it needs to be done. Giving shows your love. Thanks, if it comes, is an extra bonus. If you act out of love, you won't be disappointed when thanks don't come. This is what serving God is all about. The strength He gives us is meant for love—no strings attached.

Today, Father, lead me to do things simply because they need to be done.

H.B.F.

22.

. . . This one thing I do, forgetting those things which are behind, and reaching forth unto those things which are before, I press toward the mark for the prize of the high calling of God in Christ Jesus.

Philippians 3:13, 14

One moonless night last August, my husband and I were walking along the ocean's edge at Emerald Isle, North Carolina, where we were vacationing with our family. As we walked, savoring the magnificence of the ceaselessly thundering ocean, we became aware of an army of dark moving shapes on the sand around our bare feet. The shapes weren't moving erratically like the skittery sand crabs with which we were so familiar; they were all headed unswervingly straight toward the ocean.

Kneeling for a closer look, we discovered dozens of tiny sea turtles, no longer than my thumb. They must have been hatched that very day, from eggs buried in the dunes a few hundred feet away.

Ever so gently, I picked up one of the tiny creatures to examine him under the light streaming from the porch of a nearby cottage. How precious he was to look at, the newborn turtle that no man had ever seen. But I saw in him something even more special than the intricate beauty God has placed in all His creatures: The whole time the little turtle was in my hand, he never stopped moving his flippers in constant rhythm, as if he

148

were still heading toward the foaming ocean with every fiber of his being. Seeing that adherence to purpose in one so small, I walked back to the water's edge and set him down among his brothers.

O Jesus, let me cling as tenaciously as that turtle to the purpose for which You have placed me here. Don't let me be discouraged by any interruption in my path, but keep me moving straight toward You.

I.B.H.

23.

Blessed be God, even the Father of our Lord Jesus Christ, the Father of mercies, and the God of all comfort; Who comforteth us in all our tribulation . . .

II Corinthians 1:3, 4

It has always seemed odd to me that during her lifetime my mother never seemed to be what you'd call "religious." She saw to it that her three sons always went to Sunday school, while church for her was a Christmas Eve-and-Easter thing—except I do recall that the moment she heard the news of the D-Day invasion she got right into her car and drove around until she found a church whose doors were open. There were a number of times that I had the feeling, and it was only that, that Mother was praying. But I never asked her about this.

In her late fifties Mother developed cancer, and during the last, long months of this illness she was in severe pain. Generally I would go to see her before my day at Guideposts began, and then again in the evening. I'd sit with her, my eyes glancing from a bottle whose tablets provided her only relief, to her face, which was beautiful and strained and resolute, somehow. Often in my own concern and frustration, I'd feel like cursing. *Yet why doesn't she?* I'd wonder. I was impressed by her curious equanimity.

One evening, in a silence, our eyes met, and I knew that Mother was reading the questions in my mind. She reached out for my hand and when she could feel its warmth she said something that has reassured me ever since.

"God," she told me in a low voice, "never said He'd keep us *from* trouble, but He did promise to help us *in* trouble. And He does, you know, He does."

I know You'll be there, Lord, when I cry out.

V.V.

24. For I will turn their mourning into joy.
Jeremiah 31:13

I rushed that Sunday morning as usual. Breakfast was over, dishes done, house neat, dinner almost ready. The children had been scrubbed, dressed, combed, ready for church, and just in time. Then my youngest, helping himself to a glass of chocolate milk, dropped the carton. Milk cascaded in an arc, splashing the floor, wall, my son. That culprit stood in a dirty pool, stunned, waiting for the storm to break. Break it almost did, too. Just as I was about to explode in a tirade of angry oratory, my husband looked at the milk on the floor and said,

"Look, a picnic for the pup!"

Even I had to smile. And the children unfroze, laughed, ran to get our obliging pooch and towels to mop up. A sense of humor had saved us again.

How often a little lightness at the right moment can keep a trifle from becoming a tragedy—and even turn a tidy profit for a pup.

Father, I need to remember that You gave us a sense of humor to use. And, oh Lord, in dark moments how my children would appreciate Your reminding me of this!

L.C.

25. For where your treasure is, there will your heart be also.
Luke 12:34

The dew-streaked sign on the lifeguard station had been turned to read "Off Duty." A fat child, out by herself, was dropping last night's shells into her pail. A bent bronzed woman wandered barefoot into the edge of the ebbing waves. Except for these companions—and the strange solitary figure up ahead—I was alone on the beach that fresh Florida morning.

As I drew closer to the solitary figure I began to be intrigued. He was walking the beach in a fixed pattern, a few paces one way, turn, come back almost in his own footsteps. His eyes were fixed on a metal loop at the end of a wand which he carried in his right hand. The wand seemed to be wired to a set of earphones, clamped heavily over the man's head. Occasionally he would stop, dig at the sand with his boot, then move on.

He was a modern-day beachcomber. The apparatus indicated the presence of buried coins or metal jewelry through a series of clicking sounds in the earphones.

An interesting gadget. But in a way I pitied the man. Because, in looking for treasure that *might* be buried in the sand, he was missing the treasures of the beach which were all around him: the sanderlings chasing the tide, the wave-foam blowing, the pelicans sailing in awkward beauty.

Lord, teach me to remove from my ears my own treasure-hunting devices which keep me from hearing You; teach me to lift my eyes so that I can see the treasures You have planned for me to enjoy each day, free for the asking.

J.L.S.

26.

The Pharisee stood and prayed thus . . . God, I thank thee, that I am not . . . as this publican. . . . And the publican . . . smote upon his breast, saying, God be merciful to me a sinner.

Luke 18:11, 13

I gave a silent groan when I realized the telephone caller was Martha. I had long ago figured her problems were insoluble, mainly because of her lack of Christian principles. I had never told her that, though, because I felt awkward discussing religion. I felt it was too bad she had not had the religious exposure I had.

I was braced against hearing more about her troubles, but I realized she was talking about a camping trip, and her tone was joyous.

"You sound happier than I've ever heard you," I said tentatively.

"I am," she bubbled. "A woman I met recently gave me a Bible. It has changed my life."

I would never have thought Martha would have been that receptive to the idea of Christianity. Then I realized she was trying to tell me something.

"You don't go in for reading the Bible and going to church, do you?" she asked gently. "It really helps you see what is wrong in your life and what to do about it."

I was aghast. I had considered myself a good Christian. I started each day with reading the Bible and went to church every Sunday. But I had kept my faith a secret. And now this woman I had judged to be beyond salvation was generously sharing her new faith with me.

That night I added a new petition to my prayers:

God, please forgive me when I act self-righteous, and when I hold back from telling others about You. Strengthen my faith so that it shines for all to see.

L. P. E.

27.

The Lord is my helper, and I will not fear what man shall do unto me.

Hebrews 13:6

Great-grandfather George Sutton came from England in 1861 settling in Chicago; there he met and married pretty Dorothea Koso. Ten years later they bought a farm in Effingham County and built a two-story house. It opened onto a garden, and had space for their seventy-five books; they had jerseys and fields, and they shipped apples to Chicago on the amazing Illinois

Central that whistled through virgin woodlands. With their children Sara, Mary and Martin, they thanked God for His rich blessings.

Then the gypsies came. Camped in the valley, they begged to trade fortune-telling for food. The Suttons gave them food. A gypsy told Great-grandfather, "You will die at age 98." And he remembered this.

He was 92 years old when he went to live with my grandparents Sara and John Buchholz. Each spring he planted a garden, and carefully saved seed. Then came his 98th birthday. Each morning he wondered, "Today? How? Accident? Illness?" He planted his garden, but didn't save seed. Autumn and Christmas passed. Then it was seven days until his 99th birthday. This week death would come for him!

But it never came to pass. One year later he stood tall as his five-feet-seven would allow to greet the line of friends who came to congratulate him on his 100th birthday.

He lived to be 101 years old. The gypsy was wrong. She didn't know. Only God knows. Like us, Great-grandfather needed to search God's word for the truth. The Bible warns against soothsayers. He Who knows the number of hairs on our heads, and He only, knows the day.

God, Your word shows us the way. Forgive our foolishness when we stray from it.

Z.B.D.

28.

A talebearer revealeth secrets: but he that is of a faithful spirit concealeth the matter.
Proverbs 11:13

I sat on a moss-covered rock, absent-mindedly looking into an upside-down world reflected on the surface of a woodland pond, thinking about a couple in our congregation. *I was sure the Smiths had a perfect marriage! They always seemed so peaceful — just like this pond*, I thought.

One rumor said a triangle was involved. Some thought it was on her part; some thought, no, it was on his.

I chucked a pebble into the middle of the pond. Immediately a tiny, rippled circle appeared. It spawned other rippled circles. All grew larger and larger until the outside one slapped against the banks ringing the pond, followed by others.

Another rumor said the Smiths' trouble was finances . . .

I tossed in another pebble and the ripples again brushed each other, spoiling the peaceful picture. It wasn't until I stopped tossing stones that the pond resumed its peaceful self.

But it took time before the ripples stopped and the surface was mirror-like.

I still sat on the moss-covered rock, but I'd stopped watching only absent-mindedly, by then I was intent. Maybe God was showing me that rumors are like ripples . . . spreading . . . disturbing.

"Troubled waters" took on new significance. *Maybe the problem wasn't only the Smiths. Maybe I'd helped contribute to it. . . .*

Dear God, keep my tongue from spreading ugly rumors about Your children.

I.C.

29.

. . . How oft shall my brother sin against me, and I forgive him? till seven times? Jesus saith unto him, I say not unto thee, Until seven times: but, Until seventy times seven.
Matthew 18:21, 22

I heard a little story the other day that impelled me to take some action that I should have taken much sooner. According to the story, Clara Barton, the founder of the nursing profession, never was known to hold resentment against anyone. One time a friend reminded her of a cruel thing that had happened to her some years previous, but Clara seemed not to recall the incident. The friend asked: "Don't you remember the wrong that was done to you?"

"No," said Clara. "I distinctly remember forgetting that."

I pondered that story for a while. Then I called up a former friend who I thought had done me an unkindness, told him that I was ashamed of harboring a grudge, asked him if he would care to have lunch and resume our old friendship. There was surprise and gladness in his voice when he said he certainly would.

Lord, keep us mindful of the fact that when we use our love to forgive others we open our hearts to more love from You.

G.D.K.

30.

In your patience possess ye your souls.
Luke 21:19

Weeds are the enemy of gardeners, but this spring, working in my garden, I learned something from one. Pulling it up by its roots, I tossed it between two rows of peas. A few days later, returning to the garden after a rainfall, I noticed that although the weed was wilted, it had already sent out tiny tentacles of new rootlets, groping toward the rich soil, struggling to get a foothold again.

Gradually, day by day, the weed sent out more and more roots, digging ever deeper into the earth. Soon, it had pulled itself upright again, had new leaf growth, a bright green color, and was flourishing.

There are times when all of us feel uprooted. A change of jobs, moving away from friends and loved ones, a death in the family, can make a person feel cut off and alone. When that happens, the important thing is to reach out to the source of life that is available to all of us. A Christian can always find the courage to grow new roots. Christ is always there.

Thank You, for being the rich soil of my soul, yesterday, today and tomorrow.

P.S.

JULY 1979

S	M	T	W	T	F	S
1	2	3	4	5	6	7
8	9	10	11	12	13	14
15	16	17	18	19	20	21
22	23	24	25	26	27	28
29	30	31				

1.

. . . Whatsoever ye would that men should do to you, do ye even so to them: for this is the law and the prophets.

Matthew 7:12

One hot summer when I was young, the vegetable gardens, planted with hope, turned to dust in the scorching Missouri sun. Dogs hid under the houses, leaves hung limp on the trees, old people fanned languidly in the shade. Parents were listless and children cantankerous. That was the summer my dad sewed himself a bathing suit out of an old flannel shirt and tolled all the neighborhood kids to the Chariton River every afternoon. They trooped after him as if he were the Pied Piper as he walked down the middle of the road with that striped suit showing above his overalls.

All afternoon we cavorted about in "Bass Hole" or "Corduroy Bend," sliding down mud slides, swinging out over the river on grapevines, teaching each other how to swim or dive. Then we trooped home again, exuberantly renewed and exhausted, to

157

mothers who had relaxed on back porches together piecing quilt blocks, embroidering or just dreaming.

Then one evening Mrs. Bean, whose kids were the liveliest and noisiest of all, invited us up to her back porch for lemonade. I remember she handed my dad the first glass. "Bless you, George," she said. "You've given me a whole afternoon to be myself again!"

Wouldn't it be nice if, even once a day, each of us could lift a burden from someone else so that his true spirit could shine forth and he could come closer to being the person God meant him to be?

Lord, show me today some small way I can help another to become the beautiful person he really is.

M.M

2. There are glimpses of heaven to us in every act, or thought, or word that raises us above ourselves.

A. P. Stanley

Just out of a hospital, on furlough from World War II, I took a rowboat out on a glacial lake in Switzerland. I rowed far from the shore, took in the oars, laid myself down under the seat and just drifted for hours.

The only sight I saw was the blue, almost cloudless sky. The only sounds I heard were the gentle slappings of water against the hull and the tinklings of cowbells from the mountainsides that cradled the lake. God was giving me a tiny hint of what peace in Heaven is like.

Today, when life's pace gets too frantic, I draw upon the memory of that time and that place. I use it to calm myself—to bless and heal.

You have memories like this too.   Stop now. This instant. Choose one that still moves you. Relive it intensely. See, hear, smell, taste, touch . . . remember!

Dear Lord, when I am most needful, You comfort me with healing memories. Thank You.

M.A.

3.

. . . But that the members should have the same care one for another.

I Corinthians 12:25

I was having coffee with a friend when her neighbor came in, bringing her a lovely pink rose. Jenny thanked her, praised and admired the flower and put it in a place of honor in her prettiest vase.

"But you have so many beautiful roses in your backyard," I remarked when the friend had gone. "Why didn't you show them to her?"

"Don't take away her song," Jenny smiled. "She was so proud of her rose."

Don't take away her song! How much I need to remember the little subtle ways in which God wants us to *care one for another*! Someone tells me her grandbaby just said a word—I'm wild to tell how mine, same age, speaks in sentences. Someone tells me what a wonderful trip she's just come back from—I long to describe in great detail the even longer trip we took last summer. No, a true Christian doesn't do that. A Christian has the grace to help others feel adequate, successful, good about themselves.

Father, we all have songs to sing. Remind me that sometimes the songs that praise You the most are those that remain unsung.

L.C.

4.

(Independence Day)
Breathes there the man, with soul so dead,
Who never to himself hath said, 'This is my
own, my native land!'

Sir Walter Scott

Whenever I see our national flag, bright against the summer sky, two things come into my mind: a memory and a question.

The memory goes back to a little ceremony that took place every Fourth of July around the flagpole in my grandparents' front yard on Long Island, when I was a little girl of five or six or so. Their house was right across the street from ours, so at the crack of dawn I'd dress hurriedly and race over to ring their doorbell. Fortunately, Grandpa was an early riser. Out he'd come carrying the neatly folded flag over his arm. At the pole, he'd untie ropes and fumble with different catches and pulleys while I'd jump up and down, eager for what I considered the big moment.

Grandpa would give the rope a couple of test tugs. Then, with a nod in my direction, he'd begin to raise the flag.

"Oh, Columbia, the gem of the ocean," I'd sing out in my high, piping, child's voice, "the home of the brave and the free . . ." Grandpa always joined in the chorus: "Three cheers for the red, white and blue," while a warm breeze gently blew the flag, now flying high at the top of the pole.

After this Grandpa and I would go into his kitchen where we'd eat cereal smothered with blueberries and cream while he told me stories about life in his native Germany and how he came to the United States when he was a young boy of 14. "I'm so grateful to God," Grandpa would say, "for the privilege of living in such a wonderful country. Always remember, Eleanor, how lucky you are. . . ."

So that's the memory. And the question? It's this: Does a person have to come from someplace else to appreciate—really appreciate—all that our country's flag stands for, all that it means?

I hope not, I pray not.

Lord, hear my prayer.

E.V.S.

5. **Run! Move the stone from your brother's path before he sees it.**

Old proverb

You couldn't have found a more self-effacing person than Mother. Hers was always the smallest portion, the hardest chair. Yet one July she started saying things that were completely out of character.

"This time next week I'll be another year older."

"I see my birthday falls on a Sunday this year."

I tackled Aunt Kit. "What's got into Mother? After all these years, why on earth is she dropping hints about her birthday? It's not a bit like her."

Aunt Kit smiled. "If you think about it, it's *just* like her. Don't you remember last year? We didn't remember her birthday until the day after it had passed. How awful we felt! No, it's not her birthday she cares about; it's us. She's trying to save us from another dreadful feeling of embarrassment."

Heavenly Father, help me to love others sincerely—and with imagination, too.

G.K.

6.

Trust and obey,
For there's no other way
To be happy in Jesus . . .

John H. Sammis

When I was a very small girl, Mom took the family to the New York World's Fair. Recognizing the danger in such crowds, she gathered us together at the entrance. "Remember to stick together," she said. "But in case anybody gets separated from the rest of us, stand still. Don't try to find us. We'll come back for you."

Sure enough, it happened. Enthralled by all the exhibits, I lagged behind and suddenly found myself alone. I climbed up on a bench and scanned the crowd. The family was nowhere in sight. Which way had they gone? Terribly frightened, I was tempted to run wildly after them, but then I remembered Mom's words and stood still. For what seemed ages I stood on that bench, straining my eyes in every direction. At last I saw Mom hurrying toward me, the rest of the family following her in a line like baby ducklings. Tears of relief rolled down my cheeks as she threw her arms around me. She had found me, just as she had promised.

In my spiritual life since then there have been times when,

feeling separated, I've been tempted to search frantically in all directions for God. But I've learned how much wiser it is simply to be calm, to wait and let Him find me. "Be still," He said, "and know that I am God." Exactly so!

Lord, give the quietness and confidence that are based on total trust in Thee.

B. R. G.

7.

An acre of performance is worth the whole world of promise.

James Howell

Skipper was our first new friend at the lake. She lived just around the bend. One day, canoeing by, I admired her yard, a paradise of flowers. "Would you like some plants?" she called back. "I'll bring you some." To my surprise, she pulled up at our dock the next day with a big box of petunias, marigolds and iris roots. "Here are the plants I promised," she announced, red bandanna blowing. "Let me know if you need any more."

A few weeks later she appeared to take the children water skiing. "C'mon, kids. I said I'd be over to pull you as soon as we got a new ski rope. Who's first?"

Another time she produced the photographer we'd been looking for. A man to take pictures of the remodeling of our cabin. Thanking them both I said, "Skipper, you shouldn't have gone to all that trouble!"

"Why not?" she demanded, blue eyes puzzled. "I *said* we'd come, didn't I?"

In short, you could depend on Skipper. Unlike so many people, she didn't blurt out promises primarily to please, to make a good impression. Those "oral good deeds" so easy to forget and to hope other people will, too. Skipper kept her word.

Skipper moved away, but she had a profound effect on me. I think of her whenever I'm tempted to forego a commitment I sometimes wish I hadn't made. And I think of Jesus and the apostles. There was nothing careless or merely kind-hearted about their ministry. If they said, "We'll come," they went. When the Lord said, "I will heal your daughter," He meant it. And certainly the promises God gave us in the Bible are forever valid. They are God's own word. All we have to do is read them and believe them. We can depend on them.

Lord, today, this moment, remind me of any promise I have made to anybody, even lightly, and to act on it. Help me to keep my word.

M.H.

8.

Each man must brave the sea alone.
Sailor's proverb

From many small towns in Portugal, cod fishermen come to Lisbon each summer to sign on a large fishing vessel and sail on a far-reaching, six-month voyage. "Vá com Deus" (Go with God) their captain says to the fishermen every morning as they are lowered in their single-man dories to work their lines alone.

Each fisherman's success depends on how well he knows the sea, how faithfully he abides by disciplines passed down through generations. But, no matter how good a fisherman he is, he must be careful not to drift too far from the ship that lowered him. Any number of emergencies—sudden squalls, fog, tangled lines—can suddenly put him in need of this ship.

Life is a sea, and I am like a Portuguese fisherman. I must brave that sea alone. I have companionship of family and friends, it's true. I can draw from the experience of others who have lived before, and I can be guided by the teachings of the Bible. Yet, if I stray too far from Christ's side, I have difficulty dealing with the tangles of life, and I'm in danger of being lost. Christ promised that He will give me strength to meet the challenges of living, and that He will stand beside me in eternity. But I, alone on the sea of life, must stay close to Him.

Jesus, let me be with You.

B.R.G.

9.

. . . Stand fast in the Lord. . . .

Philippians 4:1

In the play, "A Man for All Seasons," Sir Thomas More is being pressured by an old friend to go along with the idea that Henry VIII's divorce from the queen is valid, which More has steadfastly refused to do, even though his life is in jeopardy because of it.

Exhausting logical arguments, the friend says, "Come along, Thomas, with the rest of us—for the fellowship."

To which More replies, "And when I have violated my conscience and must go to hell for it, will you come along—for the fellowship?"

I try to keep that reply in mind whenever I hear the phrase "everybody does it."

Lord, give us Your grace to stand by the truth, no matter what the cost may be.

W.D.

10.

Let those refuse to sing
Who never knew our God;
But children of the heavenly King
May speak their joys abroad.

Isaac Watts hymn

We own a summertime gift gallery in the tiny vacation paradise of Lake City, Colorado. Once it was a brawling mining community; now the permanent population is less than 200. But Lake City's four pioneer churches have survived, and summer finds them filled with vacationing worshipers. The Community Presbyterian Church we attend has to schedule three services on Sunday mornings during the summer months.

At an early service last July, I sat next to the pastor's small boy, Malin Parker. He doesn't read yet and hasn't memorized all the words to the hymns, but he didn't let those handicaps prevent him from participating. Never have I enjoyed hymns as much as that morning beside Malin as he whistled all the verses of all the hymns.

What a joyful noise he made—and I couldn't help thinking that Malin knew something that many grownups never really grasp. He knew that when we go to church, the Lord doesn't want us just to sit there; He wants to *hear* from us. He wants us to praise and acknowledge Him openly and enthusiastically, in whatever way we can.

And so in the winter months, back home in Texas, I sing a little louder in our church choir whenever I remember Malin whistling.

Lord, give us the simplicity of a child that we may offer You what we have with a glad heart.

D.M.

11.
. . .And Mary hath chosen that good part, which shall not be taken away from her.
Luke 10:42

When I was first married, I had a hard time balancing my indoor and outdoor work, especially in the summer. I'd often go outside right after breakfast, leaving the housework undone. Sometimes I'd get so engrossed in yard work that I wouldn't have lunch ready when Rex came home at noon. Fortunately, over the years I've learned to do the inside work first and *then* go out. I really do a better job of both that way, and things are definitely more peaceful at our house when I have my priorities right.

I think we Christians sometimes have a hard time balancing our inner and outer work, too. It's easy to get so busy serving on the altar guild, singing in the choir, teaching Sunday school and such that we neglect our inner house. Important as these things are, we also need time for spiritual growth, time for getting to really know the Christ who dwells within.

I think a good rule is this: always do your inner work first. If you follow that faithfully and let nothing interfere, you'll find yourself so in tune with Christ that you will know when and how to reach out, and the balance between inner and outer will become automatic.

Help me to make my inner house a fit place for You to dwell, Lord. Only then can my outer work be truly blessed.

M.M.H.

12.

**For the beauty of the earth ...
Lord of all to Thee we raise
This our hymn of grateful praise.**
Folliott S. Pierpoint hymn

During our foreign service tour in Venezuela we always attended the annual orchid exhibit in Caracas. I was impressed with the hybrids, the largest blossoms, each delicately formed and beautifully colored. Sometimes a single bloom was too big to hold in both my hands.

Then one weekend our family went camping in the mountains, near the electric company's dam. While my husband and sons played ball, I took a nature walk in the woods, gathering wildflowers to brighten our tent. High in the trees I could see the orchids growing wild, blotches of purple sticking out of the mass of tendrils encircling the tree trunks. There were no crowds, nor blue ribbons, yet God had arrayed them in all their glory for the birds and animals to enjoy. And at my feet, on what looked like a tall blade of grass, I noticed a touch of color. A closer examination revealed that it, too, was an orchid of a different variety. I plucked it and carried it back to the tent to study it closer. With a magnifying glass I discovered each tiny detail as exquisitely formed as those of its giant cousins in the show. Who but the ants and insects of the forest ever saw this beauty?

God is in all things around us, the tiny as well as the huge. Does He really care enough to provide beauty for ants? How marvelous if He does!

Father, thank You for the infinite touches of beauty in my life.

B.R.G.

13.

. . . And God shall wipe away all tears from their eyes.

Revelation 7:17

The day finally came when I had to have Suki put to sleep. Our Siamese cat had been sick a long time. She was 13 years old.

"Nothing can be done," the veterinarian told me. "She's too old." And so I took her to the animal hospital.

"It's for the best," I reassured myself. "She'll be out of her suffering."

Quickly I took her in and signed the necessary papers. But it was hard. When it was over I climbed into my car, slammed the door and began to cry.

The next day I called a close friend.

"I really didn't know how much I'd miss her," I said tearfully. "It's almost as though she were one of my children."

"Remember the good feeling we get during the holidays, listening to Christmas carols?" my friend asked gently. "Well, when something upsets me during the year, I just put on an album of Christmas records. The old, familiar songs always help."

At first I thought her suggestion strange. Whoever heard of Christmas carols in July! Still, I decided to try it. As I sat listening to the words, "Silent night, holy night, all is calm. . ." I felt the pain lessen. Slowly a sense of quiet filled me. "Sleep in heavenly peace, Suki," I said.

A reminder of Your presence brings such comfort, Lord.

D.H.

14.

Let all bitterness, and wrath, and anger, and clamour, and evil speaking, be put away from you, with all malice; And be kind one to another . . . forgiving one another even as God for Christ's sake hath forgiven you.

Ephesians 4:31, 32

At our church circle, some of the ladies started discussing an absent member. They talked about how irritable she had been lately, how many meetings she had missed, how bossy she had become. Soon, there was a full-fledged gossip fest going on. Being chairman, I called the meeting to order, heard the minutes, and asked for any new business.

I was shocked when one member said, "I move to ask Mrs. X to leave our circle, as she has gotten to be a bossy troublemaker." Several ladies seconded the motion.

My eyes met those of our pastor's wife. She was as unhappy as I. "Please, God," I prayed silently, "help us to get out of this terrible situation."

Suddenly the pastor's wife spoke out firmly. "Well, ladies," she said, "before we do something we may be sorry for I request that we all join hands and each one say something in Mrs. X's behalf. Now if there is anyone who feels they can't say something on her behalf, just say a little prayer out loud for her."

One by one, each member spoke. The first said, "Lord, You know the Xs are having marriage problems. Help us to be more understanding of why she has been on edge."

Another said, "Dear Lord, forgive us for forgetting she has never turned down a dirty job, or refused to head a committee, no matter how hard the work, or how long the hours."

"I had forgotten," said the third, "that when my husband was in the hospital a few years ago, she took charge of my house and my kids, so I could visit him each day."

Another woman spoke. "Heavenly Father, there are times when we need a bossy person to take charge, to get us moving, to get things headed in the right direction. We thank You, Lord, for sending Mrs. X to our community."

By the time we got halfway around the circle, we were all weeping.

Mrs. X? After solving her marital problems, she was given an opportunity to use her valuable talents as a worker for the church on the national level, where today she has an important administrative and managerial position.

Thank You, God, for constructing my hand in such a way that whenever I point a finger to accuse someone else, I have three fingers pointing back in my direction.

P.S.

TRAINING FOR SPIRITUAL STAMINA

I have an unusual friend named Rae—unusual because she has the ability to weather the storms of life without getting pulled under. During a crisis in my own life, I turned to Rae for help. She took a plaque from her bedroom wall and handed it to me.

"It's a program I start in the morning and continue all day," she said, explaining the list of directions on the plaque.

I copied them down—12 exercises for body, mind and soul. I changed the emphasis here and there and started using them myself. In a matter of weeks, I noticed the difference. Daily irritations no longer upset me; I gained more patience and confidence.

Perhaps you will want to use your imagination in adapting this spiritual daily dozen to your own needs.

RELAX—See your burdens dropping away.

STRETCH—Mentally reach for the good that is yours.

INHALE—Breathe in all the beauty your soul can take.

EXHALE—Expel critical and negative thoughts.

THINK—Develop one healthy, constructive thought and hold onto it all day long.

LOOK—Seek one good quality in each person you encounter.

LISTEN—Hear the voice of God in some aspect of nature.

WALK—Let your steps follow His direction.

TALK—Speak kindness to one less fortunate than you.

SMILE—And watch the effect on each person you meet.

LOVE—An all-day heart exercise with others.

PRAY—Communicate with God throughout the day.

P. W.

16.

We know nothing of tomorrow; our business is to be glad and happy today.

Sydney Smith

I'd released an undersized trout into New Jersey's Raritan River and was carefully working the pool from which he'd struck when a fellow fisherman came by.

"Anything doing?" he asked.

"Nothing much. They're spooky today."

"Yup. You shoulda' been here yesterday, though. There was a fresh hatch of mayflies, and the trout were going crazy! Got my limit in a half hour."

I could only smile. How many times had I heard the refrain: you shoulda' been here, yesterday. Or last week, or the spring, or the fall.

Horsefeathers!

Today is the day where we are. God meant for us to rejoice in it. The one trout I had lured from today's stream was nearer and dearer and far more real to me than my fellow fisherman's yesterday's limit.

How foolish it is, really, to cloud one day by comparing it to another, especially another that is past. God fills each new day with its own fresh, limitless possibilities. Why can't we settle for that?

Thank You for this new day, Father, a day unique to itself and unlike any that has come before or any that will follow.

J. McD.

17.

Behold, I have longed after Thy precepts: quicken me in Thy righteousness.

Psalm 119:40

One hot summer day our daughter placed a tall glass of lemonade, frosty and clinking with ice, next to our mailbox with a note. "Mr. Postman," it read, "this is for you. You must be very hot today." I can still remember how that postman's face looked when he saw the glass and read the note.

And I can still remember how I felt when a new neighbor went out of her way to make me feel at home when we moved to California. She brought me a map she had drawn with our house marked in the middle, and then she had me in stitches with anecdotes about the people in the neighborhood. By the time she left my fears about a strange new place had vanished.

Neither my daughter nor my neighbor became famous for these Christian acts. No ribbons for excellence, no fortune for cleverness, no acclaim for brilliance. But such small acts of kindness live in our hearts and minds forever. I wonder if God isn't trying to tell us something by what we remember?

Keep me alert, Lord, to the needs of others that I can supply.

M.T.

18.

And they shall call His name Emmanuel, which being interpreted is, God with us.
Matthew 1:23

I was sitting on a rocky cliff overlooking the stream where my menfolk fished, near Slumgullion Pass in Colorado, when another camper joined me. We visited companionably for a few minutes and then introduced ourselves. "Dot," my new friend said thoughtfully, as though the name somehow didn't fit me. "What else are you called?"

"Oh," I laughed. "Sweetheart, or Honey, or Mom. Some-times, Hey You!"

It was only a casual encounter in a beautiful outdoor setting, but I've often recalled that question. Even our unchanging and steadfast God answers to different names: Savior, Redeemer, Heavenly Father, Holy Spirit, Shepherd, Comforter, Counselor. We have only to call out to Him, choosing the name that meets our special need. And He always hears us.

Thank You for being with us Savior, Redeemer, Heavenly Father, Holy Spirit, Shepherd, Comforter, Counselor that You may bless each moment of our lives.

D.M.

19.

If I were a little twinkling star
I'd shine on the darkest night;
I'd find some little, lonely spot
And shine with all my might.
                    Old English Sunday-school hymn

When Miss Betty opened her small needlework shop in one of our town's back streets many friends shook their heads.

"You need a central site to succeed," they told her.

Undeterred, Miss Betty was early at her shop each day, dressing the window. One day the display would be of baby dresses, palest blue and pink, ready to smock in delicate silks. Another would see a flamboyant tapestry patterned with peacocks or scarlet poppies, a riotous tumble of wools heaped enticingly at the foot. At Christmas there were gold and silver stars in the window, gleaming among gift boxes of sewing aids.

Gradually people began going out of their way to see what was new in the little shop window. "Never two days the same," they told each other admiringly. Passers-by became customers, customers friends, and sales increased. Today the back-street shop is a real success.

"And if I get the window done early," Miss Betty told me, "I can sit here behind the counter later and scarely anyone notices I'm in this old wheelchair at all."

Lord, give me the courage and creativity that laugh at life's obstacles.

                                                            G.K.

20.

And God saw every thing that He had made,
and, behold, it was very good. . . .
                              Genesis 1:31

After seven months of motherhood I was fed up. The cycle of diapers, dishes and chasing a crawling child seemed tedious and often unimportant. How I yearned for an *important* job to do—one where I could make decisions that mattered and lunch with people who went places and did things. Instead, I lunched with a child who usually spilled his food.

Then I found the weed. I nearly missed it, hidden behind the grapefruit tree. It wasn't very big—50 like it would have hardly filled my palm. And yet, how perfect! A royal purple center surrounded by seven of the tiniest white petals, each as carefully designed and executed as a prize-winning rose.

God hadn't seemed to care, making that weed, whether anybody else thought it was important or not, or even whether anybody saw it or not. The important thing was to make it as perfectly as possible. Somehow, seeing it nestled in the grass behind the tree, I sensed that just making it had given its Creator joy.

Few of us are engaged in what the world calls "important" work. But God's idea of importance is so different from the world's. A tiny hidden weed receives the same loving, careful attention as a universe.

Lord, give us Your perspective on life. Show us the true meaning of "importance."

P.H.S.

21.
God takes hold when we can't go any farther.
A. P. Gouthey

The little boy was having difficulty lifting a heavy stone. His father came along and, noting the boy's struggle, asked the lad, "Are you using all your strength?"

"Yes, I am," the boy replied.

"No, you're not," the father answered. "I'm right here and you haven't asked me to help you."

Sometimes when I'm faced with a problem that seems unsolvable, or a burden too heavy, I remember that little boy and I say this prayer:

Dear Father, make me remember that You are waiting to help.

R.H.S.

22.

Jesus loves me, this I know,
For the Bible tells me so.

Anna Bartlett Warner

One Sunday I sat near a young mother and her three-year-old daughter, Cindy, at church. As the service progressed, Cindy grew more and more restless. Finally, she pulled a hymnal from the rack and it slipped to the floor with a resounding thud. Immediately, Cindy received a slap on the hand from her embarrassed mother.

A long pause followed, then Cindy whispered in a choked voice, "M-Mommy, do you l-love me?"

The mother, unable to ignore the heartbreak in the small voice, slipped her arm around Cindy and replied softly, "Of course I do. I just don't love what you're doing."

That's the same relationship I have with God, I thought. How many times do I do things that are displeasing to Him? Yet, no matter how undeserving I am, He continues to pour His love and blessings upon me. I glanced at little Cindy's face and the joy I saw there was reflected in my heart.

Thank You, Lord, for loving me even when I'm unlovable.

R. H.

23.

Ah, nothing is too late,
Till the tired heart shall cease to palpitate.

Henry Wadsworth Longfellow

When our family moved to Pennsylvania from the South, one thing that attracted us to the home we bought was the stately conifer that grew in the back yard. Up and up it went, seeming to say, "You've bought a piece of time; I've been growing for years."

But in the fall, before our horrified eyes, its needles grew dry and brittle, then began to fall until the ground was covered with their lifeless brown. Our proud conifer stood stripped and bare.

"Well, I guess it's got to come down," my husband said sadly. "When a tree that size falls, it could wipe out a whole house." But, half in sorrow and half in awe of the project, we procrastinated. When snows set in, my husband said, "I guess we better

174

wait until spring."

Then, when spring did finally come, we were sizing up our sad duty when I noticed our tree's branches had taken on a pale green cast. Impossible!

We dashed for an encyclopedia. Under conifers we found larch: "Unlike most trees with needle-like leaves, larches shed their needles every fall and go through the winter 'naked.'"

We had been too hasty to give up on our "evergreen." Thank heavens we hadn't done anything about it! Then it occurred to me that you can make the same misjudgments about people. Those who have been hurt, those who are discouraged, or those who have grown old often appear of no use to us. When you treat them this way, you can make your misjudgment come true. Has someone you know lost a bit of his "foliage"? Don't cut him down. Fertilize him with some encouragement!

Give me the grace, dear Lord, to bring out the best in those who are near me.

M.R.

24.

The fear of man bringeth a snare: but whoso putteth his trust in the Lord shall be safe.
Proverbs 29:25

It was 95 in the shade. I was laboriously treading water in a swimming pool in which a neighbor floated placidly. She looked enviably relaxed and serene.

I worked my way over to her. "I've never been able to float," I complained.

She smiled and said, "That's because you've never believed you could. If you don't trust the water to support you, then it never will. Just lie down, relax, believe it, and you'll float." She drifted off dreamily.

Hesitantly, I tried it. Amazingly, it worked.

Life in Jesus is like that. Trust yourself to Him, and He will surround and support you in peace and serenity forever.

Dear Lord, give me the faith to surrender myself completely to You.

D.S.

25.

**If I have wounded any soul today,
If I have caused one foot to go astray,
If I have walked in my own willful way,
Dear Lord, forgive!**

C. M. Battersby

The other night, watching the news on television, I saw a father pleading for information about his 15-year-old daughter. An announcer explained that the young girl, upset by being called fat by her schoolmates, had simply stepped out of her father's car and disappeared when he, too, teased her about her weight.

With tears in his eyes, the father related that he had never imagined that his thoughtless words would have such a heart-breaking effect. He was willing to stand before the world and say, "I'm sorry. I was wrong" in order to reach out to a daughter he loved.

The man was unknown to me, but I found myself praying that he and his child would be reunited. I could feel his anguish because I, too, have often been thoughtlessly unkind, especially to those I love the most. Words can be weapons, and they should be handled just as carefully.

"Let the words of my mouth, and the meditations of my heart, be acceptable in Thy sight, O Lord." (Psalm 19:14)

B.R.G.

26.

It is almost a definition of a gentleman to say he is one who never inflicts pain.
John Henry, Cardinal Newman

DeWitt Wallace, the founder of the *Reader's Digest*, is both a friend and admirer of Dr. and Mrs. Norman Vincent Peale. Since he knew that I, as one of their sons-in-law, would be joining the Peales at their wedding anniversary dinner last spring, he asked me if I would mind hand-delivering a letter of congratulation to them.

Minutes after I said I'd be glad to, his secretary brought it to

me. Then, ten minutes later, she was back with another envelope.

"Mr. Wallace said he's terribly sorry to bother you again, but
he was very embarrassed about the first letter I brought you,"
she said.

I was baffled. "Why?"

"Well, since I thought it was going through the mails, I sealed
it. But Mr. Wallace said that handing a sealed envelope to
someone for delivery is rude. It implies that you may pry into it."

I chuckled and flipped the now unsealed letter back into my
briefcase.

But then DeWitt Wallace's thoughtfulness gave me pause.
One reason for the growth and prosperity of the *Reader's Digest*
is the devotion of its staff. And why this devotion? Simple,
because its founder cares enough to be concerned if he thinks he
has given offense to one of his employees.

*Heavenly Father, make me sensitive to the little ways in which I
might wound others.*

J.M.A.

27.

**Lo, children are an heritage of the Lord: and
the fruit of the womb is His reward.**

Psalm 127:3

I just found out that my nephew's wife is expecting a baby. That's
good news! You can't tell it yet by looking at her, except that
there's a very special glow about her that seems to shine out from
within. It's kind of like the glow that surrounds you when you
carry Christ within you. At first, it's like a holy secret, known
only to a few special friends, held within and savored with a quiet
joy. But before long, the Christ within begins to grow and
develop until all who come in contact with you become aware of
the very special Presence you carry.

Try carrying Christ within you today. Add His life to your life.
When you feel tired or discouraged, when you want direction or
forgiveness, when you need help with a problem or want to help

another, remember Who lives within you. Your heart is the home of the Christ Child's love.

Thank You for Your Son, Heavenly Father. Help me to carry this Holy Child within me today.

M.M.H.

28.

So long as we love we serve.
Robert Louis Stevenson

When my four children were young they loved to play in the sand along a branch of the creek at the bottom of our hill. One day they decided to spend the whole day there and persuaded me to pack them a lunch. I watched out the window as the bicycle procession began, wondering how they would manage to carry the lunch, since none of them had baskets on their bicycles and David, who was five, didn't even have a bicycle. But there was no problem as far as the children were concerned. Gail led the procession; Linda came next, and then Kathy. And David ran along behind carrying the lunches!

When they came home, hot and happy, I asked, "Aren't you ashamed to make David run along behind? And making him carry your lunch is adding insult to injury!" I fumed. But David was aglow. "We couldn't get our lunch down there without me!" he chirruped.

And suddenly I realized something: The older children hadn't really taken advantage of David; they'd done him a favor—by making him feel indispensable.

So my prayer for today is . . .

Oh, Lord, take my love. Shape it so that I can serve, even in unexpected ways.

M.M.

29.

Jesus said unto him, Thou shalt love the Lord thy God with all thy heart. . . .
Matthew 22:37

Jenny's birthday party was special this year because her father was dead and, as her mother, I wanted to make up the loss to her. So did friends and relatives. The gifts piled high. A tiny gold bracelet with Ten Commandments charms became her immediate favorite. She wore it as she and her cousins went out to play.

"You might lose it, Jenny," I warned. *No more losses, God,* I thought silently. *We can't stand any more losses, even tiny ones.*

I joined my younger sister and her husband in the living room. They sat close together, hands entwined and smiling. The way Dave and I used to do. Their intimacy seemed complete and exclusive. I felt stirrings of pain. *They're ignoring the other guests,* I thought irritably. And then another thought came.

It isn't fair that they're together and I'm alone. There it was. Envy. The words struck like a bolt of lightning. It's not fair!

"Mom," Jenny called, running in. "The catch opened and I lost my bracelet. Help me find it, Mom."

Grateful for the chance to hide my face and feelings, I went outside and dug through leaves and flowers. We found the chain quickly, but one of the charms was missing. On my knees in the grass I hunted. At last a glimmer caught my eye. The tenth charm. I picked it up. Tiny engraved letters on gold: "Thou shalt not covet."

Everything became still. *Thou shalt not covet thy neighbor's happiness,* I thought. *Or thy sister's joy.* I walked slowly back into the living room and stood looking at them. I felt their love, and suddenly its warmth seemed to draw me in. Quickly I bent down and kissed my sister's cheek.

Lord, let the love shared by others increase my happiness not my pain.

D.H.

30. A friend loveth at all times . . .
Proverbs 17:17

The envelope tucked among my bills, solicitations, and "occupant" flyers obviously contained a greeting card. It bore a local postmark, but what could it be? Birthday? Anniversary? Holiday? No, all were past or distant. I could think of no special event. I tore open the envelope, still wondering. Graduation? Promotion? Condolence?

Underneath a clump of blue forget-me-nots, gold lettering on the card read: "This is a Special Occasion." Inside it continued, "Another chance to say 'I Love You.' " It was signed "Maxiene." I saw her every day, but my friend had felt an extra impulse to cheer me, even though there was no special occasion.

How much better to remember a friend when there's no particular reason. Often that's when a lift is especially needed. How many such opportunities I have missed! Today I'm going to pass Maxiene's message along. Before sundown I will do it. Won't you try it with some friend of yours, too?

Lord, let us express our love for one another—never waiting for the "right moment" to say it.

J. M. B.

31.

Along the cool sequester'd vale of life
They kept the noiseless tenor of their way.
Thomas Gray

On the small Hebridean island where we were holidaying, Gaelic was the main language—to us quite incomprehensible.

Outside our orange tent, pitched on the flower-starred *machair* (short turf), our gay sunchairs and picnic table contrasted brightly with the gray stone wall of the ancient island cemetery nearby.

"Is the graveyard still in use?" we asked Mrs. Mac, who "had the English."

"Indeed it is, and a fine man will be laid there tomorrow."

We knew that these were very private people. So early the next day we stowed away our gear and went quietly to the other end of the island for the day. On our return we found a big bowl of brown eggs by the door-flap. Our silent sympathy had met with a heart's response—without one word being exchanged.

Teach me, Lord, the language of the caring heart today.

G. K.

AUGUST 1979

S	M	T	W	T	F	S
			1	2	3	4
5	6	7	8	9	10	11
12	13	14	15	16	17	18
19	20	21	22	23	24	25
26	27	28	29	30	31	

1.

The more we address and commit ourselves to God, and reject ourselves, the better it is for us.

Montaigne

On a summer's night several years ago I interviewed pitcher Jerry Koosman in the locker room of the New York Mets. All around us the players were showering, hollering, suiting up, running out for batting practice, yet Koosman, with a pitcher's concentration, was telling me how God worked in his life; he was oblivious to the confusion around him.

What Koosman had to say centered around the recent day when his pride had been punctured, a day when the Mets' manager had called him in and asked that he hold himself ready to pitch in relief that afternoon. Kooz was—and is—a starting pitcher; pitching in relief, therefore, seemed like a comedown. Kooz didn't want to do it. But he did. Why?

"Before the game that day," he said, "the speaker in our weekly Baseball Chapel just happened to talk to us about man's self-centeredness. He said that sin was having our own way rather than God's way. Well, those words were all it took to make me ask myself whether I should go my own stubborn way or do what the manager figured was best for the team."

Koosman's thinking was right on the beam, and so was his pitching. It's nice to report that he was summoned from the bullpen to relieve none other than the great Tom Seaver that afternoon, and won the game for him!

Father, I'm hardly a star baseball player, but I too can understand the difference between Your way and my way, and, yes, I know which is the right way. Help me to follow it.

V. V.

2.

They shall not labor in vain... for they are the seed of the blessed of the Lord....
Isaiah 65:23

I met Juliette De Bairach Levi, author of SUMMER IN GALILEE, quite by chance in Israel one year. Her letter that fall said the rainy season was just beginning, and described the miracle that signals its advent: "In late August and early September in the full searing heat of summer a miracle occurs every year. Up through the sunbaked earth, so hard it is almost impossible to dig it with fork or spade, white lilies press in delicate spires. They grow to a height of about two feet, flowering wands covered with starry white flowers.

"Their botanical name is maritime squill, but we in Galilee call them the rain lilies, for they foretell the rains which are soon to come and take the dust from the air and the burn from the earth. The miracle is that such delicate spikes can press up through such rock-hard earth every late summer.

"The Jews decorate their houses for the Hebrew New Year with these spikes of silver-white rain lilies, and they might have been the 'lilies of the field' spoken of in the New Testament."

I believe this is true, for the land is not much changed. And it is symbolic of an even more thrilling truth: God's seed prevails. However dry and barren the landscape of our lives, or how hard the fields we have to plow, we know the time will come when both earth and heavens open. The miracle will happen. Beauty will burst forth once more to prove God's love for us.

Dear Lord, give me patience. Whenever I get discouraged, when my very faith seems to dry and wither, when I begin to wonder if anything lovely can ever happen to me again—help me to remember the lilies of the field.

M.H.

3. **Then said they unto Him, What shall we do, that we might work the works of God?**

John 6:28

I picked a heaping pan of fresh green beans for dinner. My baby granddaughter, Jenny, found me "snapping" them in the shade of an oak on our front lawn.

"I'll help you, Grandma!" she cried with delight. I carefully explained and demonstrated the process: Snap off the sharp ends. Discard. Snap the beans in pieces. Jenny watched; then how her tiny hands made those beans fly!

"I snapped these beans!" she told everyone proudly at dinner. I merely smiled, thinking how she had innocently thrown good beans away, put discards in to be cooked. Actually she made my preparation time about twice as long as usual.

Like Jenny, I tried hard to help my Heavenly Father today. And like Jenny, I'm afraid I was very poor help. When I witnessed for my Savior, the clever young man I was speaking with left me stammering helplessly with his sharp arguments. When I tried gently to point out a wrong in a friend's life, it only left her very angry. Like Jenny, I must learn better how to do His work. I must grow, pray, study the Bible and seek the Holy Spirit's help.

Surely, then, with God's help, I'll serve Him just a little better each day.

Please, Father, help us to do Your work in a way pleasing to You.
L.C.

4.

Where are the songs of Spring? Ay, where are they? Think not of them: thou hast thy music too.

Keats

With jammed keys and peeling veneer, our piano's days seemed over. We couldn't even give it away. We tried to manhandle it into a shed, but we got only as far as a corner of the orchard and could go no farther. But at least it was out of sight.

Until our daughter's seventh birthday party, we forgot all about it. I'd planned games on the lawn, but suddenly Heather and her little girl friends were lined up at the old piano's keyboard, strumming happily, apple petals starring their hair. Five small boys lined up to climb to the piano top so they could jump gleefully into the tall grass. Three cows stood wide-eyed at the boundary hedge, and a robin begged cake-crumbs from our picnic table. Then straight into the piano's torn backing the bird went, revealing to the ecstatic children a nestful of fledglings among the wires.

"That old piano gave me my best-ever birthday," Heather said.

The piano was old, it was pushed aside, and yet it was still capable of giving great joy. And what about ourselves? While advancing years may remove us from center stage, this doesn't mean that life is over. There are all kinds of ways, some of them surprising, that we can still be used. Look for them!

Lord, as I grow older, help me to find unexpected ways of giving joy to others.

G.K.

5.

Delight thyself also in the Lord; and He shall give thee the desires of thine heart.

Psalm 37:4

One day our pastor told me, "Mrs. Ball isn't feeling well. Would you go see her? She lives out at the edge of town."

During my visit with the elderly widow, she confided, "I wish I had the finances to buy a bus so all the little kiddies in town could get to Sunday school. I'd sell some of my ground, but they tell me it's too rocky to farm."

Several years later Mrs. Ball suffered a fatal stroke and our board members were informed she'd willed her home, its lot and adjoining rocky property to the church. And not many months later, our church burned.

Instead of rebuilding on the cramped city lot, it was decided to erect the new edifice on that same rocky ground of Mrs. Ball's that no one wanted to buy.

Besides, it was no longer at the edge of town. Subdivisions— dotted with unchurched children—had surrounded it. Her meager little house and lot were sold . . . to buy—not one, but two—yellow buses to pick up children for church.

Apparently the Lord had looked at Mrs. Ball's heart and saw there a desire for kiddies to get to Sunday school. In the Lord's sight she had already bought that bus because it was in her heart to do so.

Oh, Lord! Let me not belittle my—or anyone else's—heartfelt desires.

I.C.

6.

Preserve me, O God, for in Thee do I put my trust.

Psalm 16:1

When my son Bruce was very small, we used to take him to the swimming pool at the club. He delighted in standing on the edge of the pool, with his father in the water shouting, "One, two, three, go!" At the signal Bruce would hurl himself into the pool, wrap his arms around Dick's neck, and pull them both under water. They'd bob to the surface, sputtering and laughing. Though the water was very deep, and Bruce couldn't swim, he had no fear. Never once did he doubt that his father would catch him.

One day Dick's friend tried to take part in the game. "Come on, Bruce, jump. I'll catch you," he called. But Bruce wouldn't budge. Not until Dick stretched out his arms did Bruce have confidence enough to make the plunge once more. His trust was in one man only—his father.

There is a Father you and I can trust, too; One on Whom we can rely in times of doubt, fear or stress. Others may fail or mislead me, but with Him I can be sure. That security can be yours, as well. He is waiting for you to make the leap of faith, into His open arms.

Father, help me to put my trust completely and solely in You today.

B.R.G.

7.

Be not overcome of evil, but overcome evil with good.

Romans 12:21

I attended a Christian meditation retreat in the Colorado Rockies last summer, and one afternoon the whole group of us took a silent walk together through the little mountain village. As we walked, I began to notice bits and pieces of litter scattered along the graveled paths—candy bar wrappers, old cigarette packages, pieces of newspaper, pop can rings, cigarette butts—all detracting from the picture-book tranquility of the nestled village. The more I saw, the more annoyed I became. *Why do people have to clutter up everything?* I thought. *Why don't they hire someone to clean it up? What's the matter with people, anyway?*

I walked along, grumbling internally and getting more and more disgusted with people in general, when I heard footsteps behind me stepping off the road. I looked back and saw the lady behind me reach down and pick up a wadded-up paper napkin. Then I noticed that she had both hands full of litter she'd picked up while I'd been complaining to myself and doing nothing!

Whenever I feel like criticizing or complaining about others, that incident seems to come back and jab me in the ribs as if to say, "Are you sure you're doing all *you* can?"

When I am tempted to complain, Lord, put me to work making things right.

M.M.H.

8. But why dost thou judge thy brother? . . . for we shall all stand before the judgment seat of Christ."

Romans 14:10

Five of us strangers emerged from the subway exit onto the Manhattan sidewalk one morning, and, as everyone headed away, I amused myself by analyzing the success-potential of the other four people by the way they walked. The man hurrying far in front of the others, I figured, was a real go-getter. The woman close behind him was undoubtedly on the way up the ladder. The third person who strolled at a normal pace was just average. And the fourth man who idled along glancing in shop windows, I told myself, would never make it in this competitive world.

Then the realization struck me like a pail of cold water: I was the last one of all!

Lord: Forgive us for the quick way in which we judge others.

R.H.S.

9. But lay up for yourselves treasures in heaven, where neither moth nor rust doth corrupt, and where thieves do not break through nor steal.

Matthew 6:20

A beloved grandmother who became ill was taken into the home of her daughter and family and tenderly cared for. She enjoyed the bedside visits with loved ones, especially her four-year-old great-granddaughter, Jill. Jill smoothed the covers, discussed the things she and her doll Moppet had been doing, and often brought Moppet with her to visit, too.

One day, the door to the bedroom was softly closed and Jill's mother told her gently, "Grandmother just went to heaven."

"In her nightgown?" Jill exclaimed. "She should have got ready!"

What Jill didn't understand was that grandmother had gotten ready a long time before. For this great and final journey, Grandma had packed days with prayers for family and friends; she had gathered up knowledge of God's greatness and shared it with many; she had given her love, her testimony, her time and her tithes, witnessing to Sunday school classes, to strangers, and to any seeking the way. She had mended hose and hearts; had lifted her voice in songs of praise in the choir and in her kitchen.

For this journey she had joyfully "got ready"—and had left behind a clearly marked road map as to where she'd be.

May we heed Your admonitions, Lord, and lay up for ourselves treasures in Heaven.

Z.B.D.

10.

. . . So let him give; not grudgingly, or of necessity; for God loveth a cheerful giver.

II Corinthians 9:7

When I first began wage-earning, I determined to finance a "real vacation" for my mother. So, for many weeks I saved my extra dollars. At last I proudly presented a full envelope to Mom. Her moist eyes and warm hug filled my heart.

One evening a month or so later, when we sat down for dinner, I noticed that Mom looked more tired and drawn than ever. "When are you going to take that vacation?" I demanded. At first, Mom didn't answer, but after much poking and prodding she finally admitted that she had given the vacation money to Daddy "because he had desperate need of it."

Mother heard my reproaches in silence for a time. Then she

held up her hand, and with a soft smile asked, "Whom did you give your gift to?"

"That's just it," I exclaimed, "I gave it to you, not to Dad!"

"Rosie," she said, "when you give something, *really* give it away. If you had done this, you wouldn't be worrying now about how I used it."

How right she was! All too often I have tormented myself about the use of my gifts. I have fretted about children breaking *my* toys, or spending *my* money on things they'll discard the next day. I've nagged my husband for not wearing *my* cufflinks. How foolish—and how selfish!

Lord, when I give, let me separate my gift from myself so that I may take joy in whatever use is made of it. Remind me that only then am I truly giving.

R. H. F.

11.

Those who know how to win are far more numerous than those who know how to use their victories.

Polybius

I'm a great tennis fan, and I particularly enjoy women's tennis for its grace and finesse. Far and away my favorite player is Evonne Goolagong, not only because she seems the essence of this grace and finesse, but because of her attitude.

Several years ago I watched her win a grueling match that was televised from Wimbledon. When she saw how distressed her opponent had become in defeat, she burst into tears of sympathy and rushed to comfort the loser.

In a game where "killer instinct" is regarded as so necessary for success, Evonne has carved a unique niche by winning with gentleness and compassion.

In the climate of competition that we live in today, it's easy to put winning first. Nothing wrong with this, if, like Evonne, we make winning an affair of the heart.

Keep me from victories that are won without You, Lord.

J. McD.

12.

All music jars when the soul's out of tune.

Cervantes

It was a summer afternoon at the zoo. We had worked our way down the path from the lion and tiger areas to the cages of the small woods creatures. Tommy, my three-year-old, had been jittery near the big predators. He felt more comfortable among the little ones.

I lifted him up to see a porcupine. They stared at each other. After carefully sizing the animal up, Tommy made his appraisal.

"Nice kitty," he said and reached his hand through the bars. Quickly I pulled him back.

"No, honey," I told him firmly. "That kitty has prickly skin. You have to love him without touching."

Later that week I had one of those days where everything goes wrong. The last straw came when Tommy spilled a glass of colored water from a finger-painting project on the white shag carpeting in my bedroom.

"I told you never to play in here!" I could hear my own shrill voice. My nerves hummed like telegraph wires. I could feel my patience disintegrate. The little fellow trembled. Tears came.

I endured this wretched day resentfully until at last bedtime came. I saw a little boy, brown hair damp and tousled, pink cheeks, pajama'd in blue. The day's irritations at last melted away.

And somehow Tommy knew it, because when I asked for a goodnight kiss, he touched my cheek. "I don't mind now, Mommy," he said, "you've lost your prickly skin."

Oh, Lord, help me to learn to follow Your example to be "merciful and gracious, slow to anger, and plenteous in mercy." Let my son grow up in the harmony of my love, not the discords.

D.H.

13.

. . . I will bless thee . . . and thou shalt be a blessing.

Genesis 12:2

One August morning on business some years ago, I took a shortcut between two desert towns. Before I realized that I'd

192

taken a wrong turn, I had gone miles off-route. At two in the afternoon, with desert heat at 112 degrees, I ran out of gas on a sparsely traveled road. And my thermos of water was diminishing rapidly. Of course, I prayed.

You can imagine my relief when a car soon came by carrying both extra gasoline and water for just such an emergency.

When I tried to pay the motorist for the gas, he refused saying, "No, just pass it on. You see, that's what *I'm* doing—ever since a man once gave me gas when I ran out." Following suit, each time I give gas and water to a stranded motorist, I feel again the blessing experienced that August.

What kindness have you passed on to others lately? God gives us so much of His abundance. And, sometimes, we get so involved enjoying that abundance that we selfishly forget to pass any of it on to others.

Father, save us from being so satisfied and complacent in our gifts from You that we fail to pass on Your blessings to others.

J.H.

14.

If any man among you seem to be religious, and bridleth not his tongue, but deceiveth his own heart, this man's religion is vain.

James 1:26

One morning at breakfast, we were discussing the impending visit of a relative that I was dreading—he was an incessant talker, for one thing. He also had some odd speech mannerisms and, having a small talent for mimicry, I was doing my usual impression of him. My nephew, Scotty, was in hysterics, but his sister Donna, 15, wasn't amused. I was disconcerted during my performance by her solemn eyes.

"Oh, come on, Donna," I chided her. "Don't you think I imitate Chester well?"

"That's not Christian, Uncle Bill," she replied quietly, "no matter how well you do it."

"It's all in fun," I protested. "You know that. I *like* Chester; I don't mean anything by it."

But Donna seemed unconvinced. "There's something mean about it," she said. "There's something malicious under all the fun."

I . . . *malicious*? Surely not! But in that moment I looked within myself and suddenly saw in a deep, intuitive way that all too often my imitations of people were a mask for pettiness and spite. The truth was that I really didn't want Chester to visit, and this was my way of lashing out at him. How many times had I done this with other people?

All I could do was silently pray, "Forgive me, Lord. Take away the expression of ill will that disguises itself as innocent fun. Help me to be honest about my true feelings and motives."

That prayer must have been heard, because now every time I'm tempted to imitate somebody "in fun," I bite my tongue instead. And I don't even miss it; it was only a small talent anyway.

Dear Lord, help us to guard our tongues and always consider the feelings of others.

W.D.

TO RIGHT A WRONG

Every wrongdoing is a barrier separating us from God. To move closer to Him, the barrier must be removed. Restitution (described in the dictionary as "any act of restoring . . . of giving an equivalent for loss or damage") is one way of accomplishing this. It is not easy, but if you work at it, you'll find the rewards are great.

First, read the story of Zacchaeus (Luke 19) and note how he decided that before he could become a follower of Jesus he had to make restitution for his past dishonesty: "And if I have taken any thing from any man by false accusation, I restore him fourfold." Then review the Ten Commandments (Exodus 20). Make your prayer something like this: "Lord, I have done many wrong things in my life. Help me to see now which ones I can rectify. Show me how to go about this so that in a small way it will ease the hurt of mankind and glorify You."

Second, make a list of the wrongs you want to right and submit it prayerfully to God. Remember this is a private matter between you and God. Do not let anyone else see this list. Overzealousness in confessing sins is wrong if it involves someone else and hurts his or her reputation.

Third, write down after each wrong the action you feel guided to take. A letter of apology; an anonymous payment to people or concerns for items taken; or, if there seems no way to pay a person back, send an equivalent sum to a church or charity. Restoring a bad relationship is thorny; one way is to seek the other person out and personally admit your mistake. Go further and accept responsibility for things that happened which you feel were not your fault. If your effort is rejected, don't feel hurt. You tried. The wounds may take time to heal. Try again later.

Restitution is a good way to deal with an overgrown ego. It also strengthens one's faith and makes it harder to backslide. The worker who returned the equipment he had sneaked out of his company found his will to resist temptations stronger. The more so because he acknowledged his guilt to his boss and fellow workers. Restitution always costs something—money, pride, position—but the alternative is worse, an inner discontent.

Righting a wrong smooths your way to God again!

L.E.L.

16.

. . . He created it not in vain . . .

Isaiah 45:18

I sat on a Hawaiian beach in the sun, watching a boy about eleven working in the sand building a village. An ambitious project, it had rows of cone-roofed huts enclosed within village walls. A roadway with sticks, spaced along it for trees, ran through the village. Pebbles scooped into a circle—a communal fireplace, a well. The little fellow worked carefully and painstakingly for over three hours without stopping, while his little brother and sister played near him.

"That's really beautiful," I told him. He smiled at me and kept working, flattered by my watching.

Gradually the tide came in. The waves broke closer and closer. At last a single long wave rolled higher than the rest, washed over the sand village, melted away the wall, smoothed and blended the little houses into a shining, wet, gray mass.

"Oh, that's too bad!" I exclaimed, feeling almost physical pain at the destruction of his patient work. I waited for his answering response of anger, hurt or frustration.

"It's okay," he said, getting to his feet. Quickly he brushed the sand from his jeans. "Next time I'll make a better one." Then, without a backward glance, he ran after his brother, tackling him in a great lunge. They rolled together on the sand. He had created for the sake of creating. That's all. No tears. No backward glance. On to the next challenge!

Lord, let me keep the lesson in my heart. Thank You for the chance to be creative today, and the endless opportunities that lie ahead in all my tomorrows.

D.H.

17.

As we have therefore opportunity, let us do good unto all men.

Galatians 6:10

For weeks I had scrubbed, scoured, painted and varnished the somewhat drab house into which we had moved. So when I heard the doorbell ring on the day our dining-room rug was to be delivered, I was delighted. With the rug down, it would mean that one room would be completely finished.

"The rug goes in the dining room," I said to the delivery man. "I'll help you straighten it on the floor."

"Ma'am," he said, dropping the rug, "I just deliver."

"Oh," I said, "I'm sorry. I thought you were from the store." I was so deflated that I could barely smile as I handed him back his delivery slip that I had to sign.

Moments later the doorbell rang, and there he was again with another man. "Lady," he said, "if you'll show us where you want the rug, we'll lay it for you."

"Oh, my goodness!" I exclaimed. "But it means moving the table and chairs, and the hutch, too! And I know it's not your job."

"Lady," the first man said, "we know it's not our job, but to make you happy we'll be glad to do it."

What a wonderful gesture! He had seen my disappointment and decided to go the extra mile. How heartening when others unexpectedly go out of their way to bring you joy! That thoughtful delivery man did more than just lay my rug; he taught me to look for opportunities to perform favors that are not my job.

Lord, show me an opening today that I can fill with the joy of an effort that is not required of me.

M.T.

18.

And as ye would that men should do to you, do ye also to them likewise.

Luke 6:31

My mother-in-law kept bees at home, the hives placed on a wooded hill. I would watch in fascination as she strolled calmly up the hill, wearing no protective covering. As she went, she clucked softly, much as one does to chickens, and she spoke endearments to the bees which flew down to meet her. When she came down again with the treasure of golden honey, her head and arms would be covered with bees, all humming accompaniment to her sweet words.

"How do you do it?" I demanded in awe. "I would be scared to death."

"And you would be stung!" she replied. "But they know I love them, that I won't hurt them and that I don't expect them to hurt me. And they don't."

I'd still be scared to do it, but perhaps I could, if my faith were stronger. For after all, it's not courage that's required, it's trust. And trust, I've found, has a beautiful way of inspiring more trust.

Father, teach us to love one another the way You have commanded us.

D.D.**

19. Thou openest thine hand, and satisfiest the desire of every living thing
Psalm 145:16

Not long ago, I felt my life was dull routine. Let someone name a future day and time, and I could say just what I'd be doing—pushing the vacuum cleaner, returning library books, traveling the freeway.

Then one Sunday, late for church, I slipped into a rear pew. Surprisingly, everything seemed a little unusual. At first, I blamed my breathlessness. Later, I realized I was viewing the pulpit from a new angle and different people surrounded me. After the service, a woman in yellow shook my hand. For months we had traded nods in the parking lot. Now, chatting as we edged down the aisle, we became acquainted.

Since that day, I've signed up for Bible class, tried singing hymns out loud, and every Sunday sit in another pew.

Although routine is necessary to orderly existence, too much steals zest from our hours. Most of us can't vary our pace by taking off for Tahiti or buying a string of pearls, but we can discover certain freshness by altering our small ways. To grow, we must keep looking at life from new angles.

Lord, spare us the dull depression of routine. Help us to see fresh angles.

M.B.D.*

20.

... With men it is impossible, but not with God: for with God all things are possible.

Mark 10:27

"Dear God," I said one morning, "show me how to be pleasing to You today."

Later that day I sat in the shade of our walnut tree, husking corn from our garden. The ears all looked alike, wrapped in green, parchment-like leaves with silken tips frosted brown.

But when I stripped off the husks, their similarity ended.

Some of the ears were mostly cob with sparse kernels only at the base. *Is one weekly attendance at church enough to mature you?*

Other ears were well-developed on one side, but not the other. *You're content to sit. How about giving a hand in daily vacation Bible school?*

Still others had darkly-smudged kernels discolored and growing cancerous-like from dreaded smut fungus. *You listened to gossip about one of My children, then added a few tidbits before passing it on.*

What a pleasure to find perfectly-developed ears with plump, even rows all the way around. *That's the way I, your Creator, intended you to be.*

I'd glibly asked God to show me how to be pleasing to Him, but I hadn't expected Him to do it through corn!

Father, I'm thankful I'm not an inanimate ear of corn, but I'm Your child. Keep me from smudge and immaturity and other diseases and make me pleasing to You.

I.C.

21.

In every thing give thanks ...

I Thessalonians 5:18

My young son David and his two friends finished devouring the home-made pizza and orange frosties I had prepared for their lunches. "Beat you out back," David shouted, grabbing a handful of cookies before he disappeared out the kitchen door. His friends quickly followed, and I was left with dishes to clean up.

I didn't mind because I had told David I would do today's lunch dishes. But I did feel a bit ruffled because, although I enjoy making lunch for the boys, not one had thought to say "thank you." Who likes to be taken for granted?

I sighed, and began to clean up the kitchen. Then I thought of Him, my Heavenly Father. When had I last said thank You for all that He has done for me? "Thank You, Father," I said, "for hands able to cook and clean."

The basketball banged against the window. I frowned. The kitchen door flew open. "Sorry about that," a boy said. "And hey, I forgot, thanks for the great lunch!" My son and the other boy chimed in, "Yeah, us too, thanks."

"You're welcome," I said, beaming.

As the door closed, and the basketball began hitting the house again, I said, "And thank You also, Father, for a home full of healthy, happy children."

Father, keep me from taking You so much for granted that I forget to say thank You for all I have.

P.E.D.

22.

I do not love him because he is good, but because he is my little child.

Tagore

One summer evening when I was eight or so, I sat on the front porch steps with Mother. That very day I had done something that made me miserable. Instead of bringing home all her much-needed change from my grocery shopping errand, I'd spent a nickel on a candy bar.

Now I could feel God looking sorrowfully down on me from His starry kingdom. Trying to swallow away my heavy lump of a heart, I said, "Mama, when any of us kids do bad things, do you still love us?"

Without turning her head, Mother said, "With all my heart! Nobody is good all the time. Besides, love sees straight through and beyond bad deeds. And forgives."

How lovingly she closed the door on my guilty fear. Without any more hesitation I poured out my shame. And I was free.

God loves me and you, His earthly children, in the same way. Even those times when we are not living as we know He wants us to. In fact, He is so forgiving and loves us so much that He sent His only Son, Jesus, to die for our sins so that we might be rewarded with eternal life. I feel every day the glorious freedom of His forgiving love.

Because of it, I try every day to do better.

Dear Savior, help me to be deserving of Your unbelievably vast scope of love and forgiveness.

R.H.F.

23. Take therefore no thought for the morrow: for the morrow shall take thought for the things of itself.
Matthew 6:34

I have found over the years that taking one step at a time is the best means of progress. At my summer home, the garage is perhaps two hundred yards from the house. At night when it is pitch dark, I carry a flashlight to guide me home. I have discovered that the most effective way of using my flashlight is to throw its light upon the path immediately ahead of me. If I lift the light and throw it far out, its beam is soon lost and I find myself stumbling. When I am content to light up merely the next step or two, I keep on the path and come quickly and safely to the house.

When our thought is projected days, months and years ahead, personal power is gone and we stumble through life without direction. Put the force of your thought on the day at hand and the tomorrows will take care of themselves. It's an unwise burden to take the tomorrows on your shoulders today.

Father, keep us from being impatient and running ahead of You, but to learn to take one step—and one day—at a time.

N.V.P.

24. How excellent is Thy loving kindness, O God!
therefore the children of men put their trust
under the shadow of Thy wings.

Psalm 36:7

In 1966, because of my husband's assignment in the U.S. Foreign Service, we were living in Lagos, Nigeria, where life was quite different from that I'd been used to in America.

One afternoon, sitting on my patio, I watched a young barefoot native boy approach. On his head was a huge basket of vegetables to sell. It balanced perfectly as he turned to look carefully in both directions before crossing the street in front of my house. Then as he entered the yard, I noticed a tiny little girl following close in his footsteps. Concerned for one so small, I asked the boy, "Why don't you put your sister in front of you, so you can see that she's all right?"

"Oh, no, madam," he answered. "Sun, he plenty hot. I not too big; but my shadow, he plenty, plenty big. If she stay in my shade, she no get lost, and she no get tired, too."

It made me think, and taught me a lesson. God casts His protective shadow over all the earth. If I walk in His path, and stay in His shade, I have nothing to fear.

Lord, help me to walk in Your protective shadow today.

B.R.G.

25. Yet, in the maddening maze of things,
And tossed by storm and flood,
To one fixed trust my spirit clings;
I know that God is good!

John Greenleaf Whittier

On the first day of our Scottish holiday, the view from our caravan window was of sun-sparkled sea and cloudless sky, the horizon broken by the hills of a long, low island.

Next day a mist covered the scene, and our newly-arrived

neighbors were disconsolate. "Can't see a thing," they mourned. "Not even a fishing boat."

"Wait till the fog clears; you'll see the mountains of North Uist," we told them.

They were frankly incredulous. "But that's miles away. Surely that island isn't visible from here."

"Oh, yes it is. We *know.* We've seen it," we replied, and waited confidently for our words to be proved true.

God's love is like that. When I cultivate a daily awareness of His goodness I need not fear its loss, even when temporary spiritual mists cloud my vision.

Thank You, Lord, that I can say with assurance "I know that God is good," whatever the day may bring.

G.K.

26.

Make a joyful noise . . .

Psalm 100:1

Even as a child and teen-ager I liked quietness. So it was not surprising that I found myself getting angry one night. I was attending a Guideposts Writers' Workshop. Sixteen women from all over the United States were getting bedded down. My roommate and I had agreed not to talk, but to get some much needed sleep.

I was almost asleep when ringing laughter and loud conversation began down the hall. "They sound like a bunch of college girls," I muttered resentfully to my roommate. She agreed.

The commotion finally subsided and I went to sleep, still grumbling to myself about the noise:

The next morning I was curious about who the night owls were. But before I could find out, a shy looking young woman came up to me. "I hope we didn't disturb you last night. In college I never could join in that sort of thing. Oh, I always wanted to, but I stayed alone in my room and was quiet. All my life I've longed to sit on a bed with a bunch of girls late at night and laugh and talk and . . . belong. It happened to me last night."

Her eyes brimmed with joyful tears, as she asked, "Did we bother you?"

I smiled sheepishly, ashamed of the way I had felt. "No," I said, and now I meant it, "it was sort of a . . . joyful noise."

Father, help me be willing to change some of my lifetime habits and to understand people not like myself.

M.B.W.

27.

. . . Wash me and I shall be whiter than snow.
Psalm 51:7

My antique clock had stopped. It was one of those large mantel types with a ponderous pendulum and a face painted with Roman numerals. I hadn't paid much attention to its ticking until it wasn't there.

I told the jeweler, "The clock's so old, it probably can't be repaired."

But when I returned to the store, my bill was marked, "No Charge," instead of the large amount it could've been. The jeweler pulled down his magnifying eyepiece and picked up a bit of lint with tweezers. "This was the trouble."

I stared at that lint. It hadn't taken something terribly significant to block those cog-wheels—just a smidgen of fuzz, barely noticeable, which worked its way inside. I didn't know anything was there until the clock stopped.

It made me wonder if I hadn't let some lint creep into my own life. For instance, lately I hadn't felt really close to the Lord. Had I been too casual with my prayers? Had I been spending too much time at the TV and not enough with His people? All rather insignificant things, really. But fuzz.

Lord, show me the fuzzy things I've allowed to come in and stop our fellowship. And help me get rid of them.

I.C.

28.

Come unto Me, all ye that labour and are heavy laden, and I will give you rest.
Matthew 11:28

During a summer visit to a friend's farm, I sat down under a shade tree beside the dirt road, enjoying the smell of earth and the hum of the bees. Soon an overalled man came down the road, walking between two mules. On the back of one was strapped a small wooden rocking chair. He held tightly to the chair with his right hand and led the other mule with his left. Nodding a greeting, he stopped in the shade and wiped his sweating forehead on his shirt sleeve.

"Too hot to be walking today," he commented.

I agreed and asked him why he didn't ride the second mule. "I just bought this chair," he said. "Don't want it to get broken before I get home with it. I have to hold on to it."

"But it's strapped so firmly on that mule's back," I said, "there's no way for it to fall."

"No matter." He shook his head vigorously. "I don't dare turn it loose!"

How many times I have spent unnecessary time and energy clinging to my own problems and burdens. Jesus has told me to come to Him when I am heavy laden, to cast my burdens on Him. Why, then, should I cling to them?

If I am to be truly free of a load, I must take it to Jesus—and turn it loose.

Lord, help us to learn to bring all of our burdens to You and to leave them there.

D.D.* *

29.

It is the Lord; let him do what seemeth Him good.
I Samuel 3:18

Many summers ago I was painting window frames and our five-year-old son, Paul, watched with fascination as the glistening white paint glided onto wood. "Let me do it," he begged repeatedly. "Mama, please let me do it."

When I had finished and there was a small amount of paint left in the bucket, I handed Paul the brush and said, "Okay, Son. Paint the stepladder. Try not to get paint on you or your sunsuit."

When the paint was gone, he came to me—and I was appalled. His naked arms and legs were white splotched; his hair was clotted with paint. The combination of dripped paint and dry grass clippings had formed straw pads on the bottoms of his feet.

"Paul!" I said in shock, "Why weren't you more careful?"

I kept asking that question as I applied cold cream, turpentine, kerosene, Vaseline and muscle. His hide turned pink and his whimperings increased to yelps and tears. "What did you tell me yes for?" he kept sobbing.

"Honey, because you wanted to paint," I reminded him. "I'm sorry. I don't want to hurt you like this . . ."

Parents are not always wise. Human decisions are not always right. But our Heavenly Father doesn't make mistakes. He doesn't say "yes" when He knows our requests will hurt us. From the first day of creation He has done all things right. We can trust Him without question.

God, give us perfect peace in the knowledge that You're in control, and that You love us.

Z.B.D.

30.

The way of a fool is right in his own eyes: but he that hearkeneth unto counsel is wise.

Proverbs 12:15

I am a person who needs a pattern to follow. Maps. Rules and regulations. Without them I am confused and lost. I have occasionally followed my own sense of direction. That is how I learned it is not to be trusted.

One summer a few years ago, I was vacationing with my son in Hawaii. We detoured from the main road in Kauai to sightsee. Heading back, my son, who was driving, turned right. *No*, I thought anxiously. *Left*.

"It's the other way," I told him pleasantly. "No it isn't, Mom," he answered. The car never wavered from its course. Fear set in. *We'll get lost in a strange place*, I thought.

"Honey, please turn around," I begged. "No, Mom. We're going right." Fear snapped the reins of my control.

"Turn around," I insisted. My voice rose, much to my surprise and his. Fear and fury suddenly filled me. "Turn around!" "No, Mom." He looked at me surprised, concerned.

At that moment I saw a sign with an arrow. "Poipu Beach" it said and the arrow pointed the way we were going. Why, that was our next planned stop. I was stunned. I had been so sure! How could I have been wrong. But wrong I was.

Yes, I am a person who needs a map to follow. To keep from getting lost I must have direction. Knowing this, each day I have learned to stop for a moment and ask, "What way now, Lord?"

When perplexed, what do you do?

For Thy name's sake lead me, and guide me, Father. For You alone are my strength and my pilot.

D.H.

31.

Every good gift and every perfect gift is from above, and cometh down from the Father . . .
James 1:17

I've always had trouble accepting compliments on the rare occasions when they come my way. If you agree with the complimenter, you may seem conceited. If you deprecate what is said, you are labeling the other person a flatterer, or questioning his judgment. It was a real problem for me. Then one August morning, unexpectedly, I found a solution.

My sister and I were attending an old-fashioned revival meeting held on the grounds of the Methodist church in Powell, Texas. A black man stood on the handmade platform in the sweltering heat of the noonday sun. He sang in deep, vibrant tones that carried across the congregation and into the cotton field beyond. He had chosen that great hymn, "The Old Rugged Cross."

When the service ended, we hurried to the improvised altar to tell him how wonderful his singing was.

He gave us a warm handshake, a broad smile and said simply in response to our praise, "The Lord has blessed me."

How unself-conscious he was compared to many people who appear awkward when they are lauded!

I decided right then and there that never again would it be difficult for me to accept a compliment. All I needed to do would be to recognize whatever gift is mine, acknowledge it, and then return it to the Lord.

Dear God, let me know, with gratitude, that You have imparted to me and to every person a special gift, precious in Your sight, to be used in Your service.

F. F.

SEPTEMBER 1979

S	M	T	W	T	F	S
						1
2	3	4	5	6	7	8
9	10	11	12	13	14	15
16	17	18	19	20	21	22
23	24	25	26	27	28	29
30						

1.

**In His hands are the deep places of the earth:
the strength of the hills is His also.**

Psalm 95:4

The kitchen was warm and cozy as we four girls watched Mama pinch off blobs of light bread dough, sop them in grease and line them up in the bread pan. I remember the smell of soup beans bubbling and potatoes frying, and the secret smell of vanilla issuing from the sack of chocolate I was hiding behind my back.

"What did you bring for Mama's birthday?" we chorused as Daddy strode through the door, dinner bucket under his arm.

But Daddy didn't answer. He just handed Mom his crushed and leaking pit lamp still fastened to a torn miner's cap. There was an odd quirk to Daddy's mouth, and Mama's eyes filled with tears. "What happened?" she whispered.

And then Daddy told of the great rock that had fallen as he bent over to load a chunk of coal. It grazed his head, he said, peeling off his cap and crushing it with the pit lamp against the coal face.

"And you?" Mama whispered. And Daddy showed her the dried blood on his bald head. They just stood there looking at each other with a strange light in their eyes. Then Mama said softly, "It's the best birthday present I ever had!" And even I knew she meant it was God who had given the gift.

Sometimes it take a near-tragedy to make us realize how much we possess and how deeply runs the river of human love.

Lord, help me to be grateful for the things I take for granted.
M.M.

2.

Open thou mine eyes, that I may behold wondrous things out of Thy law.
Psalm 119:18

When we were visiting in Denmark, my husband's cousin, Svend, took us to an old churchyard where there was a stone well so deep and dark that I couldn't see anything at all when I looked into it. Then Svend rolled up a newspaper, twisted it, set one end on fire, and dropped it in the well. It started spiraling down into the well, illuminating deeper and deeper levels with each twirl. How thrilling to see those new depths opening up that I would never have guessed were there!

Scriptural prayer has the same kind of effect on me. I choose a very short passage, pray for God to speak to me through it, and then begin to read it, *one word at a time*, letting each word stir up as many associations as it can. I usually get through only a few verses before the inner lights start flashing and I begin to see new depths of meaning I had not guessed were there. Very often the words speak to some special problem I have or provide just the guidance or insight I need. It's as if God dropped a flame into those words, illuminating them with special significance meant just for me on that particular day.

Maybe you'd like to try looking into the well of God's word in this way. What you see may light up your life.

Light of the world, shine in my heart as I read Your word.

M.M.H.

3.
(**Labor Day**)
All true work is sacred; in all true work, were it but true hand-labor, there is something of divineness.

Thomas Carlyle

Each year when Labor Day comes around, I think of my father with affection and pride. He came to this country from Sicily when he was just a young man, married my mother, and had five children, all boys.

My father's favorite room in our house was the basement workshop. This was the place where he spent most of his "spare" time—or whatever time was left over after working as a carpenter six days a week, 12 hours a day.

Now and then in the evening he would go down to his workshop to prepare his tools for the next day's work. I especially loved to watch him sharpen a saw. He would lock the saw into a carpenter's "horse" and with a triangular file stroke each tooth at exactly the right angle. The rhythm of his arms and his careful examination of each stroke was almost like a violin virtuoso preparing his instrument for a concert.

One evening when I was about 10 years old, he looked down at me and said, "Tomorrow when I need this saw for a tough job it will be ready. That's why you should study and learn. Somewhere in you is a special talent that you must sharpen and prepare so you can handle the tough jobs in your tomorrows."

My father had a way of making a profound point with a simple illustration. So did another Carpenter who lived 2,000 years ago.

Lord, each of us possesses a special talent that You have given us. Help us to find it and make the most of it to Your glory.

S.L.

4. I built a chimney for a comrade old.
I did the service not for hope or hire—
And then I traveled on in winter's cold,
Yet all the day I glowed before the fire.

Edwin Markham

When I was growing up I knew a sweet old lady named Mrs. Dehn. From the time I can remember, the second pew on the left in our church was reserved for her. She was the happiest woman I ever knew. I never heard her give a speech, nor did she hold any high office that put her in the spotlight. Yet, still today, when I think of Mrs. Dehn, the word "Christian" comes automatically to mind.

I remember most the times she came to stay with us, whenever Mom was sick or away. She didn't wait to be asked; she just showed up, apron in hand, ready to cook, clean, mend, or do any other service she could to help. And she'd take nothing but her meals in payment. Ours wasn't the only house to have the benefit of Mrs. Dehn. Any family in town that had sickness, distress or need would find her at their door. Once when we children laughed at the town bully who came down with measles, Mrs. Dehn said nothing, but the next day, in a fresh starched apron she was at that door.

Her happiness came from knowing that she was needed, not as a leader, but as a servant. Jesus said, "And whosoever of you will be the chiefest, shall be servant of all." (Mark 10:44)

There must be someone you and I could serve today.

Today, dear Lord, to serve You, let me be a servant to someone else.

B.R.G.

5. For as the heavens are higher than the earth, so are My ways higher than your ways, and My thoughts than your thoughts.

Isaiah 55:9

I sadly drove home from Portland's airport after watching my sons' respective planes grow smaller, then disappear. The older boy was heading for a missionary flight-training school; the younger to a Bible college near Chicago.

After taking care of them for 17 and 20 years I realized, suddenly, that both were gone.

I was scared. *Small planes are dangerous*, I thought. *There's so much crime in big cities. Lord, I feel utterly helpless. What can I do when they're so far away?*

At the stop light I idly watched a Greyhound bus pull alongside, then roar off, leaving a blast of diesel odor behind, but not before I saw its slogan on the side: "Leave the driving to us."

Leave the driving to us. That was the Lord's answer to my heavy-hearted question!

God had made my sons. Christ had died for them. The Holy Spirit had promised to guide them in His ways. Three holy caretakers!

We'd taught the boys this. We all believed it. Yet it took that Greyhound's slogan to soothe the sense of loss that I was feeling.

Thank You, Lord, that You always seem to send a word of comfort whenever I need it most.

I.C.

6.

I will praise Thee; for I am fearfully and wonderfully made . . .

Psalm 139:14

"Look at me, I can do it!" the children cry as they hang by their knees, or ride a bicycle, or pull you into the yard to admire the playhouse they've built. They glory in how fast they can run, how loud they can sing. They rejoice in how they are growing, in whatever dimension. Their own bodies are a source of wonder.

We adults lose this natural delight. Bogged down with responsibilities, we go dull and take ourselves for granted. Yet how glorious it is just to *be* here on this planet, able even to cope with our labors, our very trials. What a marvel simply to exist!

Practice being grateful for every breath you draw. Rejoice and thank God for the simple act of getting out of bed in the morning.

Smell the breakfast you are cooking for yourself, or others. Be *aware* of yourself and the countless things large or small you can sense and touch and do.

Look at every member of your body with wonder. Every finger, toe, elbow, knee. How remarkable their intricate joinings, what a complex, efficient package! These arms that can lift and carry, these feet that can walk to kitchen or desk, or dance for joy. And these eyes to see, these ears to hear . . . Don't wait until they're threatened, until you're in a hospital, in fear, in traction. Bless your body and its Creator for its abilities now!

Dear God, Who designed this miracle, my body, keep me always aware of its wonders. In loving and rejoicing in my body I am showing my gratefulness to You.

M. H.

7.

But I say unto you which hear: Love your enemies, do good to them which hate you.
Luke 6:27

I had thought of every excuse to fire Toby, my assistant in a large department store advertising office. He was talented and efficient, but he and I were at constant odds, and colleagues had told me that he had even tried to undermine me with my boss. Finally, to my immense relief, he resigned.

A few years later, the president of another department store asked if I knew of a good man to head his advertising department. Though I tried to duck it, Toby's name came to mind. He filled the job description all right, but after what he and I had been through. . . .

I held a little debate with myself. *Could he do the job?*
Yes, he's a natural.
Well?

The next day I called Toby, and the day after that he had accepted the job, a very choice one. But it wasn't until Toby called and invited me to dinner that I fully realized that I had done the right thing. He confessed his former enmity and asked my forgiveness. Then, as we shook hands, he said, "Friends are better than enemies, aren't they?"

It was then that the truth of the Biblical instruction—love your enemies—came surging through. When you love them, they perform a wonderful vanishing act and then return as friends.

Lord, impress upon us that the sure way to destroy an enemy is to make him a friend.

C.M.D.

8.

Rejoice with them that do rejoice, and weep with them that weep.

Romans 12:15

A first-grade teacher I know uses the happy face symbol when grading papers. Good work is rewarded with a quickly-drawn smiling face. Sloppy work gets a face with the smile turned upside down. Her students love the symbols, and even use them in conversation.

One boy told her to "Put on a sad face. My brother has the measles." Another child said, "It's happy face time! Our cat has six kittens!"

Why do the children react so eagerly to these symbols? Isn't it because they know that words are often inadequate? A smiling face shows emotion instantly; a frown conveys sorrow. They know, too, that sorrow, shared, becomes bearable. Joy, shared, multiples itself.

Dear Lord, help us show Your love through both our laughter and our tears.

P.V.S.

9.

Hearken unto Me, My people. . . .

Isaiah 51:4

There's an old Portuguese story that my mother used to tell me about a Christian boy who had been reduced to begging on the streets. One day, the story goes, the beggar boy was mocked by the son of a wealthy atheist.

"If God really loves you," the atheist's son asked, "why doesn't He take better care of you? Why doesn't He tell someone to send you a pair of shoes?"

Sadly, the beggar boy replied, "I think God does tell people. But they're not listening."

Do you listen when God tells you about people who need help by putting them in your path? Watch today for such opportunities. Don't pass them by.

Dear Father, grant me a heart loving enough to feel what the unfortunate feel.

M.A.

10.

A talebearer revealeth secrets: but he that is of a faithful spirit concealeth the matter.
Proverbs 11:13

Some years ago a friend asked me to go to church with her. This friend was a very good-hearted lady, always willing to help someone in trouble. But she had one failing that cost her many friends: she was a compulsive gossip. Many people with whom she shared her sometimes malicious "tid-bits" tried to change the subject or disagree with her. Nothing worked.

At church that day I soon became very embarrassed for my friend. I was sure she, too, was most uncomfortable because the entire sermon was aimed at people with loose tongues, dwelling on the harm they do. I didn't say anything as we left the church, but my friend did.

"You know" she confided earnestly, "there are lots of people who gossip like that. It's really a terrible, un-Christian thing."

It came to me then that the poor lady didn't even know that she herself was guilty of endless damaging talk about others.

What a common problem this is! We all have blind spots—and when we do, how can we detect and correct our faults? Perhaps, occasionally, it would be a good idea for each of us to ask a close friend to tell us, in loving honesty, where our principal weaknesses lie. That way, we might remove some of the blocks that keep us from the persons God really wants us to be.

Dear Lord, help us see ourselves as others see us. More important, let us see ourselves as You see us—and grow ever closer to what You want us to be.

D.D.*

11.

Be doers of the word, and not hearers only, deceiving your own selves.

James 1:22

When I was in the seventh grade at North Junior High in Colorado Springs, my home room teacher was Zita Gormley. Her beautifully waved white hair made her look like a sister to George Washington, whose picture hung at the front of the classroom. Undoubtedly, Miss Gormley was an excellent teacher because I enjoyed her classes. But the one thing she taught that I've remembered through the years was not listed in the curriculum. It was "gumption."

Gumption, according to her, was a character trait to be desired, cultivated and practiced. Gumption made one try harder to excel. Gumption required one to get the assignment done the day *before* it was due. Gumption made one look for the best way, not the easiest way.

Gumption is an action word denoting courage and initiative, enterprise and boldness. It's not lazy and it's not timid.

Sometimes I'm tempted—we all are—to practice a negative kind of piety—avoiding evil by doing nothing. But faith and love demand action. Gumption, if you please. The Apostles had it. And if you consider the people you most admire you'll see it being demonstrated in their lives as they teach a Sunday school class, sponsor a youth group, deliver food for "Meals on Wheels" or quietly and tirelessly offer a helping hand where it's needed. Because "doers of the word" have the gumption to get out of their easy chairs and get into action.

Lord, give us the gumption we need to help others with love and cheerfulness.

D.M.

12.

He is closer than breathing, nearer than hands and feet.

Alfred, Lord Tennyson

A few weeks ago, as I was standing in the check-out line at the grocery store, I noticed that my purse was missing. Quickly I retraced my steps, looking everywhere I'd been, but I didn't find it. The manager announced my loss over the loud-speaker, but still no luck. I was getting a little panicky now, so I hurried out to look in the car, but it wasn't there, either. Where could it be? Could someone have stolen it? I paid for my groceries with a counter check, left my phone number, and went home in a rather frantic state of mind. The minute I walked in the door I saw it. It had been sitting on the kitchen counter all the time I was so nervously looking for it everywhere else.

Sometimes we search for God that way. We look for Him in books, in sermons, in the experiences of other people; or we think of Him as way off up in the sky somewhere, when all the time He is "closer than breathing, nearer than hands and feet." Jesus said, "The kingdom of God is within you." (Luke 17:21) He is in all of those other places, too, but unless we first find Him "in here," we'll never be able to recognize Him "out there."

Ease my frantic search, Lord, by teaching me to find Your kingdom within.

M.M.H.

13.

Greater love hath no man than this, that a man lay down his life for his friends.

John 15:13

While living in Nigeria some years ago, we enjoyed taking trips to Tarkwa Beach. Our swimming area was a sheltered cove at the tip of the mainland, just inside a rock breakwater that blocked the fury of the Atlantic Ocean. On the other side of those rocks the adventurous liked to surf.

One day a young girl, who was no match for the power of the waves, was swept away from this shore. Her neighbor, a middle-aged man, rushed into the surf to help. He managed to bring her safely to shore, but in so doing he suffered a fatal heart attack. At the funeral I saw the young girl's tears, and heard her tell the man's wife, "I'll never forget him. I owe him my life."

How would you feel if you were that young girl? Wouldn't you want your life to count for something so that the man who saved you did not die in vain?

Well, you *are* that girl. Jesus Christ died for you.

Loving Jesus, let me never forget that because of You I live, today and evermore.

B.R.G.

14.

Let not the sun go down upon your wrath.
Ephesians 4:26

I'll never forget the day my neighbor, whom I considered my friend, stopped speaking to me. We were the only two mothers in the six-apartment-building, and our small children often played together in one or the other of our apartments.

This day it was raining. I opened my door to rescue my daughter's portable swing from the back porch when I saw my neighbor Betty coming down the stairs. She seemed to have an angry look on her face. I started to say something to her when I heard a cry inside my apartment. I grabbed the swing and hurried inside. The thunder had awakened my baby from his nap, and he was crying for me.

All afternoon I remembered the angry look on Betty's face, and I wondered. What was bothering her? Since it was still raining I expected her to call and suggest the children play together. When she didn't, I began to feel sure her anger was directed at me.

Why? I had done nothing intentionally to offend her.

When my three-year-old asked to play with Betty's toddler, I answered, "No. Not today."

The next time we passed in the hall we ignored each other. It was a most uncomfortable situation. I was baffled and hurt. I considered confronting her, but her cold shoulder had chilled my feelings toward her.

Two weeks later we met again in the sunshine of our shared back yard. I started to look away, but something inside me told me this was wrong. I turned to Betty and gave her a limp smile. To my surprise she smiled back. Then she reached out her hand. "Why were you angry with me?" she asked.

"Me? I thought you were angry with me."

"No. I wasn't angry at anything except the rain that day. But you slammed the door in my face."

"No. I heard the baby cry out." Then I hugged Betty. "I'm sorry," I said. "Let's be friends again."

Many times since those two unpleasant weeks have reminded me that it is my responsibility as a Christian to reach out to an angry neighbor and ask, "What's wrong? How can I help put it right?"

Is there someone you are alienated from? Why not try it today?

Lord, teach me to respond with love even when I don't understand.

P.E.D.

15 Your Spiritual Workshop for September

PRACTICING SELF-CONTROL

Again and again I've seen that the only real freedom a person ever has comes from developing inner self-control. And how do you develop this? It's obviously a lifetime project, but if you want to begin, here are some guidelines to follow.

Take a moral inventory: Decide the areas in your life where you may need more self-control. Your job, for example. You might never steal merchandise, but do you steal time? Do you ever come in late, leave early, pad an expense account or charge a private phone call to the company? What about your marriage? Are there areas in your life—or even in your thoughts—where you deceive your married partner? And your children, do you always tell them the truth? Do you set up standards for them that you refuse to meet yourself?

Work from a spiritual base: The best base for spiritual growth is, of course, the Bible. What do the Ten Commandments say to you? Christ's Sermon on the Mount? It's vital that you know what you believe about God and how this belief relates to your life.

Concentrate on thought-control: Wrong action starts with a thought. Work at blocking those wrong thoughts before they become action. Not that you can totally prevent a tempting or destructive thought from entering your mind. But you can refuse to *dwell* on the thought and thus keep it from enlarging.

Self-denial is a must: Stop kidding yourself that you can develop self-control without giving up some of the things you like to do. Give up the movie, refuse the sweet, turn off the TV, shorten the telephone call, refrain from telling the story . . . Where will *you* start to say no to yourself? Don't consider it a decision *against* some form of fun, but a decision for some desired goal. You might even offer the sacrifice of an innocent pleasure as a prayer for another who needs God's help in some manner.

I've noticed often that the more small pleasures a person gives up to concentrate on one important task, the stronger he becomes. Jesus Christ was the greatest example of One Who depended on self-denial for strength to perform His ministry. And He put it in these words to His disciples: "If any man will come after Me, let him deny himself, and take up his cross, and follow Me." (Matthew 16:24)

Remember that the ultimate in self-control is not for you to become master of your fate, but to be able to serve a higher Master.

N.V.P.

16.

There is no spectacle on earth more appealing than that of a woman in the act of cooking dinner for someone she loves.

Thomas Wolfe

With six children, I used to spend a lot of time in the kitchen, trying to keep up with their insatiable appetites. My husband had rich variety in his garden, and the eight of us spent many happy hours around the kitchen table. Recently, however, with two of the children married and three away at school, I had got out of the habit of cooking. It hardly seemed worth the bother for my husband and me and our third-grader, Maria. We fell into the practice of eating out several times a week. It wasn't really as satisfying somehow, but it was easier. We even ate out when our college student son was home on weekends—until the Sunday afternoon when we were talking about where to eat supper before he headed back to school.

"Where would *you* like to go tonight, Dino?" We wanted him to have his heart's desire.

"Any place will do," he shrugged. "The only place I really like is too far for all of us to go." He went on to describe his favorite restaurant in his college town. "They don't serve anything very fancy," he explained. "But the food...well..." he paused, searching for the right words—"it tastes like some mother had cooked it."

We didn't eat out that night after all. "Some mother" warmed a pot of black-eyed peas she had cooked with the bone from leftover baked ham. Along with the steaming bowls of peas, there were whole-wheat crackers and cheese. For dessert, we crunched on raw carrots. And all of us agreed that it was a feast fit for kings.

O Lord, our Lord, as a homemaker let me remember that the best recipe of all is simplicity—with love.

I.B.H.

17.

Limited in his nature, infinite in his desires, man is a fallen god who remembers the heavens.

Alphonse de Lamartine

Last spring, the highlight of the titmouse family drama that unfolded outside my bedroom window was watching the mother teach her young to fly. Two caught on quickly, but a third little fellow hopped back and forth on a narrow limb, flapping and fussing, unwilling to commit himself to the air. Suddenly, his agitation caused him to topple off the branch and thump to the earth, where he wobbled along, dazed and aimless.

The mother streaked down to her fallen baby and spent an hour coaxing, chirping and demonstrating to it. Occasionally she would swoop at squirrels who ventured too close. Finally, her extra efforts paid off, and the little bird lifted off in flight beside his mother.

Nobody's perfect. That's why I've always felt the need to commit myself to Jesus. I am the reluctant little bird, and God is the protecting Force Who cared enough to send His only Son down to earth to uplift us with His perfect example. If I let Him, He can teach me to soar to the heavens. And, while I am on earth, He will keep me from those who would harm me.

Lord, I fall so often. Help me to fly by Your side today.

B.R.G.

18.

As far as the east is from the west, so far hath He removed our transgressions from us.

Psalm 103:12

I had a problem. A young woman had applied for a position in our local school. I was one of three people who would decide if she should be hired. I had known her as a rebellious, wild girl who even broke the law on several occasions. Later she had gone to college and settled down, making an excellent record. How was I to vote? I could not forget her past.

While I was pondering and praying about the question, a neighbor who sews for me prepared to make me a new suit. She asked to measure me.

"Don't you have the measurements from my last suit?" I asked.

"I've got them," she answered, "but to do things right, I must take measurements for each new one. People change, you know. And not always for the worse. For all we know you may have dropped a few inches here and there."

Not always for the worse, I thought. My decision had been made for me by my seamstress friend. I was more than a little ashamed of my narrow-mindedness. It was simple, really. If I diet and exercise, then I deserve a smarter suit. For four years this girl had worked hard to better herself, and she deserved the position.

Father, thank You for always leaving the door open to us for change and growth.

L.C.

19.

For thou hast been a shelter for me, and a strong tower from the enemy. I will abide in thy tabernacle for ever.

Psalm 61:3, 4

A recently-ordained rabbi, who didn't look much older than my own 21 years, officiated at my grandmother's funeral. By age 90 she had outlived her own rabbi and most of her friends. So the little funeral chapel in Brooklyn's Boro Park section was filled mostly with relatives, all of us feeling her loss keenly. She had come to America from Poland in the 1880s, and her struggle to give her large family the best had lasted three loving generations.

As I looked around at members of our sorrowing family, I wondered if they were sensing the same disappointment I felt at how young and unfamiliar this rabbi was. I was only half listening until I heard the words, "I feel honored to be permitted to share with you this day for *rejoicing* for Rifka Strizik." *Rejoicing*! Surely his next words would be a hasty apology. But he went on. "When a ship sets forth with precious cargo onto a turbulent sea, we worry that it may founder in a storm. When it puts into port unscathed after its perilous adventure, we rejoice. Therefore, we should expend our tears mostly at a child's birth—and least of all after ninety years of overcoming life's travails. And so I ask you to rejoice with me; Rifka is home safely at last."

Lord, help us to remember that sorrow is temporal and we may rejoice in eternity.

N. L.

20.

So many gods, so many creeds,
So many paths that wind and wind,
When just the art of being kind
Is all this sad world needs.

Ella Wheeler Wilcox

The lights went out as the wind rose, raving and screaming, battering the shutters. I shivered and tried to think where I'd put the candles. There was a knock at the door. "Who is it?" my husband called.

"Me!" came the voice of our 11 year-old neighbor, Charlie. Bounding in behind his flashlight beam, young Charlie exclaimed, "Wow, what a storm! I brought a light in case you're scared."

"We're not . . ." I started to say. But my husband quickly said, "We're not scared now that you're here."

Charlie beamed. "From now on all you have to do is call me when you're scared and I'll come right over," he said. And handing me his flashlight, he strode proudly out.

How perfect my husband's words had been, and how easy they were to say. I bit my lip to think how thoughtless my comment would have been. Then I cringed to remember how many opportunities to say a few kind words had passed me by.

Today, Heavenly Father, I will strive for a caring attitude. My prayer is that You will give me the insights to say the right thing.

R. H. F.

21.

There are diversities of operations, but it is the same God which worketh all in all.

I Corinthians 12:6

A question in our church bulletin caught my eye: "Do you make full use of your time?"

Sure, I thought to myself. I've got my job at the radio station; I'm a wife, mother, grandmother, Christian homemaker, gardener, friend . . . but before my mental argument was finished I was proven wrong.

The article instructed: "Select a large box and fill it to capacity with cannon balls. When it is full, bring a bucket of marbles. Many of these can easily fit into the spaces between the cannon balls. Now the box is full, but only in a sense. There is space in abundance into which you can place buckshot. Now the box is filled beyond question. It will not hold another marble nor even buckshot. Yet several pounds of sand can be poured into the box . . . and even then you can find room for several jugs of water."

The article continued: "Into our busiest day we can find some room for moments of prayer, little deeds of kindness, little encouragements and little sparks of great hope. It may well be that we will not be judged by the great feats but by the little things that are unseen by human eyes."

Dear God, we really haven't room enough in our lives for all of Your blessings. Thank You for showing me this.

Z.B.D.

22.

A loving heart is the truest wisdom.

Charles Dickens

The other day, in a "neatness fit," I was sorting through a drawer of precious papers I had saved. Here were children's school papers, prized because of the red "A" at the top, or perhaps treasured because of the marvelously misspelled words. Here, too, were greeting cards: each one saying, "I love you." How could I dispose of any of these?

My throw-away pile was very small when I came to the final homemade card. A childish hand had printed, "from your best child." Obviously it had accompanied a gift . . . but what? I couldn't remember. And who was the "best child" of our four now grown-up children? The writer of the card thought I would know. But the truth was, each of my children was the "best."

We each long to be singled out for special recognition, special favors and special love by our parents. And each of us yearns for a special place in the encircling arms of our Heavenly Father. Could it be that He smiles and shakes His head fondly over our egotism, murmuring, "Each one is My 'best child'"? I believe so. I know so.

Heavenly Father, I love You—from Your best child.

D.M.

23.

I love best to have each thing in its season, doing without it at all other times.

Thoreau

Summer's end. Our visitors are gone, our vacation is over and the house is too quiet. You know the feeling, particularly if you live alone and are trying to whip yourself back into a business-like schedule. A brisk after-dinner walk was my whip the evening I almost tripped over Mrs. Manners. She was kneeling at the edge of her garden, the loveliest on the hill.

"Transplanting or thinning?" I asked.

She slid over onto one hip and looked up from the chrysanthemums. "Both. Summer is such a wild confusion of growth and blooming and plants crowding each other, I think they enjoy the resting season."

She might have been describing my summer. A house full of company; all ages thrown together in a family blooming, reminding me that another generation was sprouting. Then came the thinning as everyone returned home. The analogy was so apt that I extended it further as I continued my walk. If we can think of life as a garden with its progressive seasons, each lively and beautiful with growth and experience, then we can leave each one without regret, pressing its memories into our hearts like rose petals, and move on to the next season in good humor.

Keep us strong, Lord, so we may be sturdy, blooming plants in Your garden until the day of transplanting.

M.E.H.

24.

When you look at others with their lands and gold,
Think that Christ has promised you His wealth untold.

Johnson Oatman, Jr.

Tonight my husband went through the monthly ritual of paying bills. Seated at the breakfast-room table, he spread out the notices fan-fashion and then wrote the checks, subtracting each one carefully. Then, as he always does, he placed the envelopes in the kitchen window above the sink. "Mail these tomorrow, will you, please?" he asked, and then added, "I hope the book-keeper at the bank has good eyes. Our balance is almost invisible this month!"

Maybe the bookkeeper does think we're poor. But the bank records don't show that we have three healthy children; that the car is almost paid for; that our pledge is paid up at the church. The bookkeeper hasn't met our delightful new neighbors and doesn't know that reflecting on Sunday's sermon has been a blessing all this week.

At the bank it's just as the bookkeeper thinks—we're poor. But only at the bank. At home we are very rich.

Lord, thank You that abundant living is not computed in debits and credits.

M.B.D.**

25.

Wise persons never let yesterday's mistakes use up too much of today.

Anonymous

As a very young, very sensitive, newly appointed direct-mail supervisor for a retail store's advertising department, I had approved a printer's proof of envelopes we had ordered. But when the envelopes were delivered I discovered that I had overlooked a misspelling of our company's name. All 50,000 envelopes carried the error.

In an agony of self-blame I typed my resignation, attaching one of the envelopes, and took it to my boss. He looked at it for a moment, then he smiled. "What's this nonsense about resignation?" he asked. Quickly he penciled in a design representing our company logo that would block out the error. "Take this back to the printer," he said gently, "and tell them to put our correct address below the logo. Nothing is so bad that it can't be remedied." He put my resignation in his wastebasket.

Waves of relief washed through me. *How wonderful to have a boss kind enough to forgive a stupid mistake*, I thought. Then it occurred to me that I can always count on forgiveness. No matter what I've done, I can always turn to the compassionate Christ, confess my mistake, and let His forgiving love block it out.

Lord, let me always turn to You for forgiveness when I need it.
C.M.D.

26.

To every thing there is a season . . . A time to weep, and a time to laugh; a time to mourn, and a time to dance.

Ecclesiastes 3:1, 4

I sat at the breakfast table finishing my coffee and thumbing automatically through the newspaper. Another marital argument had turned off the sun, and I sat alone in the darkness of my own thoughts. Dave had gone to work again, with a slamming of the front door.

My mind was a battleground. *All he cares about is having his own way. Being right. Making me wrong. The smiles are gone. The kisses. Why did I ever get married? I'd be better off alone!*

I was so distraught that I did something I seldom do. I found myself staring at the classified ads. My eyes roamed across the small print. I saw the words "Funeral Directors." Just above, my eyes focused on a boxed, four-line notice:

IN MEMORIAM
Robert Martin—January 16, 1978
Happy Birthday, my dear "Champ"
I miss you so very much—Love, Ellen.

I'd be better off alone? Oh, no!

I ran to the phone and called Dave's office. He had just arrived, and his "Hello" sounded gloomy.

For a minute I didn't know what to say. And then, "Dave, I just wanted you to know that I'm sorry. And I love you."

The sun came back on with the relief in his voice.

"I love you too, honey. I'm glad you called."

Thank you, Ellen, I thought, as I hung up the phone.

Let me nurture love while I may, dear God. Soon enough comes the time to mourn.

D.H.

27.

. . . And lo, I am with you alway . . .
Matthew 28:20

I need love, companionship and reassurance—without having to ask. Perhaps it's a weakness, this wanting others to sense my needs. But it's very real.

So I remember one recent incident in particular that left a lasting impression. Two of our dearest friends visited us from Van Nuys, California. The Millers never come bearing gifts and they write no out-of-obligation "bread and butter" letters. They always do the unexpected.

Our partings are always a little emotional. "See you guys!" Lucke called a little too gaily to hide her tears as Bob pulled out of the driveway. They didn't look back; and George and I blew our noses.

"Look! I found something in the cookie jar," our son Bryce called as we entered the front door.

"And what were you doing in the cookie jar?" I asked a bit irritably. He held out a folded piece of paper. "Look!"

"We love you!" And it was signed "Lucke and Bob." Immediately there was a warm glow in my heart. Then we began finding little notes everywhere. "We love you even more . . . Wasn't it wonderful? There's nothing like friends. . .God bless."

But the gesture didn't stop there. Notes beneath our pillows, one in a slipper, and (days later) one in a roll of bathroom tissue!

How rewarding when friends know you hunger for love and give it—spontaneously!

Lord, thank You for Your constant reminders of Your loving presence.

J.M.B.

28.

I, even I, am he that blotteth out thy transgressions for mine own sake and will not remember thy sins.

Isaiah 43:25

My husband, Bob, and I always enjoy pointing out our $2.00 table in our living room to guests. It is one of a few genuine antiques we possess.

A number of years ago I came across it in a transfer and storage store where it was being used to hold old newspapers and other packing material. Despite its dingy coat of white paint I could tell from its unpainted underside that it was good mahogany.

When I offered to buy it the owner casually put a price of "a couple of dollars" on it, and I took it home.

Many hours of stripping and polishing and much love of the job went into refurbishing that old table into the handsome possession it is today.

How wonderful to think that Christ sees the value in our sin-covered lives. He doesn't look just at the dingy surface. He loved us enough to give His life to strip us of our faults and claim us for His own.

We thank Thee, Jesus, for Your never-ending love for us.

D.D.**

29.

He hangeth the earth upon nothing.

Job 26:7

It was my first plane ride. "Fasten your seat belts; raise your seat backs to upright position; extinguish all smoking materials," the stewardess instructed. Then she demonstrated oxygen masks, pointed out emergency exits and suggested we read other instructions in the pocket of the seat which diagrammed flotation cushions and procedures for crashes in water.

After all this disturbing precautionary advice, the plane took off. The landscape whizzed past, then dropped away as the plane's nose aimed upward and its wheels seemed momentarily reluctant to let loose from earth.

"Your first plane ride?" my seat mate asked, pointing to my hands, still gripped on the chair arms, as if clutching a part of the plane could make me more secure when the plane itself was holding me!

"Hang on to God," people have said to me—as if my feeble clutching Him could make me more secure when He, Himself, is holding me.

There have been many plane trips since my first one. But now I've learned to have confidence in these powerful airplanes. Yet how much more comforting it is to have confidence in the One Who was powerful enough to bring the universe into being, hang it on nothing and make it stay there. He also is powerful enough to hold onto me!

You've got the whole world in Your hands, Father. I know I am safe.

I.C.

30.

**In Christ there is no East or West,
In Him no South or North;
But one great fellowship of love
Throughout the whole wide earth.**

John Oxenham hymn

That Sunday, I'd felt all alone going to Mass.

Shortly after I arrived, a young boy in ill-fitting clothes was escorted to the pew in front of me. I knew at once that he was mentally handicapped, probably retarded like some of the deaf children I'd done volunteer work with for nearly 30 years. When it came time for the greeting of peace, the little ceremony in our church in which we acknowledge our neighbors, the boy turned and looked at me. Maybe he was responding to something he saw in my eyes—I don't know—but he clasped my hand and suddenly kissed my cheek gently.

"Praise God you're here!" the boy said. "You're looking fine!" His escort looked confused. And I was sure I'd never met the boy before—where could I have known him?

Suddenly, I realized. I knew him . . . in Raymond from New Jersey, who was deaf . . . and in Gerry . . . in Bruce . . . in so many of God's special children He'd let me love and given me the privilege of knowing their love in return.

It was as if God was telling me that, no, I am not alone. My "family" is larger than those in my household. No longer lonely, I left church in joy and gratitude.

*O Lord, thank You for bringing into our lives those who,
perhaps because they are handicapped, are especially equipped
to teach us.*

M.S.G.

OCTOBER 1979

S	M	T	W	T	F	S
	1	2	3	4	5	6
7	8	9	10	11	12	13
14	15	16	17	18	19	20
21	22	23	24	25	26	27
28	29	30	31			

1.

Come, ye thankful people, come,
Raise the song of harvest home.
Henry Alford hymn

My husband Plaford was studying a sheet of paper just removed from an envelope, murmuring, "What in the world brought this on?" I could tell by his face and voice it wasn't bad news. He had a progressive grin that was spreading from cheek to cheek.

Joining him, I read over his shoulder in carefully written words, "Dear Mr. Davis: I just feel good every time I pass you." It said more good things and was by a 12-year-old, the son of friends in a neighboring town. So far as we could recall there had never been any special contact between Plaford and the youth.

Picking up the phone, Plaford called to thank him for the spirit-lifting letter. He wasn't at home, but his mother was. She explained: "Every Thanksgiving season each of our eight children write to three people who have meant something special in their lives; someone who has inspired them in an exceptional way. It's part of our saying thanks to God for all of the friends He has given us."

Since receiving that letter, Plaford has had an exceedingly warm spot in his heart for that young man.

In fact their idea was contagious. We started writing Thanksgiving messages too—thanking at least three people for something special about them that we appreciate.

And who do you think received the first letter we wrote? The parents who instilled the idea in their children—something so easy to do, so wonderful to remember the rest of our lives.

God, thank You for the adventure of finding new friends, and the wondrous gift of old friends.

Z.B.D.

2.

We are here to add what we can *to*, not to get what we can *from*, Life.

Sir William Osler

On an automobile trip last spring my husband stopped at a rural service station in Arkansas to buy gasoline. Taking advantage of the stop, I headed for the ladies' rest room. As I opened the door, I saw above the wash basin an old coffee can painted green with a huge bunch of colorful yard flowers. The presence of the big, bold flowers in that shabby rest room astonished me.

Almost immediately, however, something in me was deeply touched. Someone in that remote area cared enough about the unknown travelers to gather the flowers and put them there.

Then I saw a little hand-printed sign. "Take one," it said. So I broke a flower from the back of the bunch and carried it out to the car with me, knowing that no matter what beautiful places we might visit on our trip, nowhere would I see a lovelier scene than in that country service station's rest room.

Lord, teach us to seek ways to add beauty to the lives of others, even to strangers.

D.D.**

3.

Judge not according to the appearance.
John 7:24

Our small daughter recently borrowed my stock of canned vegetables for her pretend grocery store. Deciding that the "pretty, shiny part" would be more attractive to her make-believe customers, she stripped off the labels and threw them away. At first I was cross, but then our family made a game out of having a "surprise vegetable" each night for dinner. It was a nice change in routine, and we discovered that certain foods that I would never have dreamt of combining before actually went very well together.

The incident reminded me that all of us tend to categorize too much. We decide peas go with meat loaf just as we decide that, since Harry's the life of the party, he wouldn't have much to offer in a quiet moment. Or that Jill, generally thought to be introspective, wouldn't enjoy being included in a church social. Scripture tells us that God never looks at labels. He is only interested in the "shiny part"—the human heart—underneath.

Heavenly Father, grant me the understanding to know my friends' hearts.

J.P.

4.

What man of you, having an hundred sheep, if he lose one of them, doth not leave the ninety and nine in the wilderness, and go after that which is lost, until he find it?
Luke 15:4

Knowing that in two minutes I would cry, I fled from the Retreat House lunch table to my room. I didn't want to discuss my problems, though they were many. Half an hour later, someone knocked at my door. There was the priest, in sweat shirt and tennis shoes. He said, "You're hurting. May I come in?" Most reluctantly, I nodded. Under his gentle probing, I began to talk, then to cry . . .

Next morning, seeing Father in the dining room, I thanked

him with a hug, telling him what I myself hadn't recognized: "You are the first one who ever sought me out when I was in pain. Thanks for caring." It wasn't, I reflected later, that no one had cared, but no one had dared to come after me.

"You can't just go knocking on people's doors," someone recently objected. Yes, we can. Those in pain may not have the strength to come to us. "But I can't solve their problems. I wouldn't even know what to say." The priest didn't solve my problems. He was just there, caring. That caring was the beginning of new life for me. And as for knowing what to say, why not try, "You're hurting. May I come in?"

Jesus, give us Your courage to seek out the lost, lonely, hurting ones of our own world. Love them through us.

M.J.N.

5.

. . .I will never leave thee nor forsake thee.
Hebrews 13:5

When my youngest son, John, was just a toddler, he became separated from me in a large department store. I went from department to department, asking the clerks if they'd seen a little boy in a green and yellow "Big Bird" shirt. Time and again, they answered, "He was here a few minutes ago, calling for his mommie, but he rushed away before we could help him find you." When we finally made connections, we agreed that, if we ever got separated again, he'd stay right where he was and wait for me to find him.

That's what we need to do when we're feeling separated from God. We all have times when our prayers seem to bounce off invisible walls—times when, no matter what we do, we can't seem to feel the presence of God. It's a cold, black feeling that often makes us either pray more frantically and ineffectively or turn farther away. What we really need to do, instead, is to go within, still our clanging thoughts and wait for God to draw us gently back to Him.

Come to me in the stillness of my heart, Lord, and gather Your lost child into Your arms again.

M.M.H.

240

6.

We are surrounded by possibilities that are infinite, and the purpose of human life is to grasp as much as we can out of that infinitude.
Alfred North Whitehead

"What a waste of a gorgeous day," I growled to my wife, Judy, as I climbed into the great ark of a truck I had rented to move some furniture that had been in storage. It was a perfect October morning; there were dozens of things I'd rather have been doing.

"You never get to drive a truck," Judy said cheerily. "Why not make an adventure of it?"

"Are you kidding?" I grumbled as I clashed the gears and drove off.

I was still grumbling as I lumbered up to the toll booth at the great Verrazano Narrows bridge that spans the entrance to New York's harbor. *Adventure*, I said to myself, *what a laugh!*

But when I got on the bridge, everything changed. From the high-up cab of the truck, I could see over the retaining wall that had always blocked my view as an automobile motorist. On my right, the sea stretched in combination with the sky in an infinity of contrasting blues. And on my left, the Hudson made a glittering path between towering palisades that had been capped with the yellows and reds of autumn.

"Wow!" I said aloud. I felt as if God had reached down and tapped me on the shoulder saying, "See what I had in store for you all along!"

Heavenly Father, keep my mind open to the endless possibilities that You offer with each new day.

J. McD.

7.

Blessed is he who has found his work; let him ask no other blessedness.
Thomas Carlyle

I got to talking with Cecil at a gathering in rural Georgia one evening. Fresh-scrubbed, dressed in a short-sleeved shirt and lettuce-green trousers, Cecil was a barber. And what he had to say was interesting.

"When I was as tall as Daddy's knee," Cecil said, "the only thing I wanted was to be in his barber shop. My Daddy had to chase me out."

Cecil told how he played at barbering. He sat his friends on a low branch of a live oak tree and cut their hair. "I'll bet there's still a pile of kids' hair under that tree," Cecil said. "When my Daddy found out what I was doing he said to me, 'If you're bound to cut hair, you might as well do it right.' So he started teaching me.

"Aren't many barbers excited about their work," Cecil said happily. "But I am!"

How refreshing, I thought, *to meet a man really excited about his work*. This man will always have customers, because people are instinctively attracted to a person who likes what he does.

Dear Lord, let me find the excitement in the work that I do; it's there; I have to be reminded now and then to look for it.

J.L.S.

8. Love is an image of God, and not a lifeless image, but the living essence of the divine nature which beams full of all goodness.
Martin Luther

Just back of me lives Kathryn, a little friend of 92. And she reminds me of my Aunt Betty who is 94. Both are pleasant to be with.

I remember as a small child walking into Aunt Betty's kitchen when she was making butter and having her open up the churn and dip me out a cup of warm buttermilk. Though she was a young widow with six little children of her own, she always had time for me or for anyone. In her 70s, still unruffled, she raised a second family of four motherless grandchildren, and gave them the same Christian upbringing she gave her own children.

A study of men and women past age 95, made on the basis of a Gallup Poll, resulted in guidelines for living a long life: Eat moderately, limit indulgences, curb aggressive instincts and get enough exercise.

All of which make sense.

But when I asked Aunt Betty what she attributed her long healthy life to, she said, "Loving God and people."

Kathryn says the same.

Lord, let me learn from Your saints how to be happy and healthy.
                                                                    L.R.

9.

**Blessed is he who speaks a kindness;
thrice blessed he who repeats it.**
                                              Arabian proverb

One night when I was still young and struggling, my husband and I were waiting for our car at a parking lot. And we became aware of a lovely young girl smiling our way. Then, after conferring with her mother a minute, she rushed over and said, "Please don't think me forward, but—" and paid me a compliment. The words rushed so warmly straight from her heart that I suddenly felt like a celebrity.

Before I could even thank her properly she scurried back to her parents and into their car and sped away. But the glow of her words lingered, canceling out doubts and aggravations, adding a rare delight to the day.

How often words of admiration surge up within us, clamoring to be said. Yet, fearing to be conspicuous or misunderstood, we restrain them and go on, leaving behind the person to whom they would have been so sweet. Whose very life might have been affected.

A neighbor told me: "I'll never forget what one of my uncles said to me when I was in seventh grade: 'Betty, you grow more beautiful every year.' It was so unexpected, so sincere, and coming at a time when I felt awkward and insecure, it really thrilled me. I still treasure that memory. And had he decided *not* to say it, I would not only have missed that joy, but I really don't think I'd be the person I am now. Anyway, I make it a point to compliment others whenever I honestly can. I hope it does for them what my uncle's compliment did for me."

Pay that compliment. It is the voice of love stirring within you put there by the Lord Himself. It is the urging of His Holy Spirit. Don't be afraid to express it. It can brighten and change another life, and you may never have this opportunity again.

Lord, thank You for all the kind and generous things people have said to me. Don't let me ever be afraid to pay a compliment.

M.H.

10.

We are all in a dark room. If you know where the light switch is, share the knowledge.

Anonymous

Recently in the newspaper, I read about a little 78-year-old lady who has earned her living for many years by making and selling a marvelous kind of fudge. It is her only source of income, and you'd think she'd guard the recipe jealously. Yet when a reporter, writing a story about her for the local newspaper, asked for permission to print it, the little lady cheerfully gave not only her permission but accurate details for using it.

"The good you have is a good to share," she told him. "You never lose by sharing."

There's a thought worth carrying through this self-centered materialistic world of ours. When you share the gifts God gives you, you are really giving thanks to the Giver.

Lord, teach me to multiply Your endless gifts to me by sharing them with others. •

M.A.

11.

Therefore take no thought, saying, What shall we eat? or, What shall we drink? or, Wherewithal shall we be clothed? . . . for your heavenly Father knoweth that ye have need of all these things.

Matthew 6:31, 32

Every morning when I get up, my cat Sidney is waiting patiently for me at the bottom of the stairs. He lets out a loud *meow* or two and flirts around my slippered feet to let me know he wants to be fed. More to the point, he *expects* to be fed, and before I've had my breakfast.

Strangely, no matter how sleepy, or grumpy, or late I am, I agree in my heart to this. I know (as he knows) that he is mine, and I'm responsible for him. And by his bold, persistent approach, the cat conveys the message that he never doubts for one moment that his breakfast will be delivered on time. And it always is. In fact, so great is my concern for his well-being, that if I know we're running out of cat food, I stop off at the market that very evening so that Sidney will have his food in the morning.

It's a homely analogy, but I'm reminded that I ought to look to God with as much trust as Sidney looks to me. I ought to ask not with a question in my heart as to whether my prayer will be answered, but with a certainty, an *expectancy*, that my Master will never fail to supply my daily needs.

Oh, Lord, give us the gift of perfect trust in Your love, Your willingness and Your ability to supply our every need.

W. D.

12. I shall pass through this world but once.
If, therefore, there be any kindness
   I can show
or any good thing I can do,
   let me do it now;
let me not defer it or neglect it,
for I shall not pass this way again.
            attributed to Etienne De Grellet

Walter Knox was one of the dearest, funniest, most thoughtful men in my husband's Exchange Club. He never married, which was a loss, but he loved, aided and influenced many children.

He worked for the Chesapeake and Ohio railroad. I once wrote a column about a marvelous trip my daughter and I took to Florida on his trains. Walter missed the column, but heard about it. "I'd sure like to have a copy," he said.

"I'll duplicate half a dozen for you," I told him. But weeks passed before I got around to it. And more weeks before I finally remembered to address the envelope. Then somehow the envelope got mislaid. My husband reminded me of it, and so did my conscience—along with tender little thoughts of Walter. I *will* get it all together and have my husband carry it to the club luncheon, I kept promising myself. Next week for sure . . .

Then, suddenly, we learned that Walter had been called on a long trip of his own. One from which he wouldn't be coming back. And my heart broke. I wanted to run down the tracks waving that little offering that would have given him so much pleasure. Desperately calling, "Wait, wait!" But the train Walter had taken never backs up, never waits.

Don't put off that kind thing you really mean to do. Do it now. Today. Tomorrow may be too late.

Lord, don't let me be too busy to do the kind things my heart really intends.

M.H.

13.

If we confess our sins, He is faithful and just to forgive us our sins, and to cleanse us from all unrighteousness.

I John 1:9

It wasn't until the other day that I remembered an incident which happened when my son was four years old. He'd asked to play outside, but I didn't know he'd meant in the *mud*! At least not until he tearfully, fearfully appeared at the kitchen door.

Wet, dirty clothing outlined his yet-babyish body, showing his fat, round tummy and chubby limbs. To make matters worse, he'd tried to wash himself in a nearby puddle! I peeled him from head to toe, picked him up and leaving the sodden mess behind, carried him to the tub.

How different he looked, how sweet and clean and cuddly after I'd bathed and dressed him in fresh, clean coveralls. My pride and joy!

I'd forgotten the long ago incident until recently when in a Sunday school class we talked about a loving, heavenly Father Who cleanses us from filthy sins and clothes us in His own spotless righteousness. No matter how we try, we can never really clean up our own lives—like my child 'washing' himself in that muddy puddle.

To become His spiritual child, I must come to Him—just as I am. He'll clean me up and leave my sodden mess behind. My part is to allow Him to do so.

Heavenly Father—so often I try to clean myself, forgetting my efforts are as 'filthy rags' in comparison with what You have for me. Teach me to yield myself to Your washing.

I.C.

14.

Good health . . . if you have it praise God.
Izaak Walton

At our last church potluck, as I watched the children fill their plates, a friend ahead of me in the line remarked, "Look at those kids! They pick potato chips and pickles and hot dogs, then they pour Coke into every crack that's left. If a scientist put into a test tube what they put into their stomachs, it'd blow up!"

Later, I thought: *Isn't it the same way with spiritual food?* The Lord sets His table, fills it with choicest blessings—love, joy, peace, gentleness, goodness and all the rest—but too often I pick junk food, too, like grumbling and gossiping and complaining and wishing for things for my home here instead of my heavenly one.

Father, when I'm childlike in choosing junk foods when You've prepared such good things for me, please remind me. I really do want Your best for me.

I.C.

15 Your Spiritual Workshop for October

GET MORE OUT OF YOUR BIBLE-READING

During his long distinguished ministry, the late Dr. John Sutherland Bonnell helped thousands of people to a better, more useful understanding of the Bible with a plan he devised, the basis of this mid-month Workshop.

First: Let the Bible speak to you personally. It tells about God and what He is like; about how He deals with men and women like yourself, always confronting them, surprising them and demanding that they make a decision about Him and about what *their* relationship with Him is going to be. The feeling that you're about to make a personal discovery can make your Bible-reading an exciting adventure.

Second: Map out your reading program. Focus on one book at a time. Read in small installments. It is not the amount of reading that is important, but the insight and understanding. If you feel a meaning is not clear, discuss it with someone whose knowledge of the Bible you respect, then come back and reread the troubling section.

Third: Each day, seek out a verse that you feel might be God's "marching orders" for your day. Let it reach into every area of your life. Even better, write down the verse and carry it with you. You'll be surprised what a staff it can be for you, steadying you in trying hours.

Fourth: Commit to memory those texts that have been especially meaningful. Then they'll be available in a moment of need.

Fifth: Bible-reading will always be a more vivid experience if you can picture the Bible in time and place. Read some books about the background of the Bible, its lands, its people, the best interpretations of Biblical scholars. If you want an even more meaningful personal experience, do some reading that reflects your own interests. For instance, if you're interested in gardens, get some books about the flowers that abound in the Bible.

Sixth: Make sure that one particular volume is your Bible, yours alone. Through it a living Lord will step out of the pages to be your Friend and Contemporary.

L.E.L.

16.

. . . When I became a man, I put away childish things.

I Corinthians 13:11

Several years ago while I was visiting a church in Texas I stood in the vestibule talking with a group of four men who were discussing their college-aged children.

"Do you realize," said one man, sweeping his arm to include his friends, "that each of us has a child who has drifted away from the things we stand for?"

The stories were typical of the day. One young man was a college drop-out living in a commune; another was living with a girl he wasn't married to; another experimented with drugs; and the fourth proclaimed that every businessman was a shame and disgrace. There followed some stormy observations about the dark days we lived in, where Christian families had lost all influence on their children.

But last week I visited the same congregation again. Ten years had passed, but all four men were still there. I asked each one about his child, and I discovered an encouraging thing:

Three out of the four young people were now back on good relationships with their families. Of these three, two were raising families in conventional church-centered circumstances and a third was planning to become a missionary to Bolivia.

I was encouraged. It reminded me again that very often we parents fret too much. If we plant the right seeds in our children, chances are good that sooner or later with God's help they will blossom.

Lord, you have told us that if we train up a child in the way he should go, when he is old he will not depart from it. Give me the faith to believe this.

J.L.S.

17.

She looketh well to the ways of her household,
and eateth not the bread of idleness.
Her children arise up, and call her blessed;
her husband also, and he praiseth her.
Proverbs 31:27, 28

While I sat in the den with my husband watching the evening news, the waiting supper dishes kept nagging at me. After the news broadcast I thumbed through a magazine, still stalling to keep from facing the kitchen. And there it was, a quotation that seemed to jump off the page: "Work is love made visible."

I got up and went into the kitchen. *How true*, I thought. The stack of dinner plates meant that the family was well and able to come to the supper table. My grandmother's silver soaking in the sink represented generations of family tradition. And the pots and pans on the stove proved that we had been blessed with food in a hungry world.

I've washed many dishes since that night, but now I see them as blessings instead of a dreaded chore.

Lord, thank You for a family to care for and for the work that this entails.

M.B.D.**

18.

He who talks much cannot talk well.
Carlo Goldoni

My husband, Plaford, calls me his "storybook wife," because I want to tell him everything about everything. As news director for a local radio station, I come home filled with things to share. I not only tell him who spoke at the Lincoln Day dinner but that the centerpiece was silk violets; not only that a truck rammed a house but that it was a cement truck; that the hummingbird's wings were blue; that the congressman I interviewed wore a bow tie. I've been known to keep him awake at night to tell him one more thing.

Today we received the weekly "letter from home" from our friend Bob Hastings, author, editor and speaker from

Springfield, Illinois. He was saying, "You never learn anything when you're talking. You already know what you're telling." Bob also contended that psychiatrists are able to charge large fees because they're willing to listen.

His letter included a quote about people whose mouths work overtime. "They do not talk to you; they lecture you. They are not interested in you; they are interested in your hearing about them and their opinions. People seldom listen to one another, but instead we are like cars at four-way stop signs, each waiting for his chance to go, verbally."

I've been looking for a good place to hide Bob's letter before Plaford sees it.

Dear God, may we remember the proverb: "When you have spoken the word, it reigns over you. When it is unspoken, you reign over it." And when we have nothing to say, may we not keep on saying it.

Z.B.D.

19.

If ye then, being evil, know how to give good gifts unto your children: how much more shall your heavenly Father give the Holy Spirit to them that ask him?

Luke 11:13

As a miner's kid I would listen for the whistles that blew at 3 p.m., quitting time. One blast meant there would be no work the next day; two blasts meant some day-men would work; and three meant a full force would work. When the single whistle blew, I always felt sorry for Daddy because he didn't like it when he couldn't provide a regular pay check.

But, unlike some other mining families when business was slack, we never went hungry. Just because he wasn't in the mine didn't mean Daddy was idle. He'd work in his vegetable garden or take my brothers fishing in the summer. In winter he'd hunt and fill our larder with rabbits and squirrels. In good times he'd come home with a sack full of sweets he'd get from the grocer for paying our weekly bill.

Good times or bad we could always count on Daddy. Winters

were long and cold in north Missouri, but, one way or another, Daddy would always come whistling home with food for the next meal.

I've always thought that Daddy was a good model for me in picturing my Heavenly Father. When pickings are lean, I've learned that He, too, always provides.

Lord, give us this day our daily bread.

M.M.

20.

. . . . Thou shalt not know what hour I will come upon thee.

Revelation 3:3

A friend of ours is a truck driver. The other day I asked him, "Bill, you've only been on the job for a few years—how does it happen that you're given more routes than others who've been there longer?"

Bill said, "Because my bag is always packed. I can go whenever I'm called. Sometimes my boss has to wait for some of his drivers to pack after he phones—but he knows he can count on me."

"What's in your bag?"

"A change of clothing and a spare shaving kit. And, of course, my log book which shows what I do and where I am all the time. I don't neglect it—I always keep it up . . . the inspector might want to see it anytime."

Bill's remarks stayed in my mind. I kept wondering if my spiritual bags were packed and my log book up to date, and if I'd be ready if my Boss called.

I had to admit I might wish He'd wait until I took care of a few matters first!

Lord, show me how to arrange this day. I don't want it to close without having my bags packed and my books up-to-date for You.

I.C.

21.

I thank my God upon every remembrance of you.

Philippians 1:3

Recently my husband, a guest in a pastor's home in California, walked into the living room as the pastor and his wife were reading a letter. "Read this," the pastor said, eyes brimming with tears. "It's from our daughter. She's away at college."

The letter read, in part:

Dear Ones,

I want you to know that each year I am away, you become dearer to me. I love you for what you are and what you have helped me become! For our wonderful closeness of family ties I am very grateful. For all your warmth and sincerity, for the love you have given so greatly, for the happy and trying times we've shared, for everything you are and represent to me in high ideals and fine living I thank our Father above.

With tenderness,

Carol

As a parent, do you receive letters like that?

As a parent, do you deserve them?

O Lord, who allows me to transmit life, make me worthy of that privilege.

M.T.

22.

I am come that they might have life, and that they might have it more abundantly.

John 10:10

A small girl was given an inexpensive paper fan. Proudly she carried it in to show her father. With him was a famous artist who good-humoredly pulled out his pen. "Shall I draw something on it?"

The child snatched it away. "No!" she shouted. "You'll ruin it." And she ran from the room without knowing what she had refused.

Aren't we like that sometimes? God offers to etch something

unique on our life—a special friendship, an opportunity for service beyond our daily round, a chance to grow. And, pleased with life the way it is, we clutch it to ourselves and say, "No!" And never know what we missed.

God always stands ready to transform our ordinary lives into something very special. But only if we say, "Yes." Do we dare to take that risk? Do we dare not to?

Lord, I want to say "yes" to You today.

P.H.S.

23.

God can mend a broken heart, provided you give Him all the pieces.

Old proverb

When Aunt Kit scorched Cousin Josie's first dance dress she just sat down and cried. It was such a beautiful blue satin gown; now in the final press there was a huge brown mark on the bodice. Broken-hearted, she came round to Mother.

"And tonight's the dance," she wept. "Whatever shall I do?"

Mother never said a word about the special speaker that she had wanted to hear at Women's Guild that day. Instead, she said quietly, "Let me see if I can help." All day she stayed in her sewing room while Aunt Kit hovered anxiously; eventually she reappeared.

In place of the ugly burn a cascade of appliqued hearts flowed gently from shoulder to waist, each in softest pink outlined with blue lovers' knots.

"Oh, May, that's the *lovingest* thing," Aunt Kit said. Was Aunt Kit referring to the dress? Or was she referring to Mother's selflessness? Perhaps it doesn't matter. A really caring act always carries love's message.

Teach us, Lord, to strengthen family ties today by words and deeds of love.

G.K.

24.

**Be kind. Remember everyone you meet is
fighting a hard battle.**
T.H. Thompson

The phone interrupted my reading for the third time that evening and again it was a salesperson. The caller began telling me how happy I'd be with the new storm windows her firm was offering at a once-in-a-lifetime price.

Without even saying I already had good storm windows, I was about to slam down the receiver when something stopped me. It was a tremor in her voice. I knew it well from long-ago when with quavering heart I had walked door-to-door trying to sell magazine subscriptions. Strangely, I didn't remember the people who actually purchased subscriptions as well as the patient man who listened to my talk and then smiled, saying he was still trying to read the ones that came last year, or the lady who couldn't afford a subscription but did hand me a cold glass of lemonade on a hot day.

So I held on to the phone until the caller finished. "Thank you," I said, "we already have good storm windows. But if we didn't, I'd certainly buy a set from you. You're an excellent salesperson."

Two minutes later the phone rang again. It was the saleswoman. "I just wanted to thank you," she said, "for listening to me."

It was a nice interruption.

*Father, as I try to make my own way, remind me that others are
also traveling the same hard path.*

R.H.S.

25.

**The discretion of a man deferreth his anger;
and it is his glory to pass over a transgression.**
Proverbs 19:11

My volatile, outspoken friend was ranting and raging, telling me chapter and verse what she intended to do to get even with the landlord who had welshed on part of his contract. She had been "done wrong" and she wanted to get even. Of course she can, and probably will, sue for breach of contract, but that won't erase the frown lines anger is etching into her forehead.

Being "done wrong" seems an inescapable part of the human condition. But the response is your decision. Resentment or release? Offense or forgiveness? Pique or pardon? It's a matter of control.

Slow my anger, oh merciful God, that I may reflect Your special glory.

D.M.

26.

The first duty of love is to listen.
Paul Tillich

"Eat dinner, Wendy," I said, "not just those Oreo cookies."

Wendy slammed the cupboard door.

"What's wrong?" asked her father.

"What do you think?" she snapped. "I'm not a child anymore. Instead of all this nagging, why doesn't someone say something nice to me?"

"Your mother just did, dear, but you didn't hear her. Asking you to save room for your dinner is another way of saying 'I love you.' "

Silently Wendy studied our faces. Then, returning the cookies to the cupboard, she walked over to the table, gently kissed my cheek and sat down. "Pass the stew, Daddy," she said softly.

"Take your vitamins." "Put on your sweater." "Don't drive so fast." These are words of caring. But they're often disguised. Maybe Wendy doesn't hear them as words of love because I don't say them that way. Do I need to use a softer tone? It seems to me that perhaps both Wendy and I need to do a little looking beneath the surface.

Lord, teach me how to speak love, and how to listen for it, too.

R. H. F.

27.

When a selfish man hears another praised, he thinks himself injured.

English proverb

Carefully, I fanned a fresh supply of orange and yellow napkins on the buffet table. For two weeks I had worked hard on the retirement party under my supervisor, Elizabeth Gray's, direction. I bought supplies, designed and made the floral centerpiece, and baked the large, white frosted sheet cake that read, "Happy Tomorrow, Jim Pelton."

Now it was almost over. For the last time I replenished the punch. The party was an obvious success. My hard work had paid off.

The program began. After the usual speeches and congratulations, the big boss said a few last words:

"For all the work that went into making this an outstanding occasion, I would like us to give a hand to Elizabeth Gray." There was applause and I stood quietly, wondering where the sudden rock that filled my stomach had come from. My hands were cold and I had trouble with sudden tears. *But I was the one who did all the work*, I thought. *And they didn't even mention my name!*

As I walked despondently across the parking lot to my car, a white-haired man hurried towards me.

"I know how hard you worked," Jim Pelton said. "I'm sorry you didn't get credit for all you did. I want to personally thank you." He squeezed my hand and walked rapidly away.

I've done it again, Lord. I've let my pride stick pins in me. In my desire for recognition I almost forgot the real reason for the work I did: to make someone else happy.

D.H.

28.

Love never fails.

I Corinthians 13:8 (MLV)

Early in this century a young professor at Johns Hopkins University gave members of his sociology class an unusual assignment.

"Go into the worst slums of Baltimore," he told them. "Find

and interview 200 boys; study their backgrounds, their surroundings, their opportunities — and predict their future."

In searching out the 200 boys, the students were appalled by the housing, the environment, the broken homes, the alcoholism, the delinquency, the lack of inspiration and the absence of example. They predicted that 180 of the 200 boys would serve time in prison.

Twenty-five years passed.

The same professor assigned another class the task of finding the 200 boys and reporting on the outcome of the prediction.

They were able to find most of the original boys—but the opposite of the prediction was true; they were fine citizens. Only four had been in jail.

The next assignment was to find some common denominator in the lives of the boys that brought this about. They found it in a high school teacher, Sheila O'Rourke. Many of the boys told of Miss O'Rourke having been an inspiration in their lives. "She cared," was their summation.

Miss O'Rourke, then 70 and living in a nursing home, was told of the survey made, the predictions, the outcome of the predictions and of her influence in their lives. Asked to comment she answered, "All I can say is that I loved every one of them."

Dear God, help me to care enough.

Z.B.D.

29.

A new commandment I give unto you, That ye love one another. . . .

John 13:34

Did someone forget to mention my appointment, I wondered, as Fred Rogers, host of "Mister Rogers' Neighborhood" television program, smiled and asked, "And who are you?"

I stammered out the name of Guideposts and nervously fingered the list of questions I had prepared for the interview. I only had an hour, and I could feel precious seconds slipping away as I tried to explain my presence.

"Oh, I know about Guideposts and why you're here," Fred Rogers interrupted, his smile becoming warmer, "I want to know about *you*."

So, for about 15 minutes, I told this genial man about myself, my job, my family, even my hobbies. But I grew uneasy that the interview would never swing to its real purpose: to find out Fred Rogers' secret for relating so well to his vast television audience. Seeing me fidget, he smiled again and said, "Well, it's good to know you. Now I'll be happy to give you whatever I can."

I pulled a pencil out of my shirt pocket and was about to ask the first question when I began to smile myself.

Almost without speaking, Fred Rogers had already revealed his "secret." His formula for relating to people was simple: *care* about them.

Lord, You taught us love by Your own example; help me to make Your new commandment the first law of my heart.

E.G.

30.

Thou wilt keep him in perfect peace, whose mind is stayed on thee. . . .

Isaiah 26:3

My kids are always saying I belong to the "peace-and-quiet" generation. Well, I guess they're right. Trouble is, I never seem to find enough of it. If the TV isn't blaring, the record player is, or else there's a wrestling match on the family-room floor, or the phone is ringing or the dogs are barking or there is a group of teen-agers dancing in the basement or eating pizza in the kitchen. I learned, quite a few years ago, that if I was going to have any peace at all, I'd just have to find it on my own.

One thing that's helped me is to visualize a calm, crystal-clear lake within me and to let that symbolize the soothing Christ presence, bathing me in His peace. I just hold that picture in mind until I really feel it wash over me, and then come back to it again and again in the midst of the noise and confusion. Oh, my nerves still get a bit jangled sometimes, but now I know that peace has more to do with what's going on inside me than with what's going on around me. If you belong to the peace-and-quiet generation but live in a whirling world, you might try this way of building your own inner chapel.

Loving Christ, You are the calm center within me. Bathe me in Your peace.

M.M.H.

31. (Halloween)

He that is slow to wrath is of great understanding: but he that is hasty of spirit exalteth folly.

Proverbs 14:29

Old Mr. Pooley had a terrible temper, especially with children, and so the youngsters around Academy Circle in Madison, New Jersey, where I grew up, did their best to avoid him.

Yet, on the first Halloween that my best friend, Walter, and I were allowed out unescorted, we made a beeline for the Pooley house to torment Mr. Pooley. I was a patched together Canadian Mountie, Walter a rather wistful Sinbad. We both carried enormous shopping bags, and I had a contraption I'd made from a wire coat hanger, cardboard and some rubber bands that could be attached to a window where it would make a terrible racket.

The Pooley house had a large, multi-paned window fronting its dining room. As we arrived that evening, we could see that the Pooleys were having dinner. Perfect! We attached the noisemaker, rushed behind a tree, then pulled the thread that tripped it. To my horror, a pane shattered. Walter took off, but I stood transfixed.

Mr. Pooley, in a towering rage, grabbed me and shook me furiously. "Did you break that window?" he blared.

I was terrified. "I, I, n-no," I stammered. "I was only watching. Honest, I didn't break it."

He glared at me a long time. "Well, maybe you didn't." He strode back into his house.

Walter and I called listlessly at a few houses for treats, but my lie had ruined the fun. Finally I could bear it no longer and returned to the Pooleys' house.

When he appeared at the door, I was speechless with fright. He began to smile. "You did break it, didn't you?"

I could only nod yes.

"Well, I can't blame you for fibbing," he said. "I must have scared the honesty right out of you, the way I was carrying on. If you come over Saturday and help me rake some leaves, all is forgiven."

There's no doubt that I had been foolish and that I had compounded my foolishness with a lie. But the contrast in Mr. Pooley's first and second reactions has served as a lesson to me. When you allow your anger to speak for you in stridency or accusation, you are in effect asking for the worst from people. But when you meet transgressors openly and calmly, you are showing that you expect the best from them. So often, you get it.

Grant me a peaceful heart today, Lord, so that I may deal evenly with all those I meet.

J. McD.

NOVEMBER 1979

S	M	T	W	T	F	S
				1	2	3
4	5	6	7	8	9	10
11	12	13	14	15	16	17
18	19	20	21	22	23	24
25	26	27	28	29	30	

1.

Music is well said to be the speech of angels.
Thomas Carlyle

Everyone in our church knows "Mrs. Van." Marion Van Devanter is 85 years old, and each Sunday for nearly 60 of those years she has walked the quarter-mile from her home to sing in our church choir. Often when I see her there I think of the story that lies behind her remarkable dedication, the reason that Mrs. Van continues to pour her heart into every song she sings.

It happened a very long time ago. Mrs. Van's young husband, her beloved Jimmy, was bedridden and slowly dying of tuberculosis. Jimmy loved his wife's voice, and over and over he'd tell her, "Someday I'm going to be well enough to go to church and hear you sing in the choir." But he did not get well. On the Sunday after Jimmy died, Mrs. Van walked to church as usual, put on her robe, took her customary place in the choir loft and

263

with a voice that was firm and clear she sang more gloriously than she had ever sung before. No one has ever forgotten Mrs. Van's words when she had finished that morning:

"Now Jimmy can hear me," she said.

Thank You, Lord, for the special ways through which we can show our faith in Your word.

T.S.

2.

Strait is the gate and narrow is the way which leadeth unto life.

Matthew 7:14

My grandfather, a steam locomotive engineer, was my boyhood hero. On my 17th birthday he invited me to ride in the cab on his night fast passenger run. Watching the telegraph poles blur by I was thrilled at the speed of the roaring train. At our first stop he climbed down to oil. I followed.

"Grandpa," I asked, "how come you're a nervous wreck in your car, but in your engine, going much faster, you're so calm?"

He pointed down the shining rails in the headlight's gleam. "See that mainline, Sonny? It was laid down, ballasted, secured, and is maintained by experts who know it has to keep heavy, speeding trains like ours on the track. Even the switches to sidetracks and spurs are preset before we get to 'em to keep us going where we should go. Now, in my automobile I'm on my own, but up in my cab on the mainline I know for sure someone's always on the job looking out for us. Understand?"

I didn't then. But later I realized what a modern parable my beloved Grandpa had given me.

Lord, help us to know that when we stay on the way of Jesus You will see that we get safely to where we should go.

C.M.D.

3.

Nor height, nor depth, nor any other creature shall be able to separate us from the love of God, which is in Christ Jesus our Lord.

Romans 8:39

Last weekend while cleaning a little-used closet, I dragged from its depths a carton labeled "Mementos." Inside I discovered a dusty folder containing an 8 x 10 photograph, an old girl friend of my husband judging from the inscription although the signature was blurred.

I confronted him with the picture. "Now that we've been married twenty-seven years, do you really want to keep this?"

"Oh, what's-her-name." He studied the signature. "You know, I can't think of it."

"Do you suppose she would remember you? Look what she's written: 'All my love forever.'"

We laughed, recalling similar youthful protestations, their sincerity limited by tomorrow. Yet there is one love that time never changes: God's love. Such love never fades, is never hidden by dust. Such love is always there.

Thank You, Lord, for remembering me constantly with Your love.
M.B.D.*

4.

Every good gift and every perfect gift is from above.

James 1:17

When my first book of prayers, I'VE GOT TO TALK TO SOME-BODY, GOD, was finished, the publishers asked if I knew anyone important from whom we might get a jacket statement. I didn't. But I thought of Mary Martin, whom I've always admired, and whom we'd just seen in the play "I Do, I Do!" I knew she was a Christian and that she'd written an introduction to Tolstoy's THE KINGDOM OF GOD IS WITHIN YOU. So I wrote to her, enclosing a sample prayer.

Within a week a handwritten note came back. Warm, enthusiastic, saying she loved the title and theme. "Most of us *are* so unable to really touch and know and talk to each other! . . . We're on tour, as you know. Here is my schedule and addresses for the next few weeks."

I mailed a copy of the manuscript to her hotel and soon received another letter with a glowing recommendation for the book.

I was thrilled, of course, and moved by her humanity and graciousness. But even more significant was a letter Mary Martin wrote me later, after the book appeared. "I feel closer to you than ever, now that I'm about to be a published author, too. My needlepoint book comes out in October . . . I still have one more page to write! Been working on it for three weeks! It's something like working on one line of dialogue that should get a laugh—and you keep rethinking it, projecting it with different accents, tone—until suddenly the audience laughs! Only last night Bob Preston and I got a laugh on two lines we've been trying for over two years. It was a good feeling to hear the laughter—at last!"

To hear the laughter—at last. Mary Martin, star of countless hits that have lifted the hearts of millions and her co-star, Robert Preston, had labored two years to polish *two* lines that would bring her audience more laughter.

Surely this is the secret of greatness. This striving for perfection. To take the gifts God gives us and make the most of them. The most. The very best! And always to use them for their true purpose, to brighten other lives.

Dear God, thank You for this wonderful woman who knows the true value and purpose of Your gifts. Thank You that because of her and people like her the world is a happier place.

M. H.

5.
The love we give away is the only love we keep.
Elbert Hubbard

One of the great mysteries when I was a child centered around the problem of how to make people like me. I remember how intently I watched my teachers and classmates trying to see how they did it. Finally I made a discovery. People were always smiling at each other. Those who smiled a lot seemed to have the most friends. So I decided to smile a lot, too. I began to practice smiling often, hoping to please others, and I waited for the miracle of popularity. But all that happened was that my mouth got stiff. I remained lonely.

Years passed and those years provided me with the solution I had been looking for so long ago. I discovered that, instead of trying to please people, I should love them. Love in a person is like a light in a Japanese lantern. The surface of the shade is suffused with light. A smile is not just a "mouth" when it gets its start in love. It starts in the soul and ripples outward, flowing, washing over, touching everything. When I offer love it flows out from me to the "other" and inevitably, like changing tides, back to me.

"Do you like me?" asked the child. All you had to do, child-of-yesterday, was add one more phrase, from your heart. "I like you." Then you would have found far more than popularity.

Lord, let me learn to love others as You love me. Freely, generously, without reward. Give me the peace that such love brings.
                                                                D.H.

6.   (Election Day)
          The Lord did not . . . choose you, because ye
          were more in number than any people . . . but
          because the Lord loved you . . .
                              Deuteronomy 7:7,8

Today is Election Day. Most of us are eligible to vote for whom we want for a particular office. And those who are on the ballots today will know tomorrow whether or not we have chosen them.

It's an awesome responsibility to vote for those who will directly or indirectly affect almost every part of our lives. But in our democracy, that's our privilege.

God has given me a democratic decision to make, too. There are two names on my spiritual ballot—His and mine. With my power of choice, I can elect Him to sit in the governor's chair of my heart where He can control every part of my life. Or I can elect myself to that position of authority. If I vote for Him, He takes over and I'm His responsibility. If I vote for myself, He doesn't force Himself on me, but I become responsible for my own actions.

Father, when I sit in the governor's chair of my heart, I get myself into difficulty of every kind. Today I elect You to that position of authority over every part of my life.

I.C.

7.

Softly and tenderly Jesus is calling . . .
Will L. Thompson hymn

A friend of mine, retired from the Navy, tells about visiting the Civil Air Patrol office in a small Florida town. "They had a radio that was receiving messages from several sources at once, all in Morse code. At first it sounded like firecrackers on the fourth of July—really bedlam. But gradually, by concentrated listening, I began to pick out different signals. One was high, another low, one staccato, another slower. Through them all I eventually heard one gentle signal that was so slow even my rusty Morse code knowledge could pick it up. All I had to do was tune out the other signals, and I got the message."

We are surrounded in our lives by a lot of signals that clamor for our attention: Advertisers, family, friends, church, schools, clubs, political parties—the list is endless of people and groups sending out different messages. Through them all a gentle, persuasive voice repeatedly calls, "Follow Me. Follow Me." It's being sent at exactly the right tone and frequency. All we have to do is tune out the other signals for a moment of quiet, and we, too, get the message.

Lord, speak to me through the noise and confusion of this day. Help me tune in on Your message, and live in Your peace.

P.H.S.

8.

And the Word was made flesh, and dwelt among us. . . .

John 1:14

When I was a child I loved the fable about the prince who put on beggar's rags to go out among his people and see what it was like to be low-born and poor. The part of the story that thrilled me most was when he came back and, through some misunderstanding, was thrown out of the court as an imposter. Back again on the streets, he seemed doomed to be what his people were—frail, tired, powerless and hopeless.

Of course, the prince always managed in the end to reclaim what was rightfully his. But he was forever changed and ennobled by what he had experienced among his people. How wonderful! I loved that story.

Only recently, reading it again to my son, did the troubling thought occur to me: those people—the people who had had for a short time the veiled presence of majesty among them—did they change?

Lord, I praise Your holy name that You took on the disguise of flesh like mine and learned in pain, my pain, my hope, my need.

G.S.

9.

Fight the good fight with all thy might, Christ is thy strength, and Christ thy light.

John S. B. Monsell hymn

Some years ago I recorded this poem as a Dial-Guideposts-for-Inspiration telephone message. It was one of the most popular messages the program ever had. I don't know the author but, perhaps, if there's discouragement in your life, these lines could help:

When things go wrong, as they sometimes will,
When the road you're treading seems all uphill,
When the funds are low and the debts are high,
And you want to smile, but you have to sigh,
When care is pressing you down a bit,
Rest, if you must, but don't you quit.

Life is queer with its twists and turns,
As every one of us sometimes learns,
And many a failure comes about
When he might have won had he stuck it out;
Don't give up, though the pace seems slow—
You might succeed with another blow.

Success is failure turned inside out—
The silver tint of the clouds of doubt—
And you never can tell how close you are,
It may be near when it seems afar;
So stick to the fight when you're hardest hit—
It's when things seem worst that you mustn't quit.

Father, give us the strength and stamina today to see things through and to do our best for You.

N.V.P.

10.

A soft answer turneth away wrath. . . .
Proverbs 15:1

The waitress spilled the cream as she tried to move the pitcher closer to the man next to me at the coffee counter. I thought of how impatient I become when I must mop up the spills in my home kitchen, and braced myself for an angry encounter.

Instead the waitress just smiled and said, "My, but you have a sloppy waitress this morning."

The man looked up from his newspaper and replied, "Don't worry, you make me feel right at home."

I turned back to my own breakfast relaxed and ready for the day. *A soft answer,* I thought, *how right the Bible is!* Their cheerful acceptance of a minor inconvenience had kept it just that.

Lord, teach me not to let the spilled cream situations of daily life make me unpleasant in dealing with others.

R.C.I.

11.

The only thing we have to fear is fear itself.
Franklin D. Roosevelt

Recently, I watched a television interview between a newsman and a World War I veteran. The latter was asked, "Back in 1918, weren't you fighting the 'war to end all wars'?"

"That's right."

"Obviously it didn't work! Doesn't the present world situation make you fearful?"

"Well, it would if I spent my time looking at it. But it's like Old Nell, a skittish horse I used to have. If she didn't wear blinders to keep her looking straight ahead, she'd rear up at anything she saw on either side. Same way with me—I just put my blinders on and look straight ahead and stuff don't bother me."

I remembered the veteran's words next day at Sunday school when the lesson centered on the disciple who walked on the water to meet Jesus. (Matthew 14:26-31) Peter wasn't afraid until he looked at the waves on either side. He sank when he stopped looking straight ahead. I thought to myself, *Peter should have had some blinders on!*

Scripture is filled with comforting phrases containing two simple words, "fear not." But it took that veteran's illustration of horse blinders to remind me—it's when I look to either side that I fear. But when I face straight ahead toward the One Who said, "Look unto Me," then I don't.

Father, remind me to put on my spiritual blinders whenever I momentarily fail to keep my eyes straight upon You.

I.C.

12.

Come unto Me, all ye that labour and are heavy laden, and I will give you rest.
Matthew 11:28

My father was an old-fashioned, 24-hour-a-day doctor who made house calls to farm homes in snowstorms in the middle of the night. He was usually up at seven for surgery, and his office hours often lasted till seven or eight at night. But he always came home at noon and spent at least a half-hour of quiet time alone. I used to ask my dad what he did during this time and his answer was always the same: "I just rest and clear my mind—get in tune with the Infinite." He called this his "daily dose of silence," and I know now that it was this time of stillness and quiet renewal that gave him strength to endure the long hours and that kept him saying "yes" to life.

I used to think I didn't have time for daily doses of silence, but for the past few years I've *made* time for it, and I've found that, even on the busiest days—in fact, *especially* then—it is time *gained* rather than time lost. I accomplish *more* afterwards, because there's a kind of internal ordering that takes place during my quiet time with God that carries through to all the day's activities. My father's prescription was a good one. I recommend it. Taken once or twice a day, it can renew your strength and keep your spirit healthy.

I will keep my date with silence, Lord, for You are waiting there.

M.M.H.

13. ... He leadeth me in the paths of righteousness for His name's sake.

Psalm 23:3

A friend and I were discussing permissiveness in raising children. And some of its seeming products, the long-haired, guitar-strumming types who swarm around Dupont Circle here in Washington, D.C.

"You know what terrible traffic there is up there," she said. "Well, one day I saw a typical, bearded 'bluejeans' starting to jaywalk right into it. And I couldn't stand it, I yelled at him, 'Stop! Come back!' He turned with such a startled expression I do believe it was the first time in his life he'd ever heard a direct command.

"Then, as if he couldn't believe his ears, he turned and headed right on. But I called again, 'You'll get killed, come back!'

"And he did. I don't know whether he realized he was being foolish, or whether he was simply obeying me. Anyway, he came, looking kind of sheepish and kind of glad. I think that may be three-fourths of the trouble with a lot of kids today. They've never had people who *cared* enough about them to order them, 'Stop! Come back!' "

The Bible is full of such commands for all of us, no matter what our age. The warnings, the "Thou shalt nots" are there for our own protection. They are the words of a loving Father Who knows what can harm us and destroy the very happiness we seek. He cares enough about us to order, "Don't do this. Stop, come back!"

Dear God, help me to discipline my children with the loving firmness You show me. And when I begin to stray from Your discipline, myself, call me back.

M.H.

14.

I pledge allegiance to the flag of the United States . . . one nation, under God. . . .
Francis Bellamy

Worried about Union defeats at Fort Sumter and Bull Run and concerned about the godlessness of a nation which set brother against brother in a civil war, The Reverend Mr. Watkinson, Protestant minister of Ridleyville, Pennsylvania, decided to do something in the name of God.

On a November day in 1861 he wrote to Treasury Secretary Salmon P. Chase. "One fact touching our currency has hitherto been seriously overlooked," he said. "I mean the recognition of the Almighty God in some form on our coins. What if our Republic were now shattered beyond reconstruction? Would not the antiquaries of succeeding centuries rightly reason from our past that we were a heathen nation?"

As a result the Philadelphia mint director James Pollock was ordered to prepare a motto expressing the nation's recognition of its dependency upon God.

In 1864 the inscription, "In God We Trust," first appeared on a U.S. coin—the 2¢ piece. After 1864 the phrase appeared on many coins, but only since 1938, with coinage of the Jefferson nickel, have all U.S. coins carried this inscription.

Isn't it heartening to think that every day millions of Americans carry in their pockets this quiet affirmation of the nation's allegiance to God?

Lord, how great it is to put our trust in You.

Z.B.D.

WHAT THANKS-GIVING CAN DO FOR YOU

Giving thanks—to one's fellow man and to the Lord—is often overlooked as a powerful instrument for reaching oneness with God. From now until Thanksgiving Day, why don't you try this three-part experiment designed to increase your thanks-giving capacity.

Every day, surprise someone: How long has it been since you thanked the mailman, milkman or newspaper boy for their reliability? If you receive over-ripe fruit, do you complain to the grocer? Do you likewise tell him if it was especially delicious? Opportunities to surprise people with gratitude present themselves all day long. Most of the time you will not know what effect your thanks have on the recipients (sometimes they'll be more important than you might dream, arriving at a low point in another's life), but the effect on your own life is certain. You'll be training yourself day-by-day to seek out the good around you, rather than the more attention-catching bad.

Every day, thank God for something you have never thanked Him for—until now: It is good to start any prayer of thanksgiving to God with some statement of over-all indebtedness, "For our creation, preservation, and all the blessings of this life," as the Book of Common Prayer has it. But try to add each day some different, perhaps very tiny blessing: the gift of sight on a colorful autumn morning, warm clothes as the days grow colder. The discipline of thanking God for a different blessing each day could go on for a lifetime without repeating, but your thanks will not be confined to little things all the time, of course. There will be days when as a Christian you will be overwhelmed by the magnitude of Christ's sacrifice for You. By then, the habit of giving thanks will have been established. You'll be ready to express your deepest feelings of gratitude.

Every day, thank God for something you're not happy about: This is both the hardest exercise in thanksgiving and the one that comes closest to the heart of the spiritual life. To the oppressed Ephesians an imprisoned Paul wrote, "Giving thanks always for all things unto God and the Father in the name of our Lord Jesus Christ." (Ephesians 5:20)

Thanking God for seemingly bad events has been called the first step of faith in *action*. If you can stand before a financial setback, a disappointment, even death itself, and thank God for what in His hands these circumstances will become, you are acting out your conviction that He can bring good when you yourself do not see it.

Try these three suggestions until Thanksgiving Day—and maybe every day after . . .

E.S.

16.

How strong and sweet my Father's care
That round about me, like the air,
Is with me always, everywhere!

Anonymous

We hear so much about our environment these days. Preserving natural resources. Ecology. Thinking of this the other day, I began remembering the environment in which I grew up. I had, among other good things such as clean air, parents who raised me in an environment of love.

Love to me was smelling spicy cookies baking in a hot oven. The way little amber bubbles of sugar formed on the meringue of my mother's lemon pie. Love was the damp musty smell of laundry hanging in the house on a rainy day. Waking in terror from a nightmare to feel loving arms soothing, rocking. I could hear love in my father's voice as he read fairy tales and spun dreams while holding me on his lap. And it was the way my mother, so soft and comforting, would put her arms around me in generous, tender hugs.

I remember holding tightly to my father's hand as he pointed out wonderful things along the byways of our neighborhood. I felt love as my mother vigorously brushed my long brown hair. Love was being cared for, protected, wanted. It was being a child in a secure and happy home.

When I was grown, I took this environment with me. Love became making another home for my own husband and children. And now, since they too have gone, love has become a sunset, the purring of my kitten, the presence of my God. For it is through His promise I know that the greatest of love's experiences is still to come.

Thank You for homes, God. The home of our childhood, the home of our children, and the home of our Heavenly Father.

D.H.

17.

What wisdom can you find that is greater than kindness?

Jean Jacques Rousseau

We'd just moved back to Washington, D.C., and I was struggling to get settled in when an old friend called to say she wanted me to join her at a Bible study class the next morning. When I protested that I had too much to do, she kept insisting, saying, "I know you'll love it, May, and it would be such fun to have you in the class. I'll be by at nine-thirty."

I protested that was much too early.

"Then I'll be by at ten," she said cheerfully.

The classes were interesting, though unfamiliar to me, but I still fretted about organizing our house. *Besides,* I thought, *I've already got lots of friends in the area, and I go to Mass faithfully. Why does Joan think I need this?*

Yet I grew more and more absorbed in and enriched by the Bible study course. I could hardly wait for Monday morning, when it was held. One Monday, on our way, I told Joan how grateful I was for her persisting, even though I knew she had a secondary motive.

"Secondary motive?" she asked, looking confused.

"Yes," I said, "I'm sure you thought I needed to get out of the house and meet new people, so you used the Bible class to do it."

"Don't be silly!" she said with a smile. "It never entered my head. I just knew you'd like the course and I wanted to be with you."

Well, I could have kissed her and kicked myself. How small of me to read a motive into a simple kindness by an affectionate friend! How much better to keep an open heart and respond to a kind gesture simply and gratefully.

Lord, life is complicated enough without me analyzing a kindness. Grant me the grace to accept kindnesses with an open heart.

M.S.G.

18.

And I was afraid, and went and hid thy talent in the earth . . .

Matthew 25:25

A couple of years ago our congregation lost its skilled organist, and our hymns just weren't the same. Although our pastor made an appeal, I couldn't bring myself to volunteer. I had played the organ 20 years before, but I kept telling myself that whatever modest abilities had been mine would have become very rusty. What if I got up in front of everyone and muffed it?

Then my husband, Dick, remembered. "Hey, you used to be pretty good at the organ, didn't you?"

"Well, I could play. But I wouldn't dare try now," I replied.

"Why not?"

"Because I might make a fool of myself. I'd be much too self-conscious."

"Self-conscious?" said Dick with a smile. "Or self-centered?"

I hated to admit it, but he was right. I was thinking only of myself.

So the next Sunday I was at our church's organ. At first I was terribly nervous. But then I noticed that, whenever I hit a sour note, everybody sang louder to help me along. I was touched and heartened. Before the service was over, I was having a great time!

When God wants something done, He doesn't always call on an expert. What He does need are willing servants. So put yourself aside and use the talents God has given you to help others. If you do, they will multiply and grow. And you'll feel great!

I'm grateful for my talents, Lord, but I need You to remind me to use them in the service of others.

B.R.G.

19.

Judge not according to the appearance. . . .

John 7:24

An office manager I knew once took a dislike to our firm's cleaning lady because he thought she was glum. "Her face hates the whole world," he used to say about her.

One morning he came in late to work, looking frazzled. He had stopped smoking for a week, and his nerves were on edge. This morning, he told me, he just knew he wouldn't be able to resist a cigarette. Then he noticed a note the cleaning woman had left nestled in his unused ashtray the night before. "You've won six days straight," the note read. "Don't lose now."

It worked. He never smoked again.

How often I've made the same mistake of judging people by their faces. Don't we all?

Dear Lord, when I meet an unhappy face, give me the grace to see behind it.

M.A.

20.

. . . Let not thy left hand know what thy right hand doeth: . . .

Matthew 6:3

Being a rather shy, unathletic child, I was always uncomfortable during recesses when most of the kids played softball. One cold day in fourth grade, I was standing around feeling self-conscious when one of the most popular girls in my class came over to me. "My hands are freezing," she said, "and my pockets aren't very warm." With that, she plunged both hands into one of my pockets, held them there for a minute, then went back to the game. At noon, when I pulled my lunch money out of my pocket, there was a stick of gum in my hand—a silent message that said, "I care about you."

A small thing maybe, but I've remembered that quiet little act of kindness all these years. I think what made it so memorable was that she did it *secretly, anonymously.*

Is there someone whose life you could brighten with a little secret surprise today? An anonymous note of appreciation, a smile face drawn on a napkin, a flower on a secretary's desk, a paperback book that just "appears" on your spouse's bedside table, a piece of gum slipped into a shy child's pocket? It's a lovely way to say "I care about you."

Help me to care about others, Lord, and to show it in special, secret ways today.

M.M.H

21.

Eye hath not seen, nor ear heard . . . the things which God hath prepared for them that love Him.

I Corinthians 2:9

A German mother taught her little ones to knit as early as possible, and to encourage them she prepared a wonder ball. As she wound the ball of yarn she bound little gifts inside it, and the children learned to knit by striving for the treasures just ahead.

God has prepared a wonder ball for each of us. It's called— Life. We greet each new day with wonder and anticipation. What will it bring? Certainly little love gifts, if we'll pause to unwrap them.

You smile as you wrap a birthday gift. You can't wait to see Danny's eyes when he opens it.

With bags, you search through moldy leaves, examining old stumps and logs. Will you find mushrooms?

You re-read a letter from a soldier in Vietnam saying, "I dream of the doorknob at home. I can see it. What will it be like to close my hand on it?"

You see a farmer studying his crops and the heavens. What will be the yield?

It's the brown time of Thanksgiving and you pass ragged roadside weeds while heading home. Who all will be there? Will Mom have homemade bread?

The first snow falls and you hurry to lay the wood—eager for the family to share the quiet of a winter night, and to watch fragile, tearing flames lick a hissing log.

What greater gifts?

Oh, Lord, our God, I thank You for the countless joys You have hidden in the wonder ball of life.

Z.B.D.

22.

We have been a most favored people. We ought to be a most grateful people. We have been a most blessed people. We ought to be a most thankful people.

Calvin Coolidge

A farmer in our congregation raises pigs. One Thanksgiving afternoon his wife and I walked to a far corner of their land and watched their hogs, happily rooting beneath the trees in an oak grove, searching out acorns.

She said, "You know, I think those pigs are a lot like people in some ways. At the moment I'm not referring to their grunting and wallowing and things usually associated with pigs. But look at them eating those acorns. Not once have they looked up to see where their food is coming from! It seems to me it's sort of like not saying grace before a meal. You can't expect grace from a pig, of course. But even today, I'm sure there are many people—just like these pigs—who'll fail to look up and give God thanks before hogging down."

I giggled at her illustrations.

But then I wondered. . . . How many times have I failed to be thankful for things I take for granted?

Dear God, teach me how to give You sincere thanks from deep within my heart.

I.C.

23.

**Love divine, all love excelling,
Joy of heaven, to earth come down;
Fix in us Thy humble dwelling,
All Thy faithful mercies crown!**

Charles Wesley hymn

From the day I walked down the aisle and said "I do" I expected my husband to say "I love you" on a regular basis. Morning and night always, and during the day on weekends. He lived up to my expectations for awhile and all went well. And then I began to notice that the "I love you's" were becoming fewer. At night only, and finally not even then. He doesn't care much any more,

I decided. The honeymoon is over.

My children were born and grew up and they seldom said "I love you" either, unless I was sick in bed. And so I lived in discontent.

One day as I sat broodingly in church, suddenly the minister's words pierced my inattention. "You must learn to listen for love," he said, "because people express it in so many different ways. All of us have to learn how to watch and listen."

Being a verbal person, this was hard for me to understand. But I decided it was worth a try. And so one evening when my husband casually said, "I passed a kid selling roses on a corner but I was in the wrong lane to stop," I realized to my surprise that he had just said, "I love you." And another night my teen-aged son, slouching over his dinner, muttered, "Not bad," and my daughter winked at me. Two "I love you's" at once!

Now I hear them every day. A smile in the eyes of a friend, an arm across my shoulders . . . or God's love expressed in a glowing sunset. I find myself surrounded by love, because I've learned to watch—and listen.

Thank You, God, for opening my eyes and heart to the many evidences of love around me. And thank You most of all for the joy I find today in returning that love.

D. H.

24.

Cease from anger, and forsake wrath: fret not thyself in any wise to do evil.

Psalm 37:8

When Mama and Daddy were young they moved to a small farm, built a big chicken house and bought an incubator. My two older sisters were little girls then. They liked living on a farm and loved the idea that soon there would be hundreds of little yellow chicks and then later, all the fried chicken they could eat. There was only one fly in the ointment. Harley Stinson. He chased them when they walked to school and took their dinner buckets away and ate their cookies. He threw mudballs at them from a tree overhanging the footbridge and put garter snakes in their path. They hated Harley Stinson!

Daddy's chicken dream evaporated when the incubator over-heated and ruined all the eggs, so he told the girls to take them out and dump them.

"Wouldn't it be great if Harley Stinson came along right now?" Arleyn chirped. "We could plaster him good!"

But Nadine had a better way to vent her animosity. She picked out a big oak tree and christened it "Harley Stinson." Then she and Arleyn pelted that tree furiously with rotten eggs. By the time they had thrown half the eggs they were laughing, and when Harley Stinson actually did come along the path, they greeted him with smiles and even shared their amunition with him.

Harley was delighted. He showed them how to throw from the shoulder with a twist of the elbow so that the eggs flew straight. Then he showed them a secret place where a bluebird had her nest and another where a mother rabbit had used her own fur to make a soft nest for her babies. That night at bedtime Arleyn confessed to Mama that maybe Harley Stinson wasn't so bad, after all.

Do you have animosities smouldering inside you? If so, perhaps you should learn how to ventilate them harmlessly just as Arleyn and Nadine did, and then take another look at the person you thought you disliked. You might be surprised at what you see.

Lord, we praise You for the beauty You have placed in each human soul. Teach us, Father, to seek for it in each person we meet until we find it.

M.M.

25.

Not for one single day can I discern my way,
But this I surely know—
Who gives the day will show the way,
So I securely go.

John Oxenham

"Why did you take that picture and why do you keep it over your desk?" sometimes friends ask.

The picture is of a towering Kansas cottonwood which was struck by a dagger of lightning many years ago. In spite of being maimed, the indomitable tree pushed protective bark around its wound. But since it was only partially successful, the deep scar remains obvious to every passerby.

I snapped the picture, enlarged it and hung it above my desk.

To me, it's a lovely, courageous cottonwood. Not because the scar is beautiful—it isn't. But because the tree didn't simply give up or die when it received the lightning bolt.

At one time or another every member of our family has been hit by lightning bolts—family problems, financial difficulty, illness, death, divorce. Whenever someone thinks his or her trouble is unbearable (or if I think mine is!), we look at the picture of the scarred old cottonwood.

If an ordinary tree can survive a fearful blow, adjust itself to make a new center of balance and continue pointing up toward its Creator, then so can I!

Father, You don't ask us to bow to circumstances. You expect us to surmount them. Keep me growing, looking and pointing up!

I.C.

26.

Charity (love) suffereth long and is kind.
1 Corinthians 13:4

A college professor I heard of once told his little daughter to do something. She announced that she would not.

He sent the child to her room immediately.

Later that day, when he picked up his paper and went to sit down in his chair, he found a note on the seat. It said, "I hate daddy."

Angrily he called his wife and showed her the note. "I'm going to teach her a thing or two," he declared.

"Don't do anything rash," his wife told him. "Think about it."

With difficulty, he took her advice. He thought about it. Finally, using the same piece of paper, he wrote a note under hers, "Daddy loves you," and placed it on her pillow.

A few moments after his daughter discovered his note, she came to him with the same piece of paper. Written on the back of it were these words, "I love Daddy too."

Dear Lord, teach us to use the power of love in all our dealings with others.

Z. B. D.

27.

O come let us sing unto the Lord . . .
Psalm 95:1

Whatever assets I might be able to claim for mine, a singing voice could never be included. Yet no one enjoys trying to sing more than I! To be part of a lustily singing congregation in church delights me because I can join in wholeheartedly, certain that my noise will be lost in the volume and might even reach Heaven disguised as melodious.

I used to be envious of anyone who sang well and I still stand in awe of great soloists. But I have learned that there are very few who are called to be truly outstanding in any field. For every Neil Armstrong there are hundreds of unsung engineers, draftsmen and mechanics who put the whole thing together to make possible his footprints on the moon.

One small buttercup can't measure up to a mighty oak. But a few dozen of them nodding together in a field make a breathtaking thing of beauty.

So if you are feeling small, low, inferior and talentless, cheer up. You are much more important than you think! Why, God even knows the number of hairs on your head. (Matthew 10:30)

Take heart, join me. And if we can't carry the tune, then we'll just make a joyful noise together.

Teach us, Lord, that it really isn't the tune that counts; it's the singing.

D.D* *

28.

I would be humble for I know my weakness;
I would look up, and laugh, and love, and lift.
Howard Arnold Walter hymn

My "good china" is one of my prized possessions and leads a very sheltered life. However, despite my loving care, there have been mishaps.

The day a cup became badly chipped, and a dark crack ran down the side, it moved into a new category of being loved and used regularly. I couldn't discard it. I brought it into the kitchen to be used every day. How I have enjoyed it! Cheery violet faces cling to its sides and the handle curves beautifully. It has shared much of my planning and daydreaming; has comforted at times of disappointment. And many problems have been freed to disappear with its rising aromatic vapor.

I like to think that God uses us flawed human beings in much the same way. Despite our imperfections, He loves us and cherishes us and refuses to let us go.

Lord, thank You for using me in spite of my flaws.

M. B. D. **

29.

Rejoice!

Veni Emmanuel

I once turned my back on the famous movie actress Joan Crawford. She was not displeased; she even thanked me.

At a big New England hotel, a business associate and I met Miss Crawford during a before-breakfast walk. My friend decided to ask for her autograph to give to his teen-age daughter. He produced pen and paper and I volunteered my back as a writing desk. Graciously, she thanked me.

We apologized for forcing our attentions on her, but she only smiled, saying, "It's a beautiful day for writing my name."

I will always remember Joan Crawford, not as a celebrity, but as a lovely lady dealing graciously with two strangers who had intruded on her privacy.

"It's a beautiful day for writing my name" was Joan Crawford's way of saying, "Thank God, I'm alive."

Do you feel that way this morning? If not, perhaps you've lost something. Better look for it!

Dear Lord, let me add the quality of enthusiasm to this day You have given us.

M.A.

30.

Choose you this day whom ye will serve. . . .
Joshua 24:15

When Alice in Wonderland came to a fork in the road she asked the Cheshire cat, "Which road do I take?"

"Where do you want to go?" asked the Cheshire cat.

"I don't know," said Alice.

"Then it doesn't matter," said the cat.

Every day in some way we face a fork in the road that does matter. Shall we yield to a good impulse, resist a bad one? Shall we pass along that juicy bit of gossip or shall we keep it to ourselves?

When I face a fork in the road each day, I ask God to help me choose the right way. I think it determines whether I grow or shrink spiritually.

Lord, let me always choose the way that brings me closer to You.

S.F.

DECEMBER 1979

S	M	T	W	T	F	S
						1
2	3	4	5	6	7	8
9	10	11	12	13	14	15
16	17	18	19	20	21	22
23	24	25	26	27	28	29
30	31					

1.

O star of wonder, star of night,
Star with royal beauty bright.
                    John H. Hopkins carol

In New Mexico where I live, there is a wonderful custom at Christmas time, a tradition the Spanish villages along the Rio Grande have been carrying on for three centuries. The Spanish word for it is *luminarias*, or "little lights."

The lights—short candles placed in paper bags partly filled with sand—are placed along roads, walks and rooftops to light the way for the Christ Child. When *luminarias* are lighted on Christmas Eve, all other lights in and around the home are extinguished. The glow of the candle through the paper bag in the dark of night, multiplied by thousands of such lights, is a lovely sight.

I like to think that these *luminarias* represent all the little deeds of kindness and expressions of love that make Christmas so precious. Now, as we enter the Christmas season, I want to concentrate on these—and other—ways to light the path for Him.

Help us, Lord, to be "little lights" for Your Son this Christmas.

T.S.

2.

They helped every one his neighbour; and every one said to his brother, Be of good courage.

Isaiah 41:6

When I was a child, in our little town there was a phrase people used often. Parting at church or on the street, they would call to each other, "Come over!"

Come to see us, they meant. Come for coffee, come to hold the new baby, come so the children can play together, and the women gossip, and the men discuss politics and crops. Leave your own house and yard and draw nearer, come closer. *Come over.*

And people came. Whole families. Usually without further invitation or phoning to be sure you were there. Most people were usually home, and visitors were so *welcome* in those days.

Today how few of us dare to drop in on each other. There is the fear of intrusion. There is the competition of television. And most of us are so busy—swamped by more people in a day than our parents might see in a week. And though friendships still root and grow between individuals, it's seldom a family affair.

Maybe that's why so many people are so lonely. They are longing to span the distance, but they don't know how. They are reaching out to others, crying out inside: "Act as if you care about me. Come closer. *Come over!*"

We can't go back to yesterday. But we can turn off the TV sets and invite others, whole families, to come over. We can fill the car with children and call on someone who can't get out, whose silent house would welcome their noise. We can find ways to spend less time with people who mean nothing to us, and more with those who do. We can draw closer to people whose background and color may be different from our own; for today if we are truly to "come over" we must be willing to leave our own safe territory and cross barriers, fences that may be keeping us from some of the most rewarding people of our lives.

Dear God, thank You that we are all members of Your family. Thank You for helping us find the time to draw closer to each other, to enrich and enjoy each other. Remind us to be more willing to "come over."

M.H.

3.

This is My commandment, that ye love one another as I have loved you.

John 15:12

The telephone rang early on a dismal Monday morning, and a lilting voice greeted me, "If it were your birthday, I'd say, 'Happy Birthday,' but since it isn't, I'll just say, 'I love you, Mom.' "

Suddenly the gray day was radiant. My heart leaped with joy. My daughter had no particular reason for calling long-distance except to say that she loves me!

"Love" is so easy to say—and so often left unsaid. When was the last time you spoke words of love to your mate? To your children? To a friend? The Bible tells us that "a flattering mouth worketh ruin" (Proverbs 26:28) but genuine affection, freely given, can cheer the saddest heart.

Try it today. Don't presume family and friends know that you love them. Tell them. It will brighten their day and yours, too.

Lord, keep us aware of Your love for us and help us to share it with others.

D.D.* *

4.

Know ye not that ye are the temple of God. . . .

I Corinthians 3:16

Ages ago our three-year-old son Paul was with me, pushing through a crowd as I covered a news story. "If you were to get lost, how would you describe me?" I asked him.

"Well, I'd say she's fat, wears grandma shoes, and her hair is always dangling in the air."

Taking solace in the thought that to a child 30 is old and 140 pounds is fat, I nevertheless looked in the mirror when I arrived home. I also remembered my husband saying as he patiently waited by the car, "Zona B! You won't leave the house until every cushion is straight, then you close the door, no one sees it, and . . . everyone sees you."

Keeping a house, being a wife, mom, cook, newswoman, teaching a Sunday-school class, visiting nursing homes, tending flowers, I'd overlooked a bit the importance of self-packaging.

Perhaps many persons who wonder what happened to their romance, both men and women, need to take a long look in the mirror. Side view too. Rear, even. Is the way you look a matter of spiritual importance? We seem to think so on Sundays. But remember—there are six other days in the week!

Created in Your image, may we strive to be beautiful inside and out, dear God.

Z. B. D.

5.

. . . Verily I say unto you, Inasmuch as ye have done it unto one of the least of these My brethren, ye have done it unto Me.

Matthew 25:40

As a pre-school child I frequently accompanied my father to our tiny rural post office. At some point I began to realize I never got any mail, and complained to the postmistress.

"Why, I think I have one for you today!" she exclaimed. And reaching under her counter she handed me a long envelope.

From then on, whenever I went to the post office I got mail. It was long after we moved from there that I realized that that kind woman must have saved her "resident" and "occupant" junk mail so that children could feel important, too.

Many people feel left out in this world. Some are too old, some too young. Some have no families, some have no access to small children, some have no spouse in a couples' world, some are retarded or illiterate or just excruciatingly lonely. Each of us has some resources to share—a smile, a touch, a moment of conversation that says, "Hey, I like you, and you are important." Today, take time to include someone who feels left out in your circle of love.

Dear Lord Who reached out to touch even lepers, reach out through me today to someone who needs Your touch.

P.H.S.

6.

. . .It is more blessed to give than to receive.
Acts 20:35

One winter day I cooked a kettle of stew for a sick neighbor. I recalled the Scriptural account of Jesus' words, "It is more blessed to give than to receive," and I could almost feel a shower of blessings covering me from head to toe as I prided myself on doing such a thoughtful deed.

But as I started next door with the steaming stew, the screen door caught one elbow and the whole pan plopped flat onto the concrete steps. The impact blew the lid five feet into the air with the stew following close behind.

I'd cooked only two quarts of stew, but it seemed there were at least two gallons when it came to cleaning up the congealed, greasy liquid.

"Where's the *blessing* in this mess?" I asked myself. "After all, I tried to do this kind of thing for Him!"

But had I really? Deep inside I expected my neighbor to say, "What a thoughtful person you are!" And I remembered the proverb, "Pride goeth before destruction, and an haughty spirit before a fall." (Proverbs 16:18) With a brush and bucket of hot soapsuds on cold concrete, I finally learned not to "do good" just to "look good."

Father, thank You for Your faithfulness in teaching me those things I need to learn.

I.C.

7.

... In quietness and in confidence shall be your strength. ...

Isaiah 30:15

To help herself overcome the loss of a loved one, a friend of mine went to work in a boutique. But she soon found that she lacked confidence. Every time a customer approached her, she felt timid.

She turned to an older, more experienced clerk for help. Wisely that woman told her, "You might try something that has helped me. Before I wait on a customer, I say a little prayer."

Gradually faith replaced fear as my friend silently said "God bless you" whenever a customer came to her. Little by little her own shyness disappeared, and her sales improved. Best of all, her own sorrow became less as she tried to serve the needs of others.

Father, give us others to help when we need help ourselves.

R.C.I.

8.

The world is a looking glass and gives back to every man the reflection of his own face.

William Makepeace Thackeray

"Well, how was your morning?" my husband asked as we sat down for lunch one day.

"Oh, I don't know. John got up on the wrong side of the bed and Karen left for work grumbling. Even Paul wasn't his usual sunny self this morning."

"Sounds like you're not in a very good mood today," Rex observed sympathetically.

"Me! *I'm* all right. It's just that the kids are so moody. Maybe it's the weather."

Later it dawned on me that Rex really had spotted the trouble.

If the children were grouchy, it was because they were mirroring me. Looking back, I remembered that I *had* felt kind of "down" when I woke up. I was tired of the rain and dreading the ironing that was waiting for me. I realized, then, how just one person's sour mood can infect a whole family.

Since then, I've been taking a little time, each morning, to assess my mood and turn over to God any "clouds" that are hovering over me, before I get the family up.It has helped.You really can affect the emotional climate of your household, or the place where you work, by keeping a controlling finger on your own mood thermostat. Try it today and see.

Let my face mirror Your love, Lord, all through this day.
M.M.H.

9. Then shall the kingdom of heaven be likened unto ten virgins . . . five of them were wise, and five were foolish. They that were foolish took their lamps, and took no oil with them.
Matthew 25:1-3

It was a dark, stormy night. Alone at home with an infant I was increasingly nervous, for I am afflicted with an unreasonable fear of the dark. Suddenly it happened—a crash, and our neighborhood lights went out. Frantically I dashed for the flashlight.

But when I flicked the switch, the bulb was so dim I could hardly see it. For weeks I had intended to get new batteries. Why hadn't I? Now, when I really needed it, the flashlight was practically useless.

Isn't it true that spirits, like flashlights, need power? When we neglect to charge our batteries—through prayer, Bible study and quiet meditation—our spirits grow dim.

Father, recharge us today so that we may lighten the darkness where we are.
P.H.S.

10.

The night is far spent, the day is at hand. . . .
Romans 13:12

We own a heating company, and I take the night calls. One customer kept calling between two and five a.m., wanting a serviceman to come to her home immediately. Each time, he would find the heating unit operating perfectly, but the woman would be drunk and insistent that he stay longer. He finally told her he would not come to her home again unless she was sober.

The following morning at four, she called. This time, drunk again, she became abusive. I was tempted to hang up on her but an inner voice told me not to. Instead, I told her, "God loves you. He knows all your problems and He wants to help you."

She screamed, "Who is this? I demand to know who this is!"

I answered, "This is a friend who knows that God will move into your life, if you will meet Him halfway. I want you to know that I will pray for you."

She replied, "Whoever heard of a heating company praying for people?" Then, in a softer tone, "You sound just like me, twenty years ago. I used to pray. I used to go to church. I wasn't always like this."

I asked her, "Will you pray with me for just one minute, every midnight, for the next thirty days? You will see a great change for the better if you do."

She hung up on me.

A week later at midnight she called back. "Are you praying?" she asked curtly. When I told her I was, she hung up again. This went on for another three weeks.

One night she finally opened up and was able to talk about her problems and fears. We prayed together, and we both asked Jesus to help her and give her strength and courage.

A year has gone by. She still calls me from time to time, but now it is to tell me of the peace and joy she has found in living a sober, self-respecting, Christian life. Once more.

Thank You, Lord, for the inner voice that urges us to help people in our search for You.

P.S.

11.

To be seventy years young is sometimes far more cheerful and hopeful than to be forty years old.

Oliver Wendell Holmes

I stared in the mirror. Where did all those gray hairs come from? I hadn't noticed them yesterday. My toothbrush flew. Under my breath I mumbled, "Mirror, mirror on the wall, who is the fairest of them all." As I rinsed and dried my face, I glared at my reflection. "Don't answer that." Turning my back, I marched out of the bathroom.

In the kitchen I continued the conversation.

"You're getting old," I said to myself aloud. "No wonder you can't remember anything any more."

"Don't worry, Mom," my teen-age son cheerfully said, as he came into the kitchen behind me. "I'll take care of you when you become senile."

"That's comforting," I answered, sarcastically, making a face at him. He grinned and for just a moment I saw my mother's smile shining from his smooth young face. My mother had been gone now for over six years, but I could still hear her voice.

"It doesn't matter how long we live," she reminded me in a soft voice echoing from the past. I could almost see the upward tilt of her chin and the blue sparkle of her eyes . . . "The truth is that God intended His children to be forever young in spirit. It's up to us to believe in His intention." Mother's beautiful face had been a living example of eternal youth. White hair and all.

"Amen," I said as the eggs began to fry.

Of all the beautiful things You have given us, Lord, I thank You most of all for the gift of eternal life. And eternal youth.

D.H.

12.

The Lord is nigh unto all them that call upon him, to all that call upon him in truth.

Psalm 145:18

Two days after we moved to Kansas a blizzard struck. Frenzied snowflakes hurtled through the air, coming to rest in huge drifts that blocked the roads and locked our car in a prison of ice. We were eight miles from town, so there was no chance anyone would see us and help us dig out. Alone, cut off from everything familiar, from everyone I knew and loved, I sat down on a packing box to cry.

Then, unexpectedly, the telephone rang. "I'm your nearest neighbor," a cheery voice announced. "You can't see my house in this storm, but I'm just a ways east of you. If you need anything, all you have to do is call."

Later, I remembered other times I had been lonely or troubled and thought I was friendless. I realized that Jesus was there all the time. I couldn't actually see Him but, like my neighbor, He was ready to help. All I had to do was call.

Thank You, Lord, for Your presence. Help us remember that You are always there, waiting for us to reach out to You.

P.V.S.

13.

Be not afraid of sudden fear. . . .
Proverbs 3:25

As a tense beginner on the ski slopes, I would stiffen up each time I sensed I was going to fall. As a result, each spill hurt twice as much. One day as I was toppling toward the snow, a fellow skier flew by and yelled out, "Enjoy your fall."

At first I thought he was being flippant, but then I began to think there might be some truth in what he said. So the next time I was about to fall, instead of tightening up, I let my body go loose. And when I started "enjoying" my falls I began to ski much better.

It seems to me that life is a lot like that. When we tense up in tough situations, defeat can overwhelm us. But when we learn to relax and stop being afraid of challenges, we can take life's tumbles in stride.

Guide us, Lord, through the ups and downs of life.

T.S.

14.

Devise not evil against thy neighbour, seeing he dwelleth securely by thee.

Proverb 3:29

A night-shift worker I knew, who had to sleep during daylight hours, kept being awakened by the clatter of his neighbor's garbage can. At first he was annoyed and was going to give her a piece of his mind. But then, recognizing that the odd hours he had to keep were part of the problem, he decided to contribute to its solution. He bought her a heavy plastic garbage container.

When a neighbor irritates you, why not try attacking the problem, instead of the neighbor?

Dear Lord, show me the creative ways to handle the irritations of this day.

M.A.

IS YOUR HEART IN YOUR GIVING?

The Christmas season is the most appropriate time of all for examining one's attitudes toward giving. Below you will find a way to gauge your own sense of generosity by reflecting on the eight steps of "The Golden Ladder of Charity." This famous ladder was created by Moses ben Maimon, known to us as Maimonides (1135–1204), the Jewish philosopher-physician-astronomer-rabbi who greatly influenced the thinking and doctrine of his own religion and of Christian and Islamic thinking as well.

Read each step carefully, then think of one or more personal gifts you have made in the past year that correspond to Maimonides' definition.

The first and lowest degree is to give—but with reluctance or regret. This is the gift of the *hand* but not of the *heart.*

The second is to give cheerfully, but not proportionately to the distress of the suffering.

The third is to give cheerfully, and proportionately, but not until we are solicited.

The fourth is to give cheerfully, proportionately, and even unsolicited; but to put it in the poor man's hand, thereby exciting in him the painful emotion of shame.

The fifth is to give charity in such a way that the distressed may receive the bounty and know their benefactor, without their being known to him. Such was the conduct of our ancestors, who used to tie up money in the hind-corners of their cloaks, so that the poor might take it unperceived.

The sixth, which rises still higher, is to know the objects of our bounty, but remain unknown to them. Such was the conduct of those of our ancestors who used to convey their charitable gifts into people's dwellings, taking care that their own persons should remain unknown.

The seventh is still more meritorious, namely, to bestow charity in such a way that the benefactor may not know the relieved persons, nor they the name of their benefactor.

The eighth and most meritorious of all is to anticipate charity by preventing poverty; namely, to assist the reduced brother either by a considerable gift, or a loan of money, or by teaching him a trade, or by putting him in the way of business, so that he may earn an honest livelihood and not be forced to the dreadful alternative of holding up his hand for charity. This is the highest step and the summit of charity's Golden Ladder.

How many of the eight kinds of giving were you able to recount? Did you find your list thinning out near the end? That happens to almost everybody. But that doesn't mean that you, or any of us, should stop trying to make a success of all the ladder's rungs. And remember, gracious giving requires no special talent, nor large sums of money. The best gift is always a portion of oneself.

V. V.

16.

When thou prayest, enter into thy closet. . . .
Matthew 6:6

Sometimes my days get packed so full—don't yours?—that my time for prayer and meditation gets squeezed out. When that happens for more than a couple of days in a row, though, I begin to feel scattered and out of focus, like a movie projector without a lens.

Maybe that's why Jesus told us to go into our closet and shut the door when we pray. Public prayer is important because it binds together the body of Christ, but private prayer has a *special* power because it focuses God's force in the depths of the individual soul.

I've found that, like the lens in a movie projector, my daily time of prayer and meditation brings the rays of God's light and the force of His love to a focal point in the center of my soul. It makes my way clear and sharpens up the focus of my whole life.

Thank You, Lord, for those private moments that bring Your life-focusing love into my life.

M. M. H.

17.

. . . Suffer the little children to come unto
Me, and forbid them not . . .

Mark 10:14

It was a rotten day to go to school that Monday—wet and
grumbling sky, river road with mud to my fenders, aching head
cold that made my eyeballs cringe and fired my sinus tissue.

But I urged my mud-grumpy car out of the drive, splashing
more mud over the windshield at each pothole, across Blackbird
Creek and the Chariton River bottom, until at last I stumbled up
the steps to the trailer we used for my kindergarten classroom. I
wiped my glasses and fished for my key while rain dripped down
my collar and a wet, scroungy dog rubbed cockleburrs against
my only good pair of nylons. The door swung open and I slammed it in the dog's face.

Five minutes later the bus arrived, spilling 28 five-years-olds
into my room. My nose was running as I pulled off 56 boots, and
my tender eardrums were bombarded with voices.

"Mrs. Montgomery, know what? We've got two new kittens
and a new baby at our house."

"The dentist told my mom she has to get false teeth, and she
cried!"

"I lost my lunch money on the bus."

"Uncle Bob has to go to the Army."

Numbly I ushered the brood past a bulletin board hung with
runny tempera paintings, a fish tank with five guppies, and a
teepee made of wrapping paper held up by a broomstick
lodgepole, to the huge rug we use for "Opening Circle."

Then Carrie, standing on tip-toe beside the ant farm: "Mrs.
Montgomery, you promised we would sing to the ants today."

So we all sang, "Good Morning to You," to the ants.

Then Carrie's tiny voice again, "And the fish. . . ." So we sang
to the guppies.

And suddenly I was aware that my sinuses had cleared and my
heart had expanded. Suddenly I was smiling into twenty-eight

eager faces, and rain was playing a happy tune on the window panes.

Ever since that far off day, when I'm feeling low or sorry for myself, I try to put myself in contact with children, or at least a child. The Lord told us that's the way we'd have to become if we wanted to enter the Kingdom. What better way to conquer gloom than to reach out and touch that inexpressible joy?

Lord, I thank You for children—their effervescent gaiety; the magic of their imaginations; the joy of sharing their untarnished view of the world and their unbounding trust!

M.M.

18.

Fear not; for God hath heard the voice of the lad where he is.

Genesis 21:17

"Why are these Christmas concerts always so crowded?" I was thinking as I settled into a chair near the back of the auditorium.

The old gentleman next to me began telling me that his son was a tenor in the choir. "He's very good," the man said, "I'm sure you'll enjoy his singing."

The curtain rose revealing a choir of a hundred young men and women. They began to sing, and it wasn't long before the old man was nudging me and pointing out his son. "He sings beautifully, doesn't he?" he asked. Although I strained to hear the boy, it was impossible to single him out. Yet I'm certain that his father could.

Our Father in Heaven is the same with us. Though we are all part of the mighty chorus of believers, He hears us one at a time.

Praise be, Father, for Your infinite capacity to hear each one of us as we pray.

J.J.

19.

Joy to the world! The Lord is come;
Let earth receive her King;
Let every heart prepare Him room
And heaven and nature sing.

Isaac Watts

There was a war on, and I had four little boys to raise by myself. Money was always short, even for necessities, so I took a part-time job as a waitress, and used my tips to buy toys and clothing at the dime store, which I passed each day as I walked home. I would pick the presents out very carefully, after much deliberation, because I knew I really had to stretch the nickels and dimes, or the boys would be disappointed on Christmas morning. I would daydream how their little faces would look, as they found the gifts from Santa. I would smuggle the packages into the house, and hide them in a box in my closet.

A week before Christmas, I came home to find the sitter taking a nap, and the children squealing with delight. They had found the box, and the presents were scattered all over the house, the new clothes tossed to one side, in favor of the toys.

"Look, Mama, look," yelled the boys. "Santa was here; come and see!"

I was so upset I sat down on the bed and started to cry. I felt that our Christmas had been spoiled.

Just then, my mother came by to help me get the boys ready for bed, as she did each night, even though she had a job to go to each day, and a house to keep up. She took the situation in at a glance.

"Merry Christmas, boys. Ho, ho, ho!" she sang out. "Santa really did come last night, didn't he? Now isn't that nice? He brought the presents early, and now we can have a whole beautiful Christmas Day all to ourselves, just us and Baby Jesus to celebrate His birthday."

Forgive me, Lord, if I have turned the sacred birthday of Thy Son into a tinsely, commercial holiday. Let me give gifts of loving, and caring, and sharing, instead of plastic trinkets. And, please Lord, let the Holy Spirit of Christmas have room in my heart all year long, not for just a day.

P.S.

20.

But grow in grace, and in the knowledge of our Lord and Saviour, Jesus Christ.

II Peter 3:18

On a two-shelved rack on my kitchen wall is a collection of tiny teacups. There is one from each tea set my daughter received during her childhood Christmases.

The smallest one is unbreakable, of painted metal. It was the first. The second Christmas and the third are also represented by metal cups, successively larger. Number four is a red plastic, followed next by a delicate pink plastic. By the sixth Christmas, she understood being careful of breakage and the first china cup appears, small and heavy. By the next year, the cup was slimmer, thinner, more delicate. The last one is a beauty. It is hand-painted, almost transparent, the top-of-the-line quality.

The evidence of her growth and development is reflected in those cups, from days of clumsy grabbing at the metal ones to an ease of handling the most fragile.

I hope that as my Heavenly Father surveys the collection of days I offer him throughout my life, He will be able to discern in me just as steady growth and development in His will.

Father, we do wish to grow steadily and we pray for Your help to do so.

D.D.**

21.

A stale article, if you dip it in a good, warm, sunny smile, will go off better than a fresh one that you've scowled upon.

Nathaniel Hawthorne

My friend and I were in a fabric shop buying material. I took my bolt of cloth to the saleslady. Sternly, she began snipping away at the material. I looked directly at her, hoping I could catch her eye and say something pleasant or at least smile. She appeared utterly miserable and continued looking grimly down.

When she handed the cloth to me I wanted to smile, but her

dour face was discouraging and I felt my smile wither and die deep inside me. I took the material and quickly walked away.

My friend brought her material to the counter and the saleswoman gave her the same stoneface treatment.

But then, without warning, my friend's face burst into a joyful smile. Confidently and gloriously her smile continued. Then, accepting the material, she said softly, "Thank you so much."

The saleswoman seemed startled. Unexpectedly, almost helplessly, she began to smile also. Even her body language changed. She didn't look stiff any more. Her voice was melodic as she answered, "You're welcome. Bye."

Leaving the store I peeked back. The saleswoman still smiled as she chatted with another customer, who was also beginning to smile.

I had kept my smile inside me. But my brave friend had given her smile away, even at the risk of having it rejected. And she had lighted up the whole place.

Lord, help me share a smile with someone who looks as if he or she needs Your love in their life.

M.B.W.

22.

. . . Give place unto wrath: for it is written, Vengeance is mine; I will repay, saith the Lord.
Romans 12:19

It was December 22. My husband and I had driven eagerly to the airport to meet our daughter flying home from her faraway school. The short-term parking lot was jammed with the Christmas rush of travelers—not a single space left. Maybe there would be space in the long-term lot.

Up one row and down another—still no space. And then, up ahead, I spotted what looked like the outer edge of two vacant parking spaces side by side. Wonderful! But when we arrived at the turning-in place, the area wasn't vacant at all. A blood-red sports car was deliberately angled across the line dividing two parking spaces. The selfishness of some people!

"Oh, I'd like to smash that car to bits!" I said furiously to my husband. "Slow down, and I'll get his license. I'm going to report him. People like that should be locked up!"

My husband smiled. "Take it easy, Irene."

"Aren't you going to stop?" I cried, still steaming.

"Heavens no. He's going to get in enough trouble on his own in life without any help from you. You've got a valid gripe, sure, but you know where to send it."

My husband was right. The best thing to do about life's little injustices is simply surrender them. Rude driver crowds you out? Over to You, Lord. Boss yells at you with reason? Over to You, Lord. Injustices crowding in on your life?

Over to You, Lord.

I.B.H.

23. They also serve who only stand and wait.
John Milton

Sister Schweider describes her work at St. John's Hospital in Springfield, Illinois, as "just standing around." And her motto, she says with a twinkle, is: "Don't just do something; stand there!"

The difference between your run-of-the-mill stander-arounders and Sister Schweider, however, is monumental. She makes it a point to be standing around where there is heartbreak, loneliness, grief and pain. When patients and visitors at St. John's need a kind word spoken softly or an attentive, sympathetic listener, Sister Schweider is there.

This kind of standing around reminds me that there are times when inaction is as heroic as action, and just as helpful. Sister Schweider's example is a good one to follow when friends are going through personal crises. So often they don't need still more advice, or money, or an overly helpful hand. What they need is someone with the kindness and self-restraint to just stand there, with mouth shut, but heart and ears open.

Quiet me today, Lord, so that I may spread the peace and understanding that knowing You brings.

Z.B.D.

24.

. . . . I have called thee by thy name; thou art mine.

Isaiah 43:1

It was Christmas Eve, and in our British household seven-year-old Debby was very uneasy about moving into the guest bed with two visiting cousins. What if Father Christmas couldn't find her? What if he got the presents mixed? She solved the problem with a note pinned to the end of the bed: "Dear Father Christmas, the one in the middle is ME."

Activity, bustle and noise are part and parcel of the festive season. As you jostle in crowded shops, cater for a houseful of visitors or squeeze into the only vacant seat at the carol service, you may feel like saying, "Dear God, in all this mass of humanity the one in the middle is me."

How wonderful it is at such moments to remember that almost 2,000 years ago God made a supreme and special effort to let us know that He does recognize and care about each of us, no matter how jostled or crowded or harassed we may be. To remind us, to reassure us, He gave us His perfect Christmas gift—and laid it in a manger.

Thank You, Father, that at Christmas You loved each one of us enough to send Your own Son, Jesus, to bring that wonderful love.

G.K.

25.

(Christmas)
And there were in the same country shepherds abiding in the field, keeping watch over their flock by night.

Luke 2:8

In the twenty-odd years I've worked for Guideposts I've written a few Christmas stories of my own and edited many more. Back in 1955, when Len LeSourd was Managing Editor, he asked me to adapt a story by J. Edgar Parks for use in the December issue, and I did. I've always remembered that story, because in a small way it seemed to have the same ingredients as Dickens' immortal A CHRISTMAS CAROL.

Since Christmas is a time for story-telling, among other good things, I thought you might enjoy reading it aloud to your children. So here it is:

The Man Who Missed Christmas

It was Christmas Eve, and, as usual, George Mason was the last to leave the office. He walked over to a massive safe, spun the dials, swung the heavy door open. Making sure the door would not close behind him, he stepped inside.

A square of white cardboard was taped just above the topmost row of strongboxes. On the card a few words were written. George Mason stared at those words, remembering . . .

Exactly one year ago he had entered this self-same vault. And then, behind his back, slowly, noiselessly, the ponderous door swung shut. He was trapped—entombed in the sudden and terrifying dark.

He hurled himself at the unyielding door, his hoarse cry sounding like an explosion. Through his mind flashed all the stories he had heard of men found suffocated in time-vaults. No timeclock controlled this mechanism; the safe would remain locked until it was opened from the outside. Tomorrow morning.

Then the realization hit him. No one would come tomorrow—tomorrow was Christmas.

Once more he flung himself at the door, shouting wildly, until he sank on his knees exhausted. Silence came, high-pitched, singing silence that seemed deafening. More than 36 hours would pass before anyone came—36 hours in a steel box three feet wide, eight feet long, seven feet high. Would the oxygen last? Perspiring and breathing heavily, he felt his way around the floor. Then, in the far right-hand corner, just above the floor, he found a small, circular opening. Quickly he thrust his finger into it and felt, faint but unmistakable, a cool current of air.

The tension release was so sudden that he burst into tears. But at last he sat up. Surely he would not have to stay trapped for the full 36 hours. Somebody would miss him.

But who? He was unmarried and lived alone. The maid who

cleaned his apartment was just a servant; he had always treated her as such. He had been invited to spend Christmas Eve with his brother's family, but children got on his nerves, and expected presents.

A friend had asked him to go to a home for elderly people on Christmas Day and play the piano—George Mason was a good musician. But he had made some excuse or other; he had intended to sit at home with a good cigar, listening to some new recordings he was giving himself.

George Mason dug his nails into the palms of his hands until the pain balanced the misery in his mind. Nobody would come and let him out. Nobody, nobody . . .

Miserably the whole of Christmas Day went by, and the succeeding night.

On the morning after Christmas the head clerk came into the office at the usual time, opened the safe, then went on into his private office.

No one saw George Mason stagger out into the corridor, run to the water cooler, and drink great gulps of water. No one paid any attention to him as he left and took a taxi home.

There he shaved, changed his wrinkled clothes, ate breakfast and returned to his office, where his employees greeted him casually.

That day he met several acquaintances and talked to his own brother. Grimly, inexorably, the truth closed in on George Mason. He had vanished from human society during the great festival of brotherhood; no one had missed him at all.

Reluctantly, George Mason began to think about the true meaning of Christmas. Was it possible that he had been blind all these years with selfishness, indifference, pride? Wasn't giving, after all, the essence of Christmas because it marked the time God gave His own Son to the world?

All through the year that followed, with little hesitant deeds of kindness, with small, unnoticed acts of unselfishness, George Mason tried to prepare himself . . .

Now, once more, it was Christmas Eve.

Slowly he backed out of the safe, closed it. He touched its grim steel face lightly, almost affectionately, and left the office.

There he goes now in his black overcoat and hat, the same George Mason as a year ago. Or is it? He walks a few blocks, then flags a taxi, anxious not to be late. His nephews are expecting him to help them trim the tree. Afterwards, he is taking his brother and his sister-in-law to a Christmas play. Why is he so happy? Why does this jostling against others, laden as he is with bundles, exhilarate and delight him?

Perhaps the card has something to do with it, the card he taped inside his office safe last New Year's Day. On the card is written, in George Mason's own hand: "To love people, to be indispensable somewhere, that is the purpose of life. That is the secret of happiness."

Father, on this happy day, help us bring happiness to others.

A.G.

26.

Better is a dinner of herbs where love is, than a stalled ox and hatred therewith.
Proverbs 15:17

Night after night I listened while my seven-year-old prayed, "Let all the sick people get well and all the poor people get rich."

I felt that I should talk to him about riches but I simply didn't know the right words to say. We had to live very modestly ourselves. Besides, John is shy and I was afraid I might cause him to stop praying aloud if I handled it wrong.

One evening after this had gone on for several weeks, he came in the kitchen while I was preparing supper, lifted a pot lid on the stove and said, "Mama, did all the poor people used to be rich like we are?"

So that was what he meant by rich! He meant being like us! I felt a great surge of warmth and happiness, knowing that it was perfectly all right for John to pray for *our* kind of wealth for the whole world: love for one another, and freedom, and beef stew for supper.

Father, let our lives show that our hearts have learned to define riches aright.

M.B.D.* *

311

27.

Why art thou cast down, O my soul? and why art thou disquieted in me?

Psalm 42:5

I've often wondered just how Mary felt after the heavenly host had returned to the Father, the shepherds and the Three Kings to their flocks and thrones, and the throngs in Bethlehem to their own abodes. How did she feel after everyone was gone?

It was just last week that our house echoed with voices: "Honey, run to the store for whipping cream!" "Kids, stay out of the candy until after we eat!" "Somebody get Jimmy out of the packages under the tree!"

Now the house is empty and quiet—the excitement dissipated into slamming car doors and revving engines. What's left behind are leftovers, copying new addresses brought on by a swarm of greetings, half-price sales on cards, gift wrap and tree decorations, plus overflowing wastebaskets and empty freezers.

Did Mary also have a hard time retaining the thrill of the preceding days? Or was she wise enough to know that life is always a series of peaks and valleys, that you can't stay on the mountaintop, that you have to come back down to the valleys where life is lived and work is done. Surely that's what Mary did when she went back to Nazareth to be a wife and mother. And that's what we must do too, when the excitement of Christmas is over, keeping in our hearts the knowledge that as the earth turns the gladness of Christmas will come again—as it always has and always will.

Father, help me get through the little feelings of depression that come when a happy time is over. And thank You for the knowledge that such times will come again.

I.C.

28.

I am come that they might have life, and that they might have it more abundantly.

John 10:10

I was being interviewed by Mutual Network's Martha Dean. After the program she began telling me about interesting women who'd been on her show. "One of the nicest was Myrna Loy. This was a surprise. Remember those old movies she used to do when she was the Oriental siren or the other woman? And since then all her glamor and success? Well, she was so warm and outgoing and honest I was almost afraid to ask about her personal life for fear she'd tell me! But I knew she'd be just as interested in mine.

"And she was so generous. She was wearing a beautiful sweater, which I admired. And she said, 'Take it! I really don't want it any more.' Of course I protested. I felt like I was in one of those foreign countries where you don't dare admire anything because they'll *give* it to you. But she kept insisting, 'Really, I've had all the pleasure I'm going to get out of this sweater and I want you to have it.' "

"I didn't take it, naturally. But later I kind of wished I had. Our engineer told me I should have—because she really *wanted* me to have that sweater, it would have given her so much joy."

What is it that makes us so often reluctant to accept gifts, whether from other people or from God? Are we afraid of seeming selfish? Or do we feel undeserving? Often there is a fear of obligation: "Oh, dear, now he (or she) will expect something from me." Yet the true giver wants us to have what is so freely offered. The true giver is not sitting in judgment, finding us weak and unworthy; by the very gift he or she is saying, "I think you're great." Nor does the true giver ask or expect anything in return. His or her reward is in the sheer joy of giving.

This is true of genuinely nice people. And it is true of the God Who gave us the gift of life. He wants us to have that life in all its abundance. Jesus Himself said that was one of the reasons He came. The Christian, then, should hold out grateful hands to accept.

Thank You, God, for Your many gifts. Don't let me ever reject them.

M.H.

29.

**God's in his Heaven—
All's right with the world!**

Robert Browning

Before I left for my friend Mary Anne's birthday dinner, I took a long look in the mirror. Perhaps a piece of jewelry would add the final touch. I searched through the box until my fingers touched a golden disc. I held it beneath the lamp so I could read the forgotten inscription: "This is the day which the Lord has made, we will rejoice and be glad in it."

My fingers traced the words as though the disc were a king's ancient seal and my fingers the wax. In that moment, the thought came to me that the words *were* from a king's ancient seal: the Bible. And I *was* the wax.

All of us are the wax, you know, imprinted with God's love and truth. As we live each day according to His teachings, He sets His seal of perfection upon us.

Like the Psalmist of old, we praise God for this day, and wait for His touch upon our lives.

M.E.H.

30.

. . . But this one thing I do, forgetting those things which are behind, and reaching forth unto those things which are before, I press toward the mark for the prize of the high calling of God in Christ Jesus.

Phillippians 3:13,14

Elsie and I often have coffee together and, while she's my best friend, she often disconcerts me by quoting Scripture instead of agreeing with me when I complain.

One day I reminisced about childhood injustices. "My first grade teacher never gave me a turn to hold the flag while the rest saluted!" Then: "One of the neighborhood kids said I couldn't walk down the 'secret path' with her—she always was a pest!"

And next I said, "And one time a cousin told me she didn't like me! All those things were unforgivable!"

Elsie merely said, "If you do not forgive men their sins, your Father will not forgive your sins."

I said, "Well, of course, I've *forgiven*. It's just that I haven't *forgotten*. Every time their names are mentioned, I remember what they did."

Elsie quoted: "'I will forgive their iniquity and I will remember their sin no more' (Jeremiah 31:34) Isn't it wonderful that the Lord has not only forgiven you, but each time He thinks of you, He doesn't remember all the bad things you've done?"

Her quotes are especially comforting to me on these last days of the year. As I look back and think of the many mistakes I've made during 1979, I'm almost afraid of beginning the fresh, new 1980 He has for me. But maybe St. Paul felt the same way when he wrote the above passage from Philippians! At least, his words are a great encouragement to me. Especially today, as the year draws to a close.

Thank You, Father, that when I fall and stumble and get discouraged, Your word always picks me up, dusts me off and tells me to try again.

I.C.

31.
All through the seasons of sowing and reaping,
All through the harvest of song and tears,
Hold us close in Your tender keeping,
O Maker of all New Years!
Author unknown

One New Year's Eve several years ago my wife, Ruth, and I found ourselves in Rome. The celebrations were unlike anything we had ever encountered at home. They started about noon on December 31 with the booming of cannon and a mounting crescendo of noisemakers. As night came on, tracer flashes cut across the sky until finally, at midnight, bedlam broke out.

But that was not all. The Romans think that New Year's Eve is an appropriate time to rid themselves of the old and take on the new, not just symbolically but actually, by throwing out of the window any old or worn-out thing such as a torn dress, a frayed suit, a cracked dish, perhaps, or a dilapidated chair. Our Roman friends warned us quite seriously to stay in the hotel to avoid being hit by one of those flying objects.

The idea is a sound one, I realized, not only for New Year's Eve but for every day. The throwing away of old things might well go far beyond material objects to include the disposal of old, tired, gloomy, fearful or depressing thoughts.

Every night, if you resolve to do it and do it regularly, the ritual of deliberate thought-emptying will get the mind in good working order for succeeding days. Just summon up all the glum impressions, the jealousies and animosities, the regrets and discouragements with which the mind becomes cluttered, and visualize them passing out of consciousness. Affirm to yourself, "These thoughts are now passing out of my mind. They are passing from me right now."

Try it. The results will be a restful sleep from which you awake full of vitality and energy to keep you going the following day.

Dear Father, thank You for 1979. Now I look forward to 1980, a new year with new hopes and new challenges awaiting me.

N. V. P.

THE GUIDEPOSTS FAMILY OF CONTRIBUTORS

J.M.A.	John M. Allen	Pawling, NY. Director of Corporate and Public Affairs for *Reader's Digest*. Board member of Guideposts Associates and Foundation for Christian Living.
M.A.	Manuel Almada	New Bedford, MA. Former newspaperman. Author of over 450 magazine articles.
C.A.	Carol Amen	Sunnyvale, CA. Nurse. Most recent book: *Changing Problems into Challenges*.
J.M.B.	June Masters Bacher	Escondido, CA. Columnist, teacher (English), poet. Latest book: *Devotions for the Woman's Hour*.
K.B.	Kathryn Brinckerhoff	New York, NY. Associate Editor, *Guideposts* magazine.
J.B.	Jamie Buckingham	Melbourne, FL. Minister. Formerly an editor for *Guideposts* and *Logos Journal*. Inspirational writer. Latest book: *The Last Word*.
L.C.	Lucille Campbell	Cainsville, MO. Former teacher. Inspirational writer.
J.C.	Jo Carr	Lubbock, TX. Pastor, United Methodist Church. Inspirational writer. Most recent book: *Plum Jelly & Stained Glass & Other Prayers*.
I.C.	Isabel Champ	Mulino, OR. Newspaper columnist. Inspirational writer and teacher.
D.J.C.	Donald J. Clark	San Diego, CA. Science editor. Inspirational writer.
C.M.D.	Charles M. Davis	Waverly, OH. Retired advertising and public relations director.
M.B.D.*	Mary Bouton Davis	Canoga Park, CA. Inspirational writer.
Z.B.D.	Zona B. Davis	Effingham, IL. Newscaster. Inspirational writer.
W.D.	William Deerfield	West Orange, NJ. Assistant Editor, *Guideposts* magazine.
P.E.D.	Pat Egan Dexter	Phoenix, AZ. Inspirational writer. Most recent book: *The Emancipation of Joe Tepper*.

317

D.D.*	Dina Donohue	San Diego, CA. Contributing Editor, *Guideposts* magazine. Inspirational writer and lecturer on inspirational writing techniques.
D.D.**	Drue Duke	Sheffield, AL. Certified lay speaker, Methodist church. Playwright. Inspirational writer.
M.B.D.**	Mildred Brown Duncan	Jacksonville, FL. Medical Secretary. Inspirational writer.
L.P.E.	Lorena Pepper Edlen	Chaparral, NM. Publicist. Former stringer for *National Enquirer*.
F.F.	Faye Field	Longview, TX. Retired high-school/college teacher. Inspirational writer.
S.F.	Sidney Fields	Hastings-on-Hudson, NY. *Guideposts* Contributing Editor. New York *Daily News* columnist ("Only Human"). Articles in major American magazines.
R.H.F.	Rosalyn Hart Finch	Westerville, OH. Inspirational writer and lecturer.
H.B.F.	Hope B. Friedmann	Altadena, CA. Formerly editor of *Singles Together*. Inspirational editor and writer. Latest book: *Innerhouse*.
E.G.	Edward Gillin	Fort Collins, CO. Graduate teaching assistant, Colorado State University. Former Associate Editor, *Guideposts* magazine. Former reporter, Indianapolis *Star*.
M.S.G.	May Sheridan Gold	Chevy Chase, MD. For 30 years a volunteer teacher to the deaf. Former reporter for Atlanta *Constitution* and daily columnist, Orlando *Sentinel*.
A.G.	Arthur Gordon	Savannah, GA. Editorial Director, *Guideposts* magazine. Former staff writer, *Reader's Digest*. Novelist. Most recent book: *A Touch of Wonder*.
B.R.G.	Betty R. Graham	Alexandria, VA. Creative writing teacher. Librarian and organist for Woodlawn Baptist Church. Inspirational writer.

D.H.	Doris Haase	Burbank, CA. Inspirational writer.
I.B.H.	Irene Burk Harrell	Wilson, NC. Inspirational writer. Most recent book: *Lord, How Will You Get Me Out of This Mess?* (with Kay Golbeck).
W.H.	Will Hayes	Santa Barbara, CA. Director, Quarterback Receiver Camp. Aviation and inspirational writer. Consultant to Federal Aviation Authority.
R.H.	Ruth Heaney	Wenonah, NJ. Teacher: high-school English, community college writing. Freelance magazine writer.
M.M.H.	Marilyn Morgan Helleberg	Kearney, NE. College English teacher. Inspirational writer. Most recent book: *Your Hearing Loss.*
J.H.	Jeanne Hill	Scottsdale, AZ. Registered Nurse. Inspirational writer. Most recent book: *Daily Breath.*
M.E.H.	Mildred E. Hoffman	Seattle, WA. Secretary. Freelance feature writer.
M.H.	Marjorie Holmes	Manassas, VA. *Guideposts* Contributing Editor. Inspirational writer. Nationally syndicated columnist. Most recent book: *Lord, Let Me Love.*
C.H.	Charlotte Hutchison	Orangevale, CA. Feature writer. Newspaper and magazine freelance writer.
R.C.I.	Ruth C. Ikerman	Redlands, CA. Former storekeeper. Columnist, Los Angeles *Times.* Author of 15 devotional books for Abingdon Press.
J.J.	Jeff Japinga	Holland, MI. Journalism student. Editorial intern (summer '78) *Guideposts* magazine.
P.K.	Pat King	Kent, WA. Author, editor. Currently Editor of *Resplandor en el Spiritu Santo* (Spanish edition of *Aglow*). Most recent book: *How do You Find the Time?*
G.D.K.	Glenn D. Kittler	New York, NY. Contributing Editor, *Guideposts* magazine. Journalist and inspirational writer. Most recent book: *My First Encounter with God.*

G.K.	Gladys Knowlton	Hampshire, England. British inspirational author. Former Contributing Editor to British *Guideposts* magazine.
N.L.	Naomi Lawrence	Brooklyn, NY. Executive secretary, *Guideposts* magazine.
S.L.	Salvatore Lazzarotti	Montclair, NJ. Design Director, *Guideposts* magazine.
L.E.L.	Leonard E. LeSourd	Lincoln, VA. Executive Director, Chosen Books. Formerly Editor, *Guideposts* magazine (1951-1974). Nationally recognized inspirational editor and anthologist.
D.M.	Dot Main	Borger, TX. Batik artist. Co-proprietor of summer gift shop. Inspirational writer.
C.M.	Catherine Marshall	Lincoln, VA. Contributing Editor, *Guideposts* Magazine. Author of 14 inspirational books and novels. Most recent book: *The Helper.*
J.McD.	James McDermott	Brooklyn, NY. International Editor, *Guideposts* magazine.
M.M.	Maxine Montgomery	Novinger, MO. Former high-school English teacher. Newspaper columnist. Inspirational writer.
M.J.N.	Marilyn J. Norquist	Cortaro, NM. Roman Catholic laywoman, conducting retreat seminars and Scripture workshops. Inspirational writer.
J.D.P.	Jeanette Doyle Parr	Horatio, AR. Part-time secretary. Volunteer counselor for exceptional children. Inspirational writer.
B.P.	Benton Patterson	Denton, TX. Contributing Editor, *Guideposts* magazine. Journalism professor, North Texas State University. Formerly an editor of the *New York Times Magazine* and associate editor of *The Saturday Evening Post.*
N.V.P.	Norman Vincent Peale	Pawling, NY. Minister, Marble Collegiate Church. Founder and co-publisher and editor of *Guideposts* magazine. Internationally

acclaimed lecturer and writer. Co-founder of the Institutes of Religion and Health. Founder of the Foundation for Christian Living. Author of 19 inspirational books of which the latest is: *The Positive Principle Today.*

R.S.P.   Ruth Stafford Peale   Pawling, NY. Co-publisher and editor of *Guideposts* magazine. General Secretary and editor-in-chief of the Foundation for Christian Living. Member, Board of Directors of the Institutes of Religion and Health. Nationally syndicated columnist and lecturer. Most recent book: *The Adventure of Being a Wife.*

M.R.   Marian Rettke   Charlotte, NC. Part-time community college and educational television English teacher. Inspirational writer.

L.R.   Laverne Riley   Sun City, CA. Freelance magazine and inspirational writer.

R.D.R.   Ruth Dinkins Rowan   Jacksonville, FL. Former college teacher. Inspirational writer. Most recent book: *Helping Children with Learning Disabilities.*

E.St.J.   Elaine St. Johns   Arroyo Grande, CA. Contributing Editor, *Guideposts* magazine. Former newspaperwoman. Inspirational lecturer and writer. Most recent book: *Prayer Can Change Your Life* (with William R. Parker).

E.V.S.   Eleanor V. Sass   New York, NY. Assistant Editor, *Guideposts* magazine.

R.H.S.   Richard H. Schneider   Lincoln, VA. Contributing Editor, *Guideposts* magazine. Managing Editor, Chosen Books. Most recent book: *I Dared To Call Him Father* (with Bilquis Sheikh).

N.S.   Nita Schuh   Dallas, TX. Retired Captain, U.S. Navy. Inspirational writer. Most recent book: *After Winter, Spring.*

P.V.S.	Penney V. Schwab	Copeland, KS. Freelance writer. Inspirational writer.
D.S.	Dorothy Shellenberger	Waco, TX. Playwright. Short story and inspirational writer.
E.S.	Elizabeth Sherrill	Chappaqua, NY. Contributing Editor, *Guideposts* magazine. A founder of Chosen Books. Most recent book: *Return from Tomorrow* (with George G. Ritchie, M.D.).
J.L.S.	John L. Sherrill	Chappaqua, NY. Contributing Editor, *Guideposts* magazine. President, Chosen Books. Most recent book: *My Friend The Bible*.
A.L.S.	Anne Lorimer Sirna	Paoli, PA. Weekly newspaper columnist. Inspirational writer.
G.S.	Gary Sledge	Pleasantville, NY. Articles Editor, *Guideposts* magazine.
T.S.	Toby Smith	Albuquerque, NM. Contributing Editor, *Guideposts* magazine. Staff writer, Albuquerque *Journal*.
P.H.S.	Patricia Houck Sprinkle	St. Petersburg, FL. Freelance magazine writer.
P.S.	Pat Sullivan	Chicago, IL. Freelance writer. Newspaper columnist.
M.T.	Mildred Tengbom	Anaheim, CA. Inspirational writer and lecturer. Most recent book: *Especially for Mother*.
V.V.	Van Varner	New York, NY. Senior Staff Editor, *Guideposts* magazine.
L.W.	Lynn Wahner	New York, NY. Editorial Assistant, *Guideposts* magazine.
P.W.	Phyllis Walk	Colorado Springs, CO. Magazine writer. Poet and former creative writing teacher and instructor in Christian meditation.
M.W.	Madeline Weatherford	Bronx, NY. Administrative secretary, *Guideposts* magazine.
M.B.W.	Marion Bond West	Lilburn, GA. Inspirational writer. Latest book: *Two of Everything But Me*.